Communicating
in
Organizations

Gerald M. Phillips

THE PENNSYLVANIA STATE UNIVERSITY

Communicating in Organizations

Macmillan Publishing Co., Inc.
NEW YORK

Collier Macmillan Publishers
LONDON

Macmillan Publishing Co., Inc.
866 Third Avenue, New York, New York 10022

Collier Macmillan Canada, Inc.

Library of Congress Cataloging in Publication Data

Phillips, Gerald M.
    Communicating in organizations.

    Includes index.
    1. Communication in management. 2. Communication in organizations. I. Title.
HF5718.P52   658.4'5   81-12379
ISBN 0-02-395160-5   AACR2

Printing: 1 2 3 4 5 6 7 8   Year: 2 3 4 5 6 7 8 9

Preface

There is an old saying that "those who can, do, and those who can't, teach." One of the main problems with teaching organizational communication is that writers of textbooks tend to base their ideas on what they see in the university. While many text writers have had contact with corporations and public organizations as consultants, they have not been resident employees in organizations, and hence, miss many of the subtleties of operation, as well as some of the points so obvious that no one talks about them. This book is designed to present a realistic view of communication requirements in complex organizations, from the point of view of the employee who wants to do what is necessary to "make it."

We offer no definition of "making it." Some will want to do as well as necessary to keep their jobs so that they can use their salaries to support their other interests. Some will want to make as much as they can, or rise to the highest possible position. Others will want to use the organization as an outlet for their creative skills. For all of them, the organization must be taken as a living thing, for organizations are made of people and their goals. Within the organization we find the combat of life with all its ramifications; deceit and loyalty, wisdom and folly, love and hate, imagination and pedantry, courage and trepidation. Each individual in the organization has his or her chance to succeed, whatever the individual definition of success. For some, hopes will be dashed for the whole organization will fail.

Others will be carried to the top in spite of themselves by being lucky enough to land a job with an organization on the rise. People in government and charitable institutions will be prisoners of both the economy and political trends. All will find it extremely difficult to balance personal and corporate interests.

Success is made up partly of luck, partly of competence and partly of others knowing of your competence. It is the third component with which this book deals. There is no employee, however, isolated, however segregated from the whole who does not communicate with others. There is no employee who can avoid writing and talking about the work she or he has done, or is doing, or plans to do. Few employees can resist contributing to the general good of the organization by making suggestions or participating in planning, and as an employee rises to the top through more and more responsible supervisory and administrative positions, the stakes in communication get higher and higher.

In the simplest possible sense, employees give instructions, persuade others of a point of view, assign tasks, make suggestions, ask and answer questions, and talk sociably with the people around them. Each of these tasks demands considerable skill to catch the attention of those who make the important decisions. Once in a position of power and influence, the consequences of ineffective communication are monumental. Leaders rise and fall on their ability to communicate clearly and persuasively with people they direct and for whose fortunes they are responsible.

This book provides basic instruction in why and how to communicate in speaking and writing. The information is basic enough and simple enough so that it can be useful to anyone, regardless of their position or their ambition. It was built out of two and one half decades of contact with corporate life. The writer began his scholarly career as a part-time academic and a full time corporate employee. Experience in marketing, sales, personnel and public relations over several years are reflected in the practical realities of this book. Experience as a consultant for public and private organizations in production, planning, and problem solving provide the subtleties. A long and varied academic career as a teacher of public speaking, group discussion, interpersonal skills, and basic writing provide the "how to" components. Students and colleagues who criticized and suggested sharpened the final product.

Special thanks are due to some of those who provided the most exciting experiences for me as a consultant: Alan Wolf, Sister Joan Chittester, Roth Wilkofsky, Terry West, and the staff of Penn State Continuing Education. Also, to the Accurate Parts Manufacturing Co., Pennsylvania Rubber and Supply, Badger Bearing, and the Premier Autoware Co. for paying me while I made my mistakes. Kent Sokoloff, my former consulting partner, and the students who interned with me and piloted much of this material, "Buddy" Good-all, Lynne Kelly, Cindy Begnal, Chris Waagen and Katie Volpe deserve extra special thanks for trying very hard to make things work and reporting honestly when they did not. Special thanks to my student, the talented Susan Getis, for her cartoons.

Textbooks ought to do some good, enough to warrant chopping down the trees to make the paper on which they are printed. It is my earnest belief that this book will "pay its way," if you, the reader, try its ideas in the real world.

Gerald M. Phillips

Table of Contents

Chapter **9**
Basic Writing in the Organization   264

Appendix **A**
Oral Reading 302

Appendix **B**
The Porto Bar Co.: An Experience in Communication 307

INTRODUCTION

WHAT THIS BOOK IS ABOUT

This book is designed so that students who will someday work in our businesses, educational and social institutions, and government can learn and practice the skills they will need to do well at their jobs. It is about how to be an effective employee and how to succeed in complex enterprises where advancement is based on merit and available only to the most competent employees. Its central theme is that if you already have technical and professional competence, the ability to communicate effectively is the most important criterion for advancement on the job. Recent surveys of top executives demonstrate this. If you can do the job you were hired to do, your ability to communicate in speaking and writing will determine how far and how fast you advance.

In this book we present ways of speaking and writing to accomplish the goals common to most complex organizations. It deals mostly with formal situations in which you will be required to prepare your presentations carefully when there is a great deal at stake. We describe many of the situations you are likely to encounter, and we provide you with procedures by which you can prepare yourself for them. In short, this is a book about survival! In a shrinking economy, there is increasing competition for the top positions, and the person who knows what to do and can demonstrate that he or she is doing it will be the one who "makes it." This book is about how to become so competent that top management will not be able to resist your claim to advancement.

This is a realistic and practical book that operates from the premise that the way large organizations operate in our democratic society is legitimate. There is no critique of organizational life. Moreover, we do not gloss over the pitfalls and perils that await those who work in large organizations. We take into account both the noble and the base potential of human beings.

The first chapter explains how complex organizations are run and how communication is used to hold the parts together. It makes clear what you can gain from having communications skills and what you can lose if you do not have them.

Chapter 2 is about interviewing. It deals with ways to ask and answer questions both to gather information and to get a job. Job interviewing is discussed from the standpoint of both the interviewer and the interviewee.

Chapter 3 is the first of three chapters about presentational speaking. In it we explain how to gather and present information and technical data and how to adapted them to your audience.

In Chapter 4 we present several patterns for the organization of formal presentations. Chapter 5 explains how to prepare and defend a proposal and how to oppose one constructively.

In Chapter 6 we discuss some of the personal issues involved in organizational communication. We deal with relatively informal situations like orientation as well as with managing social relations and dealing with gossip and rumor. Of particular interest are methods of handling "bad news" interviews and managing stress.

Chapter 7 is about group problem-solving and the skills required in this activity.

Chapter 8 deals with the characteristics and behavior of leaders and discusses the relationship of administration, management, and leadership.

Chapter 9 is a brief summary of the techniques of producing the kinds of written documents required on most jobs.

We conclude with a model task, a simulation that will require you to use every skill you have learned in this book.

For those who wish to study the theory of organizations, we provide brief reading lists at the conclusion of each chapter. We also include references to practical discussions in current books and periodicals.

Your success in using this book depends on doing. Only by performing the tasks as you encounter them and using the techniques provided for you will you acquire the practical skills you need on the job.

Chapter 1

Communication and Organization

TO BE HUMAN IS TO BE ORGANIZED

Organization is the opposite of confusion. Humans discovered at the beginning of their existence that they had to organize to protect themselves from the elements and from predators. Because human infants cannot survive unless they are protected and cared for, humans were driven together. It is a basic principle of contemporary sociobiology that the drive to organize is inherent in humans.

Organization implies both specialization and exchange. The reason we organize is that we are simply not able to care for ourselves without help. Each of us, however, can develop a specialty and perform some service that others need in exchange for rendering services that we need. In order to manage these exchanges, decisions must be made about who is to do what and how valuable each task is to be. As soon as several people are associated according to a set of rules, there must be a leader to coordinate the activity. Paramount is the decision about how to keep order. It is safer to talk about problems than to resolve them by physical force. Furthermore, if a group of people can keep from tearing each other apart while they set up an organization, they put themselves in a position to handle catastrophes and assaults, as well as to provide the means by which information can be passed from generation to generation. The history of humanity is the story of the formation of complex organizations, their rise, their prosperity, their troubles, and their eventual dissolution.

Organizations are held together by communication. Dennis Fry, in his book *Homo Loquens: Man the Talking Animal* (Cambridge: Cambridge University Press, 1977), says that humans developed the ability to speak because they had to in order to form and sustain organizations. The simple signals of animals were not sufficient to hold together the complicated arrangements humans had to make in order to stay alive. Humans developed symbol systems, which enabled them to exchange information, communicate with future generations, make plans, give directions, inspire, amuse, study, and learn, as well as to expostulate and to complain. Perhaps the most powerful ability that communication conferred on humans was the ability to study information from the past in order to plan more effectively for the future. Sadly, humans are able to transmit not only sense but nonsense from generation to generation.

In addition, symbol systems enabled the human to form a personal identity, to understand mortality, and to develop a sense of time. The understanding that we will all someday die makes it urgent that we accept our mission to build a world fit for humans to live in, so that we can be sure our children will not be placed in great peril. It is no accident that the biblical story of the Tower of Babel tells how God ended human aspirations to immortality by "counfounding their speech." We may no longer want to build a tower to the heavens, but we continue to struggle for peace, security, economic well-being, and personal pleasure through our associations with one another. Each of our organizations is dedicated to at least one of those purposes.

THE CHARACTERISTICS OF ORGANIZATIONS

Any time that two or more people are required to share time or space, goods or services, an organization is formed. Every relationship between people is characterized by having three elements of organization: (1) a way to make plans; (2) a way to carry them out; and (3) a way to resolve disputes about carrying them out. You may recognize these three elements as the basic powers in the American Constitution: the legislative, executive, and judicial powers.

If people cannot agree on these three components, they cannot stay together. They fight. Thus a formal organization must make these elements specific. There must be a person or a group with the power to decide on goals and on ways to achieve these goals. There must be someone with the authority to carry out legitimate activities, and there must be some method of resolving conflict and handling grievances. Formal organizations publish these rules either as constitutions or as manuals of procedure, and those who participate in the organization and share its benefits are bound by them. Because violations threaten the organization, violators must be punished. In governmental units, violators are regarded as criminals or rebels. In a commercial organization, those who cannot follow the rules are denied benefits or they are dismissed from the organization.

This book is about communicating in formal organizations of a particular type. When we use the word *organization* in this book we are not referring to a social club or a family. The formal organizations we deal with here are voluntary. People must formally affiliate with them to be bound by their rules or share their benefits. Usually these people are paid for doing something on behalf of the organization. Their activity is directed at attaining organizational goals, although by doing so they also seek to attain personal goals of wealth, fame, power, security, or love. By serving the organization, people are provided with a limited system in which to act. The rules are relatively clear, and the ways to success, though difficult, are available to all. The organizations we consider here exist in democratic societies. While they may have some undemocratic features, their structure is essentially democratic.

There are some personal goals that are not legitimate in formal organizations. Love and nurturance are rarely to be found, though the economic gains achieved through work in the formal organization can be used to support intimate units outside the organization. As the saying goes, money can't buy love, but it can certainly help to create a feeling of security in which love is possible.

People seek their goals both inside and outside organizations by communicating. Skillful talk and writing are required to carry out most jobs. In order to integrate technical and professional skills, directions must be given, questions must be asked and answered, problems must be discussed, and proposed solutions must be defended. In addition, human needs are met through talk. Encouragement and reward can be provided through careful and considerate management of talk. Any time that an employee of an organization makes contact with another employee for any purpose whatsoever, skillful talk and writing can make the difference between success or failure in whatever the contact is about. That is why skill in communication is essential to the person who wishes to achieve her or his goals in the organization, whatever they may be.

Organizational goals guide the behavior of the people associated with the organization. For example,

1. Governments seek to maintain order by controlling the behavior of citizens, by protecting them, by keeping the peace, and by regulating the distribution of goods and services.
2. Businesses seek a profit by selling goods for money or by providing services for a fee.
3. Social service organizations seek to provide care for those who need it.
4. Schools seek to disseminate knowledge or to train people to perform legitimate tasks.
5. Clubs and fraternal orders seek to provide recreation and personal fulfillment for their members.
6. Political parties seek to elect candidates and maintain control over the regulation of society.
7. Research groups seek to discover and disseminate knowledge. As we become more specific in our identification of organizations, the goals become more specific.

- The Boeing Company seeks to make a profit through the construction and sale of aircraft.
- The U.S. Department of Welfare seeks to distribute money and services to a defined group of the eligible needy.
- The South Hills School of Business seeks to make a profit by training students in business and commercial skills for a fee.

Whatever their goals, organizations are made up of people coordinating their efforts to accomplish those goals. For individuals, the main goal is to preserve their jobs by preserving the organization. From there, they may seek satisfaction, advancement in authority, salary increases, the excitement of competition, and many, many other intangibles. When the individual goals of the people in the organization are properly orchestrated so that efforts are synthesized with the accomplishment of the organizational goal, the organization is usually successful.

Most of the material in this book is drawn from organizations in which people are paid for their services. Though we do not consider voluntary organizations directly, we call your attention to Theodore Caplow's premise, "All human organizations resemble each other so closely that much of what is learned by managing one organization can be applied to . . . any other organization" (*How to Run Any Organization*. New York: Dryden Press, 1976, p. 5). We use here the terminology of business, government, and education. We discuss supervision, management, employees, clients, and customers. The words can be translated into less formal terminology to fit voluntary organizations, where people are compensated for their time and effort by goodwill and good feelings.

ISSUES COMMON TO ANY ORGANIZATION

An issue is a problem that people talk about in order to solve it. An issue can be how to use a thing, or what may be the consequences of a situation, or whether or not to take a particular action, or even what the value is of the behavior of an individual. If an issue is about the legitimate business of people in the organization, it can be considered an organizational issue. Each organization has its own special issues, such as how to package products or how to supply a particular service efficiently, but all organizations must deal with *structural issues, lines of authority,* and *procedural issues.*

Structural issues involve the substance of the organization. They include what rules should govern the organization and the procedures for carrying out the rules. Limitations and powers are also structural issues. Governments have formal constitutions in which their structure is defined. Corporations must be chartered, and other organizations have by-laws to specify the formalities of operation. Every formal organization resolves its structural issues in the form of a document that describes how it is to be run and that serves as the basis for the settlement of disputes about what is legal and/or permissible in the organization.

Lines of authority are established by this document. They govern the way people participate in making rules, carrying out rules, and adjudicating disputes. Most organizations are run by officers, each of whom has a particular responsibility for carrying out the organization's mission, or by boards that have the authority to establish goals or to lay out broad lines of policy. Under each of these are an array of administrators responsible for carrying out directives and implementing programs designed to achieve organizational goals. Lines of authority establish the structure of the organization and stipulate who can tell whom what to do and who has the responsibility for carrying out various tasks.

Procedural issues relate to the techniques and methods by which programs are carried out. Basically, they include the types of talk and writing exchanged by employees, including directions, discussions, disputes, reports, evaluations, and plans. Most organizations have manuals of regulations and procedures, files of minutes, and records of decisions that serve as a basis for the day-to-day action of the personnel. In addition, every organization has some informal sources of communication, such as gossip, rumor, and the folklore about who behaves in what way. The talk and writing that people do to carry out their tasks shape the operational character of the organization. Individuals in the organization become part of the process when they can follow the regulations and communicate in ways that are approved by the rest of the people in the organization. Individuals who cannot follow formal rules of operation are usually dismissed, and those who cannot follow the social rules are usually ostracized.

Affiliation with formal organizations is voluntary. Even citizenship can be changed if an individual wants to move. The act of joining an organization is a voluntary sacrifice of freedom. Before you affiliate, you are not bound by any of the organization's rules, nor can you share in its benefits. Once you are committed to the organization, you are required to surrender your personal freedom in specified ways, in exchange for which you derive economic and social security. Most people prefer to be governed, for they are thus protected from disasters that they cannot handle alone. Affiliation with a commercial organization confers the ability to purchase food, clothing, shelter, and the amenities of life. The exchange is personal freedom for economic security. The organization can also confer other benefits, however. Most important is personal identification. Most people, when asked to identify themselves state their occupation or name the company for which they work. The distinguished American psychiatrist, Harry Stack Sullivan, pointed out that human personality is developed through the responses others make to your regular habits of communication. Your membership or employment in an organization provides you with a culture in which you can grow and develop your personality. Without formal membership and people you see regularly, it is very difficult to acquire the skills needed to accomplish your goals successfully. Thus, success in organizations means more than purchasing or administrative power. It means personal power, as well.

Affiliation means acceptance of the rules, and the first problem faced by a newcomer is learning the rules. Once the rules are mastered, the individual has a place. An identity is conferred by employment. The job to be done specifies a role by which you are known. This identity generally leads to an easy and comfortable relationship with your colleagues.

Most of each day in an organization is spent dealing with operations. Operations are the tasks that must be done: they are the business of the day. Issues that grow up around them represent the substance of most communication within organizations:

- What should we do? What are the tasks that must be completed in what time period?
- How should we do it? Who will pay? Where should it take place? Who will do what? What materials are needed? What is the sequence of steps? How shall we distribute it?
- What should we say about it and to whom? What must our colleagues know? What must our supervisors know? What must our employees know? What must the public know?
- To whom are we responsible? What are the limits on our operations? What must we do? What are we not permitted to do? What is our responsibility to the larger society: stockholders, community, and government? What are our obligations to morality or common decency?

As you examine the list of questions, you should be able to see how they represent the substance of what people communicate about in organizations.

The word *organization* is an abstraction. Organizations have no real form. They exist on paper or in people's minds. The organization is not the buildings and the machinery and the people who do work. Organization is an intangible. As a noted jurist once said, "It has no legs to be broken or soul to be damned!" But though organization is an intangible, the work done by people in organizations is very real. The activities carried on and the talk about them really represent the substance of the organization. People's lives can be made rich and bountiful or utterly miserable depending on what is said, to whom, and how. Societies can bc blessed with prosperity and peace if things go well for organizations; blighted, if they go sour.

As humans, our lives are spent in organizations. We communicate with each other to make organizations run. One person alone rarely has the power to shape the destiny of an organization. It is not possible for an organization to achieve its goals without the dedicated efforts of many human beings. The world has changed a great deal since an imaginative entrepreneur could invent a new product, produce it, and become a millionaire, all alone. Today the operation of organizations is essentially corporate in nature.

THE NATURE OF CORPORATE BUREAUCRACY

We occasionally use here the word *corporation* synonymously with *organization,* for most organizations are structured in corporate fashion, even those owned by one person or by a partnership. A corporation is a legal fiction that permits a group of people to operate an organization. The charter that establishes the corporation says that a group of people will come together to carry out some specified activities without interference so long as they obey the law and pay taxes. Formal corporations restrict financial liability so that personal income and property are not threatened if the corporation should go bankrupt or lose a lawsuit. The effect of this kind of legislation is to permit the relatively free operation of businesses, service organizations, public agencies, school districts, and various other types of organizations in a thoroughly democratic manner without making individuals responsible for what is done by the whole.

Governments confer the power to vote on people holding citizenship. Governments also have the power to decide who shall be a citizen. Corporations confer the power to vote on those who hold a special kind of status, either as stockholders, citizen clients, or members of a board of directors. Huge corporations operate by having stockholders confer proxies, or the right to vote, on a few directors, who serve as a legislature. Smaller corporations may have stockholders' meetings periodically to gain approval for major policy decisions.

The legislature, in whatever form, appoints a group of executives to see that proper business is done. The executives are responsible, in theory, to the legislative body, but often, because of their mastery of the details of operation, they attain enough power to stand on their own, much as the president of the United States counterbalances Congress. Throughout the organization, contracts of employment, union contracts, and applicable legislation provide a judicial system to protect workers from exploitation, safety hazards, or unfair treatment.

Most formal organizations are made up of suborganizations. Large conglomerates are made up of several companies, each operating on its own but responsible to the larger legislative body. Within each company, there are separate divisions, each charged with a responsibility. Within each division, there is a means of enacting "legislation," that is, of making decisions about what needs to be done, and in each case, there is an executive charged with the responsibility of seeing that it is done. Organizations that are structured on this model are referred to as *bureaucracies*. They are characteristic of the type of formal organization that operates in contemporary society.

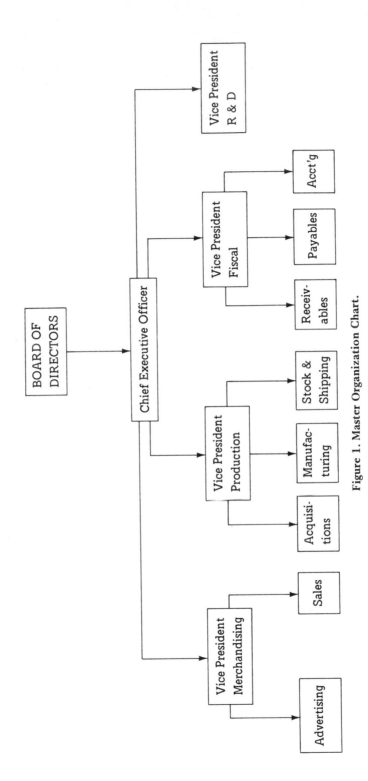

Figure 1. Master Organization Chart.

12

The word *bureaucracy* is not a bad word. A bureaucracy is merely an organization so complex that it requires suborganizations to implement the work that must be done. A privately owned shoe store with three employees functions as a bureaucracy when one person buys and stocks the shoes, one sells the shoes, and one keeps the financial records. Multiply these functions by the number of things that must be done in an organization, and you will get a sense of how a bureaucracy operates. Each component performs a specified task, integrated according to a master organization chart (Figures 1, 2, and 3).

Figure 1 shows the overall administration of a small manufacturing company. The four vice presidents report to the chief executive officer. Each of the vice presidents, in turn, delegates authority to departments or divisions, which in turn are divided into subdivisions. Figure 2 shows how the Stock and Shipping Department is subdivided into four sections. Stock and Shipping is headed by a supervisor, each of the subdivisions by a foreman. The stockroom foreman divides his operation into three segments, each having an assistant foreman in charge. Presumably, each of the assistant foremen has workers to whom he or she assigns duties. Delegation of authority according to this kind of pattern is characteristic of bureaucracy.

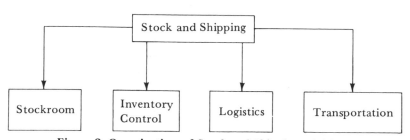

Figure 2. Organization of Stock and Shipping Division.

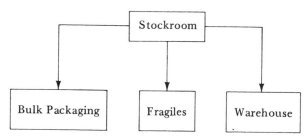

Figure 3. Organization of Stockroom.

Because the divisions and subdivisions are not directly connected, communication links must be maintained. If the communication links are effective, the various components of the operation know where they fit; that is, they know who is dependent on them for what. Stock and Shipping is vital to Sales, because if Stock and Shipping does not perform well, the work of the salespeople will be impaired. The connection between the divisions must be maintained by the various supervisors, and the chief executive officer is responsible for overseeing the communication links between all of the components of the organization. A brief look at the organization chart of any company or agency will reinforce the importance of communication to maintaining the smooth operation of the organization.

THE REASONS FOR LEARNING
ORGANIZATIONAL COMMUNICATION

This book is addressed to you as a potential employee. It is really about your ability to prosper in an organizaiton. We have already shown you that an organization is an abstraction. Its reality lies in the connections between the people that do its work. An abstraction cannot be concerned about your personal welfare, advancement, or success, but the people with whom and for whom you work must be concerned about you. Because your success on any job depends entirely on the people with whom you work, your ability to influence those people is crucial to your success.

Your first concern, of course, should be about your ability to do the work you were hired to do. Often your work will demand considerable education and training. However, a great number of people are hired to do work that requires only communication. Salespeople, supervisors, planners, and expediters all put their skill to work through communication. There is virtually no one in any organization whose work is so solitary that it does not demand some speaking and writing with others. In addition to doing what you were hired to do, you must make it clear to others that it has been done. You must draft and submit reports, ask and answer questions, work out problems with others, make proposals and requests, and deal decently with the people around you.

Communication skills are so important that they are the most frequent concern of executives looking for talented people to advance in the company. An ancient Roman educator once described the great orator as a "good man who speaks well." The successful employee could be defined as the "competent person who communicates well." In brief, whether you are seeking fame, money, power, prestige, or just satisfaction with the work you do, your ability to pursue happiness depends on your ability to speak and write effectively.

Formal training in oral communication skills is not commonly included in most technical and professional curricula. Most writing courses are quite general. In the book, we focus what we know about speaking on the kinds of situations you are likely to face on the job. We also include a brief chapter on the most important kinds of writing you might be asked to do. We believe this approach is important in light of the trend in education to go "back to basics." The distinguished scholar Robert Maynard Hutchins, the founder of the Great Books concept at the University of Chicago, remarked shortly before his death:

> The barbarism, "communication skills," which is the contemporary jargon for reading, writing, figuring, speaking and listening, appears to have permanent relevance. These arts are important in any society at any time. They are more important in a democratic society, because the citizens of a democratic society have to understand one another . . . they are arts shared by people everywhere. Without them, the individual is deprived and the community is too. In a technical age these are the only techniques that are universally valuable; they supply the only kind of vocational training a school can offer that can contribute to vocational success. They are the indispensable means to learning anything. They have to be learned if the individual hopes to expand his individuality or if he proposes to become a . . . member of a . . . community. (*Center Magazine*, "The Schools Must Stay" Vol. 6, No. 1, January/February 1973, pp. 18-19)

This book is primarily about speaking, with some directions about writing, as it is done in complex organizations. It consists of instruction in asking and answering questions (interviewing), making presentations (public speaking), participating in group problem-solving (discussion), practicing human relations, exercising leadership, and writing basic documents. You will be provided with techniques of analysis, preparation, and practice that can be applied to any organization.

THE DIFFERENCE BETWEEN SPEAKING AND WRITING

Writing was invented when humans discovered how frail their memories were and needed a way to keep records. In a formal organization, you write for two basic reasons: first, because what you want to communicate is too detailed for talk, and second, when you need a record of what you have communicated. You write when

1. You want to provide detailed information that your reader can refer to again, if necessary.
2. You wish to confirm some agreement or decision that was made orally, or you wish to record your understanding of something.
3. You need to leave a "paper trail," that is, a record of what has been done and what happened as a result.
4. It is required by a law or an internal regulation that formal records be kept.
5. You think that what you have to say is important enough for the next generation to read.

Writing is both formal and precise. It takes time to do well. Thus it should be used sparingly, as bad writing can cause more trouble than no writing at all. A confusing or foolish document with your name on it will outlast you in an organization. Write only when the issue is important enough to warrant taking the time to write well.

At the moment, our society is suffering from a paper glut. So much has been written that it is virtually impossible for people to process it. Even with computer storage and retrieval, we are overwhelmed with things to read. As a service to those who come after you, take care to make your writing useful and skillful.

Speaking is the method by which work is done on a day-to-day basis. It is actively oriented to the moment. It is essentially simple and suited for dealing with practical concepts. It is very difficult to deal with abstract concepts and detailed theories in talk, although it is possible to talk about abstract concepts and detailed theories once they have been written down.

Speaking is particularly useful when you want to get something started and you need to give instructions or orders.

1. Share a personal experience with someone.
2. Make an immediate comment about something that is going on.
3. Involve a number of people in pooling their ideas.
4. Involve a number of people in solving a problem or making a decision.
5. Inspire people to action, pay them a compliment, or reprimand them.
6. Carry on casual socializing.
7. Explore some ideas tentatively before making a commitment.
8. Present an argument on behalf of a point of view.
9. Criticize or object to a point of view.

There are estimates that most technical, professional, and supervisory personnel devote about 80 percent of their communication each day to speaking. In addition, most supervisory and executive positions involve little more than speaking. There are few jobs, except routine assembly-line work, that exempt you from face-to-face contact with others. Most jobs also require at least some writing on a daily basis.

THE ADVANTAGES OF SPEAKING WELL

As a summary of the importance of learning to speak well—once you become a skillful speaker you can

1. Discuss your concerns and problems with other so that something can be done about them.

2. Advance in the organization by letting others know of your competence.
3. Gain satisfaction from participating in accomplishing organization goals.
4. Be satisfied that you have done your best in trying to influence decisions.
5. Make rich and rewarding human contacts.

THE DISADVANTAGES OF SPEAKING POORLY

The other side of the coin is the impression people have of people who cannot speak effectively. For example,

1. If you cannot state your case competently, you may appear to be a whiner and complainer.
2. You can make yourself look incompetent by saying irrelevant or foolish things.
3. You can deny yourself important information if you cannot ask intelligent questions.
4. You can make people suspicious of you by gossiping or spreading rumors.
5. You can appear to be a heckler.
6. You can impair your credibility by being too complicated or by appearing to be patronizing.
7. You can lose important arguments by being unable to present your case well.
8. You can be identified as a bore.

SUMMARY

Organizations or groups of people who have a formal relationship that begins with a common goal. People work together to implement organizational goals. They can seek personal rewards and satisfactions, but they must do so in harmony with what the organization seeks.

There are many kinds of formal organizations identified by their goals: profit, control, social service, raising funds, making scientific discoveries, providing pleasure, or giving instruction or training. Whatever the goal, formal organizations have common problems. By learning about the problems in most complicated organizations, those that pay people for their services, you will understand how communication operates in simpler kinds of organizations as well.

Among the issues that organizations must deal with are those of structure (that is, how the organization is held together), lines of authority (the organization chart), and procedure. Organizational purposes are carried out in speech and writing on all levels. Each organization has its own unique operations and techniques for accomplishing its goals, but communication is intrinsic to all of them. People in organizations must talk about the basic questions: What should we do? How should we do it? What should we say about it and to whom? To whom are we responsible?

Virtually all organizations are set up as bureaucracies; that is, they are composed of suborganizations. Each does a task important to the whole, but often it is preoccupied with its own task, to the detriment of other organizational operations. It is the purpose of management to communicate with the components to integrate their activities into the smooth accomplishment of organizational purposes. When bureaus or divisions interface, they must solve problems together. Thus every organization has a form of governance: a way to make rules, a way to carry them out, and a way to achieve equity. Organizations depend on cooperation between people, which can be accomplished only with skillful communication.

Communication skills are a main criterion for advancement in most organizations, provided, of course, the individual first has basic technical or professional competence. There is a great deal a person can gain through skillful communication and a great deal that can be lost through incompetence.

THE USE OF THIS BOOK

As you proceed through this book, you will find it helpful to think about what you will be doing five years from now. What, exactly, will you be doing during the workday? Who will you be doing it with? Who will you have to talk with and for what purpose? What kind of writing will you be doing?

Consider the special things you are learning now and try to relate them to the work that other people do. By raising that question, you will be guided to an understanding of the role that communication will play in your organizational life. As you work through this book and perform various exercises, remember that there is no value whatsoever in mastering ideas and concepts about communication unless they result in some improved performance on your part. For this reason, it is important that you experiment with everything we offer. The most effective experimentation will be in your own career area.

READINGS

There are some good books on organizational theory. When you study human communication in organizations, be careful to distinguish books that deal specifically with *communication* as it is practiced in organizations from those on organizations, in which communication is mentioned incidentally. The following books are about how organizations work. They can serve as an excellent introduction to your study of communication.

Kenneth J. Albert *Handbook of Business Problem Solving.* New York: McGraw-Hill, 1980. Written by a distinguished management consultant, this book introduces most of the kinds of problems that affect contemporary organizations and provides an excellent overview of what people talk about.

Robert F. Allen, *Beat the System.* New York: McGraw-Hill, 1980. This book looks to the future and gives advice to people who plan to work in organizations about how to maintain personal identity while supporting organizational goals. It is a good little handbook on how to get things done, and it introduces a number of topics about which you will have to talk on the job.

Theodore Caplow, *How to Run Any Organization.* New York: Holt, Rinehart & Winston, 1976. In this book, a distinguished sociologist explains the relationship of management and leadership to the operations of organizations and sets the standards to which managers and leaders must conform in order to do their jobs effectively.

Beverly A. Potter, *Turning Around: The Behavioral Approach to Managing People.* New York: Amacom, 1980. Dealing with people is the issue addressed by this book. It is a very recent statement by the American Management Association on how people operate in organizational settings and how they can be led to accomplish both personal and organizational goals.

Everett M. Rogers and Rekha Agarwala-Rogers, *Communication in Organizations.* New York: Free Press, 1976. This book is a careful statement from the management perspective about what communication ought to accomplish in organizations and about situations in which difficult communication problems are likely to be encountered.

J. Clifton Williams, *Human Behavior in Organizations.* Cincinnati: South-Western Publishing, 1978. This book is written from a psychological perspective.

It is about the range of responses displayed by people confronted with organizational demands and stresses.

Organizational patterns are changing rapidly. To keep in touch with the realities of organizational life demands keeping posted on a rapidly unfolding future. The following books introduce the future as it affects organizational operations.

Gary Dessler, *Organization Theory: Integrating Structure and Behavior.* Englewood Cliffs, N.J.: Prentice-Hall, 1980. Structural and behavioral points of view are integrated to introduce contemporary organizational issues and to project their consequences into the immediate future.

Frank Feather (Ed.), *Through the 80s: Thinking Globally, Acting Locally.* Washington, D.C.: World Future Society, 1980. The result of the combined efforts of over a hundred authorities, this book is the result of the First Global Conference on the Future in Toronto held in the summer of 1980. It covers the major issues confronting governments and organizations and has a particularly strong section on managerial responsibilities in the future.

Neil Postman, *Crazy Talk, Stupid Talk.* New York: Delacorte, 1976. Although this book is not strictly about the future or about organizations, it introduces the major problems that humans confront in their communication and suggests that impending problems in society might well be remedied by changes in communication styles.

As this book was going to press, there was a flurry of articles in the business magazines about Japanese management and how it was superior to American practices. An excellent and brief overview can be found in Steve Lohr, "Overhauling America's Business Management," *New York Times Magazine,* January 4, 1981. The current bestseller on the issue is William Ouchi, *Theory Z: How American Business Can Meet the Japanese Challenge.* Reading, Mass,: Addison-Wesley Co., Inc, 1981. The July, 1981 Issue of *Technology Review* (Vol. 83, No. 7) contains a brief review by Robert Cole, "The Japanese Lesson in Quality" with comments by Ouchi.

A definitive review of how communication training affects hiring and advancement in organizations, including a review of the communication skills required in many occupational designations, is found in James H. McBath and David T. Burhans, Jr., *Communication Education for Careers.* Falls Church, Va: Speech Communication Association, 1975.

Chapter 2

Questions and Responses

DEFINITION OF INTERVIEWING

"Interviewing is when someone tries to make you say something that makes you look bad." "Interviewing is the way they psych you out to see what is wrong with you." "Interviewing is how they get you to expose yourself so they have a reason for not giving you the job." "Interviewing is what cops and reporters do when they want to get the goods on somebody." "Interviewing is like what they did in the Spanish Inquisition, only I want to say that interviews are worse for me than the Spanish Inquisition. When people ask me questions, I hurt." These are some answers given by students to the question, "Interviewing is . . . ?"

The preceding attitudes may not be typical, but many people do believe that interviews are generally tense situations. It is very hard to find people who like to be interviewed. It is equally hard to find people who know how to interview well. It is the purpose of this chapter to offer you some techniques for performing interviews as well as methods for performing successfully in an interview.

Most organizational communication textbooks describe interviewing by identifying types. See Randall Capps, Carley H. Dodd and Larry James Winn, *Communication for the Business and Professional Speaker*. (New York: Macmillan Publishing Co., Inc., 1981), pp. 81-89. The authors identify an information-giving interview, an

information-gathering interview, an employment selection interview, a disciplinary interview, a problem-solving interview, an employment interview, a job appraisal interview, and a data-gathering interview. These designations are useful for classification purposes. In this chapter, however, we intend to provide you with some techniques designed to accomplish the basic purposes of interviews. For this reason, it is important for you to understand some of the basic features of interviews as well as the contexts in which they can occur.

First, the definition: *Interviewing is a process in which one person seeks information from another by means of preplanned questions.* When people sit around and exchange such questions as "Where are you from?" "What kind of work do you do?" and "Do you like the weather?" they are not interviewing. Interviewing is a *persuasive* process in which skillful interviewers employ carefully worded questions to motivate someone with information to present it in a useful way. Sometimes the answers to questions are embarrassing, but embarrassment is not the purpose of an interview.

● *Interviewing is not an adversary process.* What goes on in a court of law is not interviewing. It is "examination" and "cross-examination." Its purpose may be to elicit information, but it does not proceed from the same assumptions as an interview. The questioning in a court of law follows a carefully regulated set of rules. Violation of the rules invalidates the questioning. Nonpertinent answers are ruled out. Sometimes questioners are permitted to regard the respondents as hostile and to use pressure in their questions to

force the proper information out of the respondents. People who do not answer legitimate questions in a court of law are punished, and those who answer falsely are punished severely.

• *Interviewing is a voluntary process* that proceeds from four simple premises:

1. There is a person who needs information.
2. There is another person who has information.
3. The two of them agree to meet and engage in an interview in which the individual seeking the information asks a series of planned questions of the person who has the information.
4. The quality of the information received is no better than the quality of the questions asked.

The person being interviewed is entitled to ask for some exchange for providing the service. In employment interviews, the chance of being hired is sufficient motivation. In other cases, the *quid pro quo* or exchange may be nothing more than feeling useful or earning respect, although often experts are paid for responding to questions. Generally, some negotiation must be conducted to convince the person with the information that there is some good reason for giving up the time it will take to answer the questions.

KINDS OF INTERVIEWS

Interviewing is most commonly associated with job seeking. Although this is an important use of the interview, there are many other purposes for which systematic questioning can be used to obtain useful information.

• *Experts can be interviewed for their unpublished ideas and attitudes.* People whose job it is to discover knowledge are usually quite careful about what they put in print. Before an article is submitted or a book written, the expert must test and retest the information and ideas until they are able to withstand critical reading by other experts. However, an expert's thoughts in process can be very valuable, for applications and examples can be discovered and new ideas can be considered tentatively.

Congressional committees rely heavily for information on testimony from experts at formal hearings. The congressional hearings

widely broadcast on television are not typical of the regular congressional business of information gathering. In most cases, the writing of a law is preceded by the systematic examination of facts, much as we advise in Chapter 7. One of the most efficient ways of getting current and important information is to invite people who have it to come and be questioned. The expert functions as a kind of oral library. There is virtually endless information she or he could give, but the quality of the information is determined by the expertness with which people ask questions.

• *People can be interviewed to explain or clarify something they have previously said.* Not everything put into print is easily understood, nor can everything be said accurately on the first try. Sometimes people are unclear about the meaning of memos and reports. In these cases, it is useful for the people involved to get together and ask questions. Direct questioning can correct the record and help achieve accuracy or make it clear that the person who wrote the document was unclear about what he or she wrote in the first place.

• *Experts can be asked to offer opinions on technical matters on which they have not previously commented.* It is often useful to have technical or scientific personnel attempt to apply their knowledge to the solution of practical problems. The process of consulting characteristic of contemporary business is nothing more than experts answering questions put to them by companies (for which, incidentally, they often command very high fees.) Sometimes it is very helpful to solicit recommendations about the choice of options from people who have been successful in similar circumstances. For example, when designing a factory, it is not unusual to call in various kinds of specialists to share their experiences in designing other factories. Experts can also be used to resolve conflict. Sometimes people argue simply because they do not have enough information to break the deadlock. The expert can be asked if there is any information that would take a dispute out of the realm of conjecture and move it into the domain of certainty.

• *People who express opinions can be asked to provide the data on which they based their opinions.* Experts are sometimes wrong. Often, well-informed people can offer opinions that appear peculiar, dangerous, or just unclear. By inquiring about the data on which the opinion is based, you can develop your own opinion about whether the expert is coming from "left field" or operating from sound and intelligent premises.

• *People from whom information is not commonly forthcoming can be asked for their ideas.* Often a piece of information that is desperately needed, or the best idea for the solution to a problem, lies with an "ordinary" employee whose opinions are not commonly solicited. By devising ways of asking questions of these employees, as well as by providing channels into which they can put information (like a suggestion box), an organization can encourage them to participate more directly in the exchange of information.

• *People cooperate best when they have had a say in what they are doing.* One of the best ways to get people to commit themselves to participating in activities and projects is to give them a hand in planning and designing them. An interview process that reassures people that their ideas and interests are being considered is highly persuasive. It tells them that they are important enough to be considered and that their contributions are welcome. As a result, even when the final program is not at all what they wanted, they seem to participate energetically in implementing it.

• *Interviewing is widely used by social scientists to obtain the data from which they draw conclusions.* The ever-present opinion poll is a form of interviewing. So is the census. The "ratings" that determine success or failure for television programs are based on

forms of interviewing. Sociologists and social psychologists, particularly, use a variety of interview devices to get information on such topics as normal behavior, political choices, product preferences, sexual behavior, and economic plans. This kind of interviewing operates on the basis of a "protocol," that is, a standard list of questions that are asked of everyone so that the answers are cast in the same form. Interpretive and numeric techniques can also be used to derive information from the answers. Written self-report questionnaires are also a form of this kind of interview process. The principles and techniques of using these kinds of interviews are taught in courses in research methodology. The process is very complicated and should be used with great caution.

• *Interviewing is used to facilitate the selection of employees.* This use of interviewing is considered in a separate section later in this chapter. However, employment interviewing is based on the same principle as all other forms of interviewing, that is, that the quality of the answer is shaped by the quality of the question.

THE INFORMATION SEEKING INTERVIEW

There are two major problems in any kind of information-seeking interview. First, you must be sure the person you interview has the information you want, and second, you must be sure that your questions will get the information you seek. Interviewing is carefully restricted by the available time. Hardly anyone worth interviewing will give you all the time you want. Most of the time you will have to get everything you are after in half an hour or less. Therefore you must carefully consider the questions you ask and the order in which you ask them.

The time you spend analyzing your respondent and the situation in which you will interview him or her will have high payoff. Employment interviewers, particularly, must be very careful in designing questions because they are now regulated by the Equal Employment Opportunity Laws, and inappropriate questions can cost the company considerable money in lawsuits. Because employment interviewing is competitive, the same questions may be asked of every candidate so that comparisons can be made.

Information-seeking interviews are not competitive in the same way. In those interviews, the questioner fights the clock. For that

reason, you must decide what kind of an answer you need to get so that you can phrase the question accordingly. If you have to ask the same question three or four different ways before you get what you want, you are not using your time effectively.

There is no guarantee that your subject will know what you want; therefore you must guide her or him through your questions. If you want technical details, for example, you must ask technical questions. If, for example, you want an expert to tell you something in particular about the details on which he based a conclusion, you must pinpoint the question and ask about the substance of his work. "Tell me more about the information on which you based your conclusion" will not get you what you want, except by accident.

If the respondent answers your questions in excessively technical language, you may not be able to use the information. If the respondent answered with "I used a multidimensional scaling procedure and derived factors through a varimax rotation and then worked discriminant analysis into the paradigm," you might wish you had never asked a question. If, on the other hand, you asked, "Can you explain how you identified and named the factors you reported in your conclusion?" you might get the answer you want. In order to get what you want, you must be sure that your question pushes the answer into the proper form. Keep in mind the following questions to guide the development of your interview protocol:

1. What information do I need?
2. Who has the information?
3. How can I persuade that person to provide the answers?
4. How can I phrase the questions to get the answers I want?

The preparation process consists of three parts:

1. The selection and analysis of the respondent and the situation.
2. The preparation of the questions.
3. The use of effective interview technique.

The following questions will be useful in helping you to plan your interview.

1. How much time is allotted to me by my respondent?
2. How long would it take to get a proper answer? How many questions can I get in?

3. Where will the interview take place? Is there anything in that situation that will interfere with asking and answering questions? If there is, how can I overcome it or compensate for it?
4. Are interruptions likely? How can I make up for the time lost during interruptions?
5. How communicative is my respondent? Does he or she talk fluently or respond in monosyllables? What are the chances that she or he will trap me into a digression?
6. What can I offer my respondent as compensation for his or her time and effort? Is he or she likely to be concerned about being threatened or embarrassed?
7. How will I keep records of my answers?

The answers to these questions should help you anticipate the problems you may experience during the interview. If you recognize the chance that things may not go smoothly, you can focus more intensely on the careful phrasing of your questions, and you can establish priorities so that you can be sure to ask your most important questions first. You must also understand that your respondent may have some preferences in the way that she or he wishes to present the information to which you might have to adapt. It also helps to know how communicative your subject is. Chances are you will have to try the first question a few times before you accommodate to your respondent's style. You should then be able to adapt the subsequent questions. Most interviewers prepare "probes," that is followup questions that gently prod the respondent toward the information they are seeking. Employment interviewers must be very cautious in their probing, however. If they ask one candidate questions not asked of others, they may violate fair employment regulations. Thus planning probes is a matter of real concern. In most cases, probes are nothing more than simplified and focused repetitions of the original question.

It is important to have a good idea of what a satisfactory answer might sound like. A general question like "Whom did you study and how?" might get a long, drawn-out answer. If, however, you know the specifics you want, you could ask, "What categories did you group your respondents into? How many were there? Where did you interview them? How many questions did you ask?" Such questions can help your repondent select the information most useful to you.

You should exercise care in selecting the type of question you ask. Short questions that can be answered "yes" or "no" usually do not result in much information. Excessively broad questions are not use-

ful either, as they permit the respondent to take any direction she or he chooses, usually a direction not useful to you. The most productive types of questions are short-answer forms. For example:

> UNPRODUCTIVE: Did you interview eyewitnesses?
> Tell me about how you conducted your investigation?
> PRODUCTIVE: Please describe your sample: that is, what categories of people did you question, and how many were in each category?
> What questions did you ask? Do you have a copy of the list?

You can then prepare probes to ask why each component of the sample was selected or what the purpose of each question was.

If you know a little about your respondent's communication style, you can adapt your questions and probes accordingly. However, if your respondent is a total stranger, you may have to prepare different sets of questions, one set for a talkative person and one set for a reticent person, one for a person who beats around the bush, another for a person who is very direct. Once you discover the response style, you can shift to the most promising set of questions.

It is important to anticipate potential interruptions. If your respondent is ordinarily located in a noisy place, try to find a location where you don't have to compete with external noise. If your interviewee is constantly interrupted, you will have to pace your question so that you can get faster and shorter answers. Interviewees will rarely cut off their regular phone calls for an interviewer, so you must simply prepare yourself for not having all of the time you were allotted.

Finally, keep uppermost in mind that your respondent is doing you a courtesy by making time for you. Even if your respondent is being paid for his services, you must be respectful of his time. One way to show your consideration is to guarantee your subject that you will prepare a transcript of the interview so that she or he can check it for inaccuracies and incompleteness. This means that as quickly as possible after the interview, you must write up your notes and prepare a neat draft for the respondent to review. This kind of offer serves two purposes. First, it makes your respondent feel more confident in you, and second, it gives you a greater guarantee of accurate information. Answers to questions in interviews are sometimes given off the top of the head, and consequently, a careful editorial

review of a transcript provides the greatest guarantee of fairness to your respondent and accurate information for yourself.

Your first problem is to discover the most important questions. You can do this best by specifying what answers you need. Next, prepare a separate question for each component of the answer. For example, if you want to know *where* a specialist got his or her data, start with multiple-choice questions:

1. Did you get your information from observations, interviews, or a review of literature?
2. What and where did you observe? Whom did you interview? What literature did you review?
3. Did you perform an experiment? What was your hypothesis? How did you test it? What was your conclusion?

Make sure your questions follow a logical progression. If you jump around in your questioning, you may confuse your respondent, or worse, he or she may become suspicious that your purpose is to confuse.

If you are concerned about the qualifications of the authorities cited, you can have probes prepared about their background and training, but be sure to ask the probes following the main question about the authorities. If you return to it later, you will throw your respondent off the track. If you are dubious about anything that may be in print, make sure that you get a full citation so you can go and look it up. Whatever your doubts, it is not useful to argue with the person you are interviewing. The minute you confront your respondent about anything, you forfeit the remainder of the interview. Your purpose is not to prove her or him wrong, but to get information. If you feel that the information is erroneous, you can make this comment when you put it to final use.

It is useful to write out your questions. Sometimes it helps to send them in advance so your respondent will be prepared. In fact, the respondent may have some written materials for you that would spare you the necessity of asking some of your questions, enabling you to focus on other questions. It flatters your respondent when you show that you have prepared carefully for the interview. It is annoying to someone if you appear unprepared and incoherent in your questioning. Be sure to write out your probes following the main questions you ask.

Avoid making statements and asking your respondent to agree or disagree. If you have preconceptions about what your respondent ought to be saying, try to lay them aside for the purposes of the interview. It may be convenient for your respondent simply to agree with you, but your statements may shape the interview to suit your wishes, and thus you may sacrifice accuracy and honesty. Your interview will be short enough as it is, so asking the subject to ratify your ideas will be a waste of valuable time.

Avoid challenging the respondent. If you say to her or him, "Give me one good reason for believing your conclusions," the situation is no longer an interview but an argument. It is not necessary for your respondent to know your biases, and you will be most effective if you can avoid making any commitment during the interview at all. A respondent who thinks you are against him or her may restrict the information given or even deliberately mislead you. A respondent who thinks you are on his or her side may stack the deck to suit your biases. Loaded questions like "When did you stop falsifying your data?" signal the interviewee to stop cooperating.

Be sure to have some plan for recording the answers you get. Making a tape recording is most accurate, but it is not courteous to bring in a recording device unless your respondent gives permission. Furthermore, even if your subject is willing to be taped, audio machinery is sometimes very intimidating, and taped interviews frequently seem stilted and artificial. A person who believes he or she is talking for posterity is much more apt to restrict the information given. People tend to be very tense if they think someone else will hear their errors.

Jotting down notes is the most useful method. If you have questions prepared in advance, you can anticipate the form of the answers and prepare worksheets so that your notes can be recorded with the fewest possible moves. Try not to look away from your subject when she or he is responding. It is very distracting to a person answering interview questions to look at the top of your head while you are trying to write a verbatim transcript of his or her remarks.

Don't rely on your memory. Only in the extreme case where note taking completely throws your respondent should you wait to make notes, but if you wait, be sure to write your notes as soon as possible after the interview. The transcript procedure protects you from inaccuracy. Arranging to have your respondent review a transcript also removes some of the pressure from note taking and enables you to listen more attentively to the responses.

If the subject is willing to check your transcript, this is like giving you additional interview time. As the respondent checks the record, she or he may also give you further information. When you transmit your record of the interview, be sure it has been typed neatly. It is customary to note places where you were unsure of what the respondent said or to call his or her attention to places where his or her further comments are essential.

Once you have prepared the questions you want to ask, make a quick check to see if there is any other way to get the answers. There is little sense in using valuable interview time to get information that is already available. It is not fair to impose on someone's time only for a review of what she or he has written elsewhere. The interview should be used only to get information you cannot get elsewhere and to have new ideas opened up for you. The hope is that your respondent will tell you something important and unexpected. If you confine the interview to a review of what he or she has already said, the chances of getting new information are materially reduced. By the same token, it is also important not to permit yourself to be distracted by new information that has nothing to do with the information you are seeking. Sometimes respondents can make irrelevancies seem so interesting that it isn't until the interview is over that the questioner discovers that she or he did not fulfill the purpose of the interview.

The interview situation is tense for both parties. Regardless of how much goodwill there is, the respondent runs the risk of being embar-

rassed, and the questioner may be frustrated by not being able to accomplish his or her goal. For that reason, maximum courtesy must prevail between interviewer and respondent.

Respect for time is most important. If you want to have access to the respondent again, it is particularly important that you come on time and leave when your respondent indicates that the interview is over. In fact, it is useful to end the interview a minute or two early so that farewells do not further interfere with your respondent's schedule. You will need to pay attention to civil greetings but be careful not to get involved in random small talk that might intrude on time better spent in the interview itself.

It is unethical to use interview time for ulterior purposes. Some unscrupulous investigators attempt to use interviews to obtain confidental information. They depend on inadvertent slips or on what they can pick up on the periphery of the situation, much as an investigator does. The ethical code that prevails, however, is that the respondent should know the purpose of the interview and should have the privilege of withholding some information and providing information "off the record" that is, for the benefit of the interviewer but not to be published.

The respondent's wishes about how she or he is to be identified should also be respected. She or he may wish to be known by name and title, but sometimes respondents ask to be identified only as "a reliable source," or by some other euphemism. Sometimes interviewers do not want their names mentioned and want to be identified merely as "an officer of the company" or "a professor of biology." Questioners who violate this convention usually find themselves unable to get other interviews.

The preceding sounds much more ominous than it is. Most information that is exchanged in interviews is not incriminating or embarrassing. Most of it is technical and generally uninteresting to the public at large. However, because interviews are characterized by the unexpected, the questioner must maintain a constant watch for controversial or provocative material and take care to protect it by discussing with the respondent how he or she wants it released, or if he or she wants it released at all.

Avoid badgering your respondent. A private interview is not a courtroom cross-examination or a session of "Meet the Press." Whether you agree with your respondent or not, you have no right to harass or argue. Sometimes respondents can be pompous, foolish,

or even insulting to the interviewer. Still there is no place for attack or arguement, as nothing will be gained even if you win.

If you are responding to an interview, you need to understand your privileges.

The interview should be conducted calmly, with as few digressions as possible. You may be tempted to engage in social conversation with your subject, but if you do, it will take time from the interview. And as a final note, respect whatever rule on smoking your respondent appears to have. If there are no ashtrays visible and she or he does not light up, you should curb your urgency. Do not even ask if you can smoke. In most cases, nonsmokers find that question intimidating.

1. If you are a public figure, there is no way to escape being interviewed.
2. If you are paid to give information, then you can anticipate being questioned.
3. Before you volunteer for an interview, be sure you know the questioner's purpose and be sure that you can be of some use. There is no need for you to take time to answer questions that will turn out to be irrelevant.
4. You are obligated only to answer the investigator's questions. You need not struggle to find out what information the questioner wants.
5. If there is something you think is important to say, you have the right to ask the interviewer to listen to you.
6. You have the right to ask for a transcript. Both you and your questioner are obliged to be accurate, and you have a particular right to be represented accurately.

THE EMPLOYMENT INTERVIEW

Employment interviewing is a delicate process. Even before the Equal Employment Opportunity Act, employment interviewers were responsive to the tension and stress characteristic of job seeking. With the coming of equal-opportunity hiring, interviewers were required to police themselves to guarantee fairness or run the risk of lawsuits or prosecution. Employment interviewers must be professionals. They must prepare their questions so as to serve the interests of their organization and to comply with the law, and their style of questioning must not discriminate among the interviewees. It is par-

ticularly important to treat all candidates alike. This means that they should be asked the same questions, preferably in the same setting. Sometimes, in large companies where several people are interviewing, the sameness in the situation cannot be maintained, but identical questions can be used by a number of interviewers. Above all, the interviewer must avoid forbidden ground under Title VII, of the Equal Employment Opportunity Act, which deals with ensuring that rights to employment are not abridged for reasons of race, age, national origin, sex or marital status.

To a degree, equal-opportunity hiring makes it difficult for interviewers. On the other hand, maintaining constant conditions ensures fairness in the interviewing process and usually results in good hiring decisions. Hiring becomes something like a controlled experiment: the people who evaluate the responses need not agonize about the effects of unusual circumstances because they are comparing candidates reasonably, under the same conditions.

An employment interviewer should be entirely clear on what the company is looking for. Questions should be carefully selected to help evaluators to obtain information not included on the application blank, on the résumé, or in reference letters. Some interviewers act like voyeurs. They shoot from the hip with questions like, "What do you really think of yourself?" or "Do you really see yourself doing any good in the world?" Questions like this are supposed to gain information about the character and personality of the respondent. Unfortunately character and personality are so complicated that adequate judgments probably cannot be made based on the limited time available in an employment interview. As a matter of fact, reference letters usually point to flaws in personality and character, for they commonly report misconduct or blatant unpleasantness. Questions seeking information about personality and character should be avoided unless the interviewer can specify and defend his or her judgment of what a good answer would be.

Questions about life history are answered on the application blank and the résumé. Interviewers are not allowed to ask questions about marital status, racial or ethnic background, religious affiliation, or family status or anything that would reveal information on which biased decisions could be made. The application blank provides an employment history and a school record, both of which can be corroborated, if necessary. Job descriptions and rates of pay can also be checked. People who act as references may be asked for statements

on quality of performance, and employers may solicit information from former supervisors or teachers, provided they stay within the restrictions of the Buckley Amendment which guarantees people access to their employment records. (Prospective employers can solicit and obtain a waiver of this right on references letters, and it is common practice for employers to alert reference-letter writers to the fact that their letters may be available to the candidate.) The most cogent advice to offer employment interviewers is to find out enough about the law so that they can avoid breaking it.

Useful Information from an Employment Interview.

An employment interview can give you a sense of how the candidate responds to social stress. If the job requires meeting the public or is characterized by tense social situations, it is important to know how well the candidate behaves under pressure. All candidates should be able to meet and greet their interviewer comfortably and exchange the usual polite remarks at the opening of the interview.

The interview can also be used to check general oral skills. The candidate should be able to sustain conversation, to respond to questions in something more than a monosyllable, and to sustain talk without a great number of "and, uh," and "y'know" interruptions. Furthermore, the candidate should be able to discuss his training or past experience. A good job interviewer can use some open-ended questions to get a sense of communication facility, for example,

1. What were the most controversial issues in your specialty that you studied at school? What is your point of view and why?
2. What is your attitude toward the . . .? (The questioner should select some well-known controversy in the area in which the interviewee is seeking a position.)
3. How would you handle a situation like this? (Outline a relatively common problem situation in the area in which the candidate is seeking a job.)

Questions like these will enable the interviewer to assess how competent in communication and how informed she or he is about the ideas of the professional or technical field.

Interviewers can also gather general information about the subject's interests and commitment to the community. Questions like "What do you do in your spare time?" or "What community activities are you involved in?" will give some insight into the range of the candidate's interests. It is also important to get information about the candidate's attitude toward the company and toward work, in general. Questions like the following will provide indications of whether the candidate is risk- or security-oriented, has done his or her homework about the company, and has a good sense of his or her own abilities.

1. What would you like to know about our company?
2. What kind of supervision suits you best? What form do you prefer criticism to take?
3. What particular qualifications do you have that will contribute to your success on the job?
4. What company benefits are most important to you?

The attitude the interviewer takes toward the candidate is particularly important. He or she must keep in mind that job seeking is a painful experience, especially for those who are looking for their first job. For that reason, exceptional courtesy and tact are required. The employment interviewer is powerful enough to destroy a person's chance at a good job. There is nothing Title VII of the Equal Employment Opportunity Act can do to prevent tension from injuring the ability of a job seeker to present herself or himself well. Subtle differences in the manner of asking questions cannot be detected unless the interview is videotaped, and even then, it is difficult to connect them causally to the candidate's responses. Regardless of their attitude toward the candidate, ethical interviewers try to remain supportive of her or him throughout the interview. It is impossible for the interviewer not to have an attitude toward the interviewee, but a professional interviewer will be able to maintain the same demeanor to all. The questioner should be very careful to make sure the candidate understands each question, and to allow sufficient time for the candidate to say everything she or he thinks is necessary.

Sometimes attempts to put the candidate at ease backfire. Self-conscious jokes that do not evoke laughter can increase tension. References to what the candidate is wearing or the candidate's hometown can be embarrassing. There is little point to discussing the nice restaurant in the candidate's hometown, particularly when it is possible that the candidate never had enough money to go there. Topics other than those relevant to the interview proper are best avoided.

The most important part of the interview comes before the first candidate appears. The interviewer and those who are to judge the results must have a clear idea of what constitutes an acceptable answer to the questions that are asked. Job candidates are not trained seals charged with performing before an unresponsive audience. Interviewing designed to prod and provoke the candidate is archaic and unproductive. In order to compare candidates fairly, the interviewer should be briefed on what to consider in her or his evaluation of candidates. For example, if the interviewer asks the candidate what he or she thinks of a particular professional issue, the following criteria could be specified:

1. The candidate will demonstrate that he or she has heard of the issue.
2. The candidate will think for a minute before answering.
3. It is desirable for the candidate to ask the interviewer some questions either about the situation or about the kind of comment the interviewer wants.
4. If the candidate offers an opinion, he or she will offer at least one piece of evidence to support it.

If the candidate is asked, "What form do you prefer criticism to take?" the criteria might be:

1. The candidate will demonstrate that she or he understands that employees are criticized on occasion.
2. The candidate will be able to cite one example of criticism that she or he finds helpful and one example of harmful criticism.

The necessity of defining criteria for judging answers will help interviewers confine themselves to questions that produce important information and will deter them from violating the candidate's privacy.

Ways to Do Well in Job Interviews

From the applicant's point of view, an interview is an extraordinarily tense situation. Her or his self-esteem is on the line, and success or failure has important economic consequences. The typical candidate knows, intellectually, that she or he is not going to be offered every job applied for, but hope springs eternal, and any rejection, even for a job one doesn't really want, can be depressing. An interview need not be a spontaneous event, however. The candidate can prepare for it in a number of ways.

Preparing a Good Résumé. There are a number of books and articles that can help you in preparing a résumé. In Chapter 9 of this book, we present with a model résumé. Your résumé is your first advertisement. It must be appealing and informative but not overpowering. It is important that you not oversell yourself and make claims about your competency on which you cannot deliver. The résumé contains the basic information that is found on any application blank. Obtain a copy of a typical application blank before you compose your résumé, and use it as a guide to the information you include.

1. Provide personal information like your address and phone number. Be sure to include an alternate phone number if there is a possibility that no one will be available to answer your phone during working hours. Employers will not normally call you in the evening.
2. Do not provide information excluded under equal-opportunity provisions. Employers are not permitted to seek information about age, marital status, religion, race, or health (unless it is relevant to the job).
3. If you have been in military service, offer a brief statement about your branch and the nature of your discharge.
4. Present a brief employment history, including the name and address of each employer, the type of work you did, and the name of a person who can verify your work record. Some applications ask for the amount of your salary and your reason for leaving. Most companies check this information carefully, so be sure you are accurate on both your résumé and the application blank.
5. Offer a complete record of your schooling, starting with high school. Provide the name and address of the school and designate someone who can verify the information. State the degree

obtained, the date, and your major and minor where important. Be sure to make a special note of any training that particularly qualifies you for the job for which you are applying.

6. Provide the names of three references: a work reference, a school reference, and a character reference. Indicate that more references can be supplied, if this is the case. Be sure to ask your references' permission to use their names.

7. Summarize your community service and activities, but exclude any that might identify your race or religion. Make note of special accomplishments and honors, and anything else relevant to the job for which you are applying.

It is worth the money to have a professional résumé service help you to prepare this document, as it represents your first contact with a prospective employer and makes the difference in whether you will be invited for an interview. It is often persuasive to prepare an individualized résumé for specific jobs in which you are particularly interested. If the prospective employer recognizes that you have done this, she or he may be more inclined to give you an interview.

Obtaining Information About the Company. One of the important things you can do in an interview is to show some knowledge about the company interviewing you and to be able to ask some questions about it. ("What does the company do?" is not a good question because it could be asked about any company. "When did you begin manufacturing the L-44 product?" is a good question because it is specific to the company and shows some sophistication on your part.) Virtually every interviewer asks, at one point or another, "What would you like to know about our company?" A good answer to this question is very persuasive. You should be able to ask something about products, distribution policy, or financing, or to refer to anything newsworthy about the company.

1. You can get information about the size of the company, its financing, its type of business, and its form of organization both from company stockholders' reports and from references like the *Thomas Register* or *Dun & Bradstreet.*

2. The advertisement that led you to apply for the job should specify the position available. You should be prepared with questions about what skills are required, what conditions you

would work under, how you would be supervised, and what the training period consists of.

3. Information about possible relocation and travel should be available. If you have a preference about relocation and travel, you should state it, but only if it would determine whether or not you would take the job, if offered.

4. You are entitled to ask about chances for advancement, pay increase and training opportunities. You can also inquire into turnover in the position. If there has been a "revolving door" in this particular job, you should ask why.

5. It usually impresses interviewers if you can ask intelligent questions about the financial stability of the company and can inquire about future expansion plans. Check *Fortune Magazine, Business Week, The New York Times,* and *The Wall Street Journal* for a few months preceding your interview to see if the company has made news. If it has, be sure to ask about it or mention it to demonstrate that you are interested in the company. To get an idea of the company's size, check the *Fortune 500* list.

6. You should ask something about company benefits. Most companies have standard packages, and excessive attention to benefits may convey the impression that you are excessively security-conscious. On the other hand, benefits like tuition payments for professional advancement might influence your decision about the job.

Preparing Answers to Interview Questions in Advance. Most interview questions are standard. They differ only in their wording; their content is the same. It is sometimes useful to start interviewing with the companies in which you have the least interest so that you can cultivate skill in giving answers to interview questions. If your school has a placement service, they can usually schedule you for several interviews. Once you have gone through three or four interviews, you will be able to spot the similarities between them. Here are some of the questions most frequently asked in job interviews.

1. What educational achievements in high school or college make you a particularly good candidate for this job?
2. What special qualifications do you have for this job?
3. Why are you particularly interested in this job?

4. What are your hobbies and outside interests?
5. What books have you read recently? What plays and concerts have you attended?
6. What periodicals do you read regularly?
7. What have you learned from your work experience?
8. What special contribution do you think you can make to the company that hires you?
9. How would the job for which you have applied help you to achieve your long-term vocational goals?
10. How have you demonstrated your maturity? Your leadership ability? Your creativity and originality? Your interest in important issues in your field?

Most questions are variations on these themes. Be sure to be equipped with specific statements about what you have learned and done. Name courses, skills you have learned on the job, and special experiences you may have had. Be careful on questions about books, magazines, plays, and concerts. Don't try to bluff; your interviewer has probably done a good deal more than you, and she or he will be able to detect a bluff.

Don't talk about how badly you need or want the job. Your interviewer will not be impressed. Do not talk about how superior you will be to other candidates ("some people might say . . ." is a phrase that should never be used). Be prepared to answer questions about weaknesses in your record. Most interviewers will ask you to justify low grades or explain weaknesses displayed in references.

Confine your answers to the questions that are asked. Your interviewer probably has a good reason for the order of questioning he or she uses. Avoid digressions; if you go off on a tangent, you may suggest to your interviewer that you cannot sustain your attention.

Interviewers will evaluate your general communication skills, including your fluency, your loudness, your expressiveness, your handshake, and whether or not you use jargon ("y'know," "like," and so on). They will check on promptness, responsiveness to social cues, and politeness, particularly at the beginning of the interview, and your ability to adapt to changes in the pace and pattern of the interview. The content of what you say will be evaluated for directness, documentation, economy of expression, and ability to stay on the track. Content will also be examined for whether you know something about the job for which you are applying. A limp handshake, an inability to sustain eye contact, fidgeting, aggressiveness, and excessive shyness will work against you.

Dressing Properly. The first visual impression in an interview is very important. Try to avoid appearing overly casual. Interviewers look for a businesslike demeanor from both men and women. The safest bet is a relatively conservative, but not somber suit.

It is important to avoid communicating unintentional messages. Excessive attention to modishness or a display of any kind that calls attention to sexuality will probably have an unfortunate effect. Although a great deal of advice has been given to women about how to dress, it should be noted the potential employers are also very sensitive to "macho" cues from men. Clothing should not be overly tight. Clean clothes, neatly pressed, and colors nicely blended are most appropriate. The idea is not to distract. If the interviewer notices your clothing at all, it will work against you.

Avoiding Illegal Questions. Review the questions that employers cannot ask. Questions about your mental and physical condition are particularly sensitive. Some companies effectively discriminate against women by raising questions about physical strength and stamina. Inquiries into your emotional condition are sometimes used in the same way. Employers can only ask about physical and mental condition only when they are demonstrably relevant to the particular job.

Interviewers may ask you if you were ever convicted of a crime. They cannot ask if you were arrested or accused. They may inquire into your use of drugs and alcohol. They cannot ask about anything related to national origin, race, or religion. They cannot get such information through devious channels by asking questions about your relatives' citizenship or about what your name was before you changed it. Women cannot be asked for their maiden name.

Women, particularly, must understand that they cannot be asked questions about their marital status, like "Will your relationship with men interfere with the job?" "Are you free to travel?" and "Do you have periodic health problems?" For example, employers cannot ask if a woman's family commitments (children) would prevent her from traveling. If the job requires travel, they can specify this requirement and permit a person to withdraw the application if necessary.

Questions about sexual preference (homosexuality) are not illegal, although some local jurisdictions have ruled them out.

Employers can ask questions about your character and interests.

Illegal questions place you in a peculiar position. If you refuse to answer, the interviewer may see you as resistant or uncooperative. Because it is very hard to prove discrimination, you need to have a personal policy on what you will do if you are asked a question that you need not answer. Merely complying often places you in a compromising position. Before you go to the interview, decide whether you will simply answer if asked or whether you will make a statement about why you choose not to answer. If you take the latter course, the simplest way to handle it is to say, "I would prefer not to answer that question because it is ruled out under the Equal Employment Opportunity Act." Don't confront the interviewer or appear argumentative.

The Notification Procedure

Before you leave an interview, you are entitled to ask how the decision will be made, by when, and how you will be notified. It is not useful to keep calling the personnel department to find out what is happening. If the company gives you a date for the decision, however, and the response is delayed, it is helpful to call and ask if the date has been changed and when you can expect to be notified. If you are offered a job and would prefer to wait until you hear from another, more attractive employer, you will have to be quite diplomatic. Do not tell the employer who offers you the job that there is a job that you would like better. You can ask how long you have to make up your mind. If there is no time allowance, then you must decide whether to take the job or turn it down. Accepting a job and then rejecting it when the preferred job comes through usually works against you. If a period of time is allowed for you to make up your mind, it is entirely legitimate to call the employer you would prefer and inquire when they will make a decision. They may ask if you have been offered another job. If so, you can so inform them. If they do not ask, however, it will work against you in most cases if you tell them you have another job offer and want to know where you stand with them.

There is no way to avoid feeling stress in an interview. You have a great deal at stake. You can help keep your tension under control by being well prepared. Practice job interviewing with others. Ask information of others who have been through interviews. After you have been through a few interviews, you will feel confident in your abilities. We should caution you, however, that the best of interviews rarely compensates for an inadequate record. Attention to accomplishments in the classroom and on the job will provide you with your most persuasive arguments at the interviews to follow.

SUMMARY

Interviewing is a process by which a person seeking information not available elsewhere asks questions of the person who has it. Interviews are used to get information used in planning, preparing, analyzing conditions, and making decisions. They are used extensively in personnel selection and sometimes in research. An interview is a persuasive process in which a questioner seeks to motivate a respondent to provide useful information.

Interviewing can be used to obtain new information, an elaboration of existing information, opinions, and the reasons for opinions. Interviewing is also used to provide a data base for scientific information and to obtain information about prospective employees.

Successful interviewing requires a prepared interviewer. Preparation includes selecting the proper person to ask and structuring questions so that the maximum of useful information is obtained in the available time. The information must be recorded accurately. The respondent may review the transcript to correct the record. Courtesy is an important part of the interviewing process. Because the purpose is to gather information, care should be taken by both parties to avoid contentiousness and embarrassment.

Employment interviewers must take care to stay within the limits of the Equal Employment Opportunity Act. Questions should not ask again for information already on résumés or application blanks. Care should be taken to ask all candidates similar questions under similar conditions, so that fair comparisons can be made. The criteria for judging responses should be specified in advance.

Candidates for employment can prepare in advance by writing a

Table 1. Effective Interview Strategies

Interviewer	Respondent
Be clear in your questioning. Phrase your questions to elicit useful responses. Make sure the respondent understands the question.	Be sure you understand the question before you answer. Ask for clarification when you are unsure. You have the right to refuse to answer illegal questions.
Questions should be related to the topic of the interview. It is especially easy to get off the subject in employment interviews. Irrelevant questions waste time.	If the interviewer wanders from the subject, remind him or her. Do not be tempted to dwell on irrelevancies, however interesting.
Phrase your questions to get the type of answer you want. Don't demand a yes or no answer to a complicated question.	Don't let the way a question is phrased force you into giving an inappropriate answer. Insist on answering to suit your needs. (In employment interviews, answer persuasively.)
Don't argue with the respondent. In an employment interview, particularly, the candidate is not an adversary.	Don't anticipate the interviewer's intent. Don't regard the interviewer as an enemy. Remember that you are providing a service. If the interviewer is rude or contentious, you may end the interview.
Be courteous at all times. Avoid interruptions where possible. The candidate for a job is entitled to attention. In other cases, remember you are there at the respondent's discretion.	Remember that the interviewer's time is valuable. Avoid interruptions. Do not victimize the interviewer. If you run out of time, terminate the interview courteously. In employment interviews, termination is the interviewers prerogative.
Give the subject a chance to review your notes and correct the record. In employment interviews, permit the candidate to explain any black marks on his or her record.	You can insist on the privilege of correcting the record. Ask for a transcript. In employment interviews, be prepared to explain negative aspects of your record.

47

résumé and by rehearsing answers to the questions likely to be asked. The interview is not effective when it becomes a combat.

The respondent's position is always voluntary. Even in an employment interview, the respondent chose to come. For this reason, interviewers must be respectful of the rights and the time of their respondents and must remember that the information they seek is the property of the respondent and that it will be released only through his or her goodwill.

Table 1 gives a summary of effective interview strategies from both the interviewer and the respondent.

READINGS

There are two good sources of information on interviewing technique: John W. Keltner, *Interpersonal Speech Communication: Elements and Structures.* Belmont, Calif.: Wadsworth, 1970. Pages 260–285 present a review of the functions of interviews and provide some formats for asking questions.

Hugh C. Sherwood, *The Journalistic Interview.* New York: Harper & Row, 1969. This book offers a thorough statement of how to prepare for an interview and especially how to probe for important information. Another good book from a journalistic point of view is John Brady, *The Craft of Interviewing.* Cincinnati: Writer's Digest Books, 1976.

Some standard information about employment interviewing can be found on pages 78–96 in Randall Capps, Carley H. Dodd, and Larry James Winn, *Communication for the Business and Professional Speaker.* New York: Macmillan, 1981; and Abne Eisenberg, "Surviving the Interview." In *Understanding Communication in Business and the Professions.* pp. 134–178. This article offers a psychologically based analysis of interview procedures, with emphasis on how people from other cultures must adapt in order to succeed at interviewing. A self-analysis form for preparation is provided.

Detailed information on affirmative action can be found in Jennie Farley, *Affirmative Action and the Woman Worker.* New York: AMACOM, 1979. The author gives a thorough explanation of how affirmative-action legislation has affected recruitment, selection, and training. For detailed information on how effective affirmative-action programs work, check Helen J. McLane, *Selecting, Developing and Retaining Women Executives.* New York: Van Nostrand Reinhold, 1980, pp. 14–35.

The standard books on job seeking and interviewing are Richard Nelson Bolles, *What Color Is Your Parachute?* Berkeley, Calif.: Ten Speed Press, 1978; and Tom Jackson and Davidyne Mayleas, *The Hidden Job Market.* New York: Times Books, 1978.

Chapter 3

The Presentation
of Ideas in Public

THE COMPONENTS OF PRESENTATIONAL SPEAKING

The *Book of Lists,* by David Wallechinsky, Irving Wallace and Amy Wallace (New York: Bantam books, 1978, p. 469) says that "public speaking" is the number one fear of American adults. The idea of speaking in public frightens many people because they believe they will reveal their ignorance or appear foolish to others. Some people are made uncomfortable by being so public. They shy away from presentations because they think public performance would make them look pushy or overaggressive. They prefer not to be quite so visible.

On the other hand, most of us like to influence what goes on around us—at least, to have some power over the things that really affect us. But the only way we can influence events is by being public. People who are not willing to express their ideas publicly cannot complain when their wishes are ignored. Even worse is the frustration of the individual who really wants to have a say, but when speaking out does so poorly that he or she is ignored. More than the fear of embarrassment or discomfort about being too public, the fear of being ignored intimidates most of us into silence.

But poor performance is one thing we can do something about. In order to get people around you to regard you as competent and worth listening to, you must motivate them by skillful talk addressed to their interests as well as your own. People will think of you what you persuade them to think of you. If you appear to be well organized, to present useful information, an to address some problem that concerns your listerners, they will be very likely to accept what you have to say. A competent speaker can be identified by the following characteristics:

• *An idea worth talking about.* You can identify an idea worth talking about by the fact that it relates to concerns of your listeners. A worthwhile idea can be new information, a new interpretation of old information, an evaluation of something that matters, a new way of doing things, a reliable way of doing things, a question that will help people decide intelligently, or a statement that will make people feel good about themselves or committed or ready to do well.

A good idea has appeal to listeners. Just because a speaker thinks an idea is good is not sufficient justification to try to get people to sit and listen to it. Good public speaking is done because the audience needs the ideas. If a speaker insists on talking only about what interests him, the audience will respond accordingly and ignore her or him. If a speaker believes that what interests him or her will also interest an audience, he or she must phrase it in such a way that the audience will be persuaded and convinced that they will benefit from listening. One of the main reasons for failure at public speaking is the attempt of a speaker to force the audience to listen without regard for what their needs are. An idea worth talking about is an idea that matters to the people who listen! Basically, if you promise your audience money, useful information, suggestions for survival or success, or fun, you can be pretty sure that you have an idea worth talking about.

• *Information that supports the idea.* Another way to identify a worthwhile idea is that it does not depend solely on the word of the speaker. Although we are sometimes tempted to accept on faith what speakers say, where dollars and cents are involved, listeners must always be suspicious of what is said to them. Some speakers want us to approve their ideas for their personal gain, and sometimes their gain means our loss. The best way to identify good ideas is that they are based on evidence and intelligent reasoning. Effective speakers are able to justify their opinion, present examples to illustrate their points, and relate what they say to material that is familiar to the audience. In Chapter 4, we will show you how to select and use evidence well.

When you assume responsibility for a block of audience time, you

ompaign is beginning or when an important new product is intro-
uced. A large block of time is mapped out, a dinner or reception is
rranged, and entertainment is provided—all of which focuses on the
nain presentation about the nature of the campaign, its promise and
pportunities, or the merits of the new line. (Sometimes, when a new
roduct is being introduced, these kinds of sessions are used to kick
ff a series of workshop meetings in the technical details and selling
eatures of the new product.)

Proposals

Proposals for new products and services or for major projects are
important features of contemporary organizations. A proposal
itself is really an extended written document. Oral presentation has
the advantage of gathering all interested personnel together in a situation where ideas can be exchanged and the main elements of the
proposal can be made clear. Not everyone is an organization is
affected by innovation in the same way. Holding a meeting at which
proposals are presented orally guarantees that the employees involved have a common pool of information about which they can
talk.

The result of a proposal presentation can be acceptance and
scheduling, total rejection, criticism with a directive to revise, or
referral to a task force or committee. The person presenting the proposal is commonly the one in charge of developing it or is a representation of the group from which it came. The presentation consists
of a statement about the problem the proposal is to solve, the main
components of the proposal, and a defense of its capability. Generally
this is all connected in a forensic pattern, which we discuss in detail
in Chapter 4. Oral proposals are carefully coordinated with written
documents that provide the fine details of the proposal, its defense,
and the plan of operation.

Evaluations

Formal evaluations of people and programs are required so that organizations can discover what should be commended and where the
problems are. Most recommendations for innovations and revisions

must have your best material ready. Even if you are the chief executive officer of a company, you cannot expect your employees to
understand you and believe you if they cannot see a good reason for
doing so. In their eyes, the only reason you would take their time
would be to provide them with something that will enable them to
be better employees and thus, of course, earn more money for the
company. Remember that in the world of work, hardly anyone speaks
spontaneously. Because documentation is so important, be sure to
schedule your speaking so that you have time to prepare carefully.

● *Coherent organization.* Presentations cannot come off the top
of your head. In the late 1960s, it was considered "manipulation" to
plan what you said. Today's speaker plans carefully out of respect
to the audience. The first concern is to make the main ideas clear and
to help the audience understand by carefully organizing the proofs.
Once you have decided on the idea you want the audience to receive
from your presentation, you must organize it so that the idea is
presented clearly, unambiguously, and succinctly, in a form your
listeners can remember. The last element is particularly important, for
sustaining attention to a speech is very difficult unless the audience
can follow it easily. Audiences remember the details of only the
clearest speeches.

must have your best material ready. Even if you are the chief executive officer of a company, you cannot expect your employees to understand you and believe you if they cannot see a good reason for doing so. In their eyes, the only reason you would take their time would be to provide them with something that will enable them to be better employees and thus, of course, earn more money for the company. Remember that in the world of work, hardly anyone speaks spontaneously. Because documentation is so important, be sure to schedule your speaking so that you have time to prepare carefully.

• *Coherent organization.* Presentations cannot come off the top of your head. In the late 1960s, it was considered "manipulation" to plan what you said. Today's speaker plans carefully out of respect to the audience. The first concern is to make the main ideas clear and to help the audience understand by carefully organizing the proofs. Once you have decided on the idea you want the audience to receive from your presentation, you must organize it so that the idea is presented clearly, unambiguously, and succinctly, in a form your listeners can remember. The last element is particularly important, for sustaining attention to a speech is very difficult unless the audience can follow it easily. Audiences remember the details of only the clearest speeches.

• *Intelligibility*. In the simplest possible terms, you are required to talk in a way that your audience can understand. You must use words and phrases that have meaning to your listeners. Slang and jargon will annoy and confuse them. In fact, speaking about highly technical topics or complicated philosophy is pointless. There are some ideas so involved that they can be understood only after a careful reading. Speaking is sometimes designed to inspire. One legitimate objective for a presentation might be to inspire the audience to do some of the reading.

Your words should be guided by the natural language of your listeners. You insult them if you talk to them like children, and you bore them if you try to impress them by demonstrating that you know more than they do. Careful analysis of the audience will help you select the words and phrases best suited to your message.

• *Ability to be interesting*. You can have a great idea, perfectly organized with the best proofs, and phrased to perfection, but if you deliver it in a monotone or say your words as if your mouth were filled with pebbles, the audience will simply stop listening. Speech is an economical way to get ideas to people only if they listen. It is the speaker's obligation to motivate the audience to listen. The only real obligation that listeners have is to be polite. Most people know how to be polite with their eyes open all the time. Speakers are responsible for managing their voices so as to be heard, saying their words so as to be understood, and punctuating their ideas with inflection, facial expression, and gesture so that the audience knows what is important. A display of energy in the delivery of a speech tells the audience that the speaker is interested in them.

• *Quality of performance*. A formal speech is not the place to be chatty and conversational. Actors know that their obligation is to catch the empathy of the audience, to put on a display designed to get and keep their attention, and to keep a distance from them so that they remain respectful. Presentational speakers have essentially the same obligation. They must develop their ideas with the audience's concerns in mind; they must present their ideas in an interesting manner; and they must maintain control over the situation so that the audience does not presume to take over. It is important to acquire training and experience in the basic skills of speech delivery if you expect to become an effective presentational speaker. Preparation is not enough. Preparation plus performance equals presentation!

PURPOSES OF PUBLIC SPEECH IN ORGANIZATIONS

Information

It is often important to an organization that everyone have the same information. The publication of instructions or handbooks makes the information available, but it does not guarantee that people will read it. When there is information that everyone *must* have, a public presentation is the most effective way to be sure that the main points, at least, have been put in front of everyone. It is usually not possible to handle the details in a public presentation, but a speech has the effect of making sure that everyone knows where the details can be found. Furthermore, by making a public presentation, a manager is justified in holding everyone responsible for having the information essential to the performance of his or her job.

For example, such issues as the revision of company benefits, merit-rating procedures, changes in safety regulations, and the institution of time-and-motion studies are often exposed for the first time in an oral presentation to dramatize their importance. Usually the oral presentation is followed by the distribution of reminder sheets and the relevant written documents, like copies of the new regulations, handbooks, instructions sheets, and formal memos giving directions. The oral presentation is used mainly to inform the employees how important it is to have the information and what major changes they can expect in the way things are done.

Inspiration

Occasionally it is important to remind employees how important their work is or to commend them for some meritorious act. Such occasions are used very much as a coach's halftime speech to the players is: as a chance to tell them to "get out there and fight" or "keep up the good work." There is no real information disseminated in speeches like this; instead, they have the effect of underlining the importance of the employees. If the "boss" takes their time to tell them how much she or he thinks of them, then they can be secure in their importance.

Sessions like these are often used for sales forces when a major

compaign is beginning or when an important new product is introduced. A large block of time is mapped out, a dinner or reception is
arranged, and entertainment is provided—all of which focuses on the
main presentation about the nature of the campaign, its promise and
opportunities, or the merits of the new line. (Sometimes, when a new
product is being introduced, these kinds of sessions are used to kick
off a series of workshop meetings in the technical details and selling
features of the new product.)

Proposals

Proposals for new products and services or for major projects are
important features of contemporary organizations. A proposal
itself is really an extended written document. Oral presentation has
the advantage of gathering all interested personnel together in a situation where ideas can be exchanged and the main elements of the
proposal can be made clear. Not everyone is an organization is
affected by innovation in the same way. Holding a meeting at which
proposals are presented orally guarantees that the employees involved have a common pool of information about which they can
talk.

The result of a proposal presentation can be acceptance and
scheduling, total rejection, criticism with a directive to revise, or
referral to a task force or committee. The person presenting the proposal is commonly the one in charge of developing it or is a representation of the group from which it came. The presentation consists
of a statement about the problem the proposal is to solve, the main
components of the proposal, and a defense of its capability. Generally
this is all connected in a forensic pattern, which we discuss in detail
in Chapter 4. Oral proposals are carefully coordinated with written
documents that provide the fine details of the proposal, its defense,
and the plan of operation.

Evaluations

Formal evaluations of people and programs are required so that organizations can discover what should be commended and where the
problems are. Most recommendations for innovations and revisions

start with evaluations. The identification of good performance helps the organization to develop a pool of effective ideas. The identification of a good performer enables the organization to decide who is to be rewarded and considered eligible for advancement. Poor performance, on the other hand, can lead to decisions about transfer, retraining, or, in extreme cases, dismissal, and poor programs may be revised or replaced. Decisions about the quality of personnel or program performance are usually made by individuals or committees based on data presented to them by evaluators. Immediate decisions are infrequent. The most likely outcome of an evaluation presentation is charging a committee to make recommendations for action.

Briefings

Busy executives and supervisors need information. They usually do not have the time to concentrate on extended narratives or complicated reports and explanations. In order to keep posted on current information, they use briefing reports. In a briefing, the person responsible digests the information found in a complicated document and presents its main heading orally. The person presenting the briefing usually knows enough to handle questions from the person being briefed often executives call in department heads to brief them on the events in their departments over a period of time. The person receiving the briefing can then give instructions about which documents she or he wishes to examine more carefully.

Social Events

One responsibility of occupying an important position in an organization is to appear and speak at formal occasions like honor awards meetings, testimonial dinners, and retirement ceremonies, or to serve as toastmaster at major social engagements. These situations are useful in generating goodwill. If done well, the speaker can create a bond between himself or herself and the listeners that will be useful on the job. Presentations of this kind usually consist of standard statements and clichés, but when presented well—and *briefly*—they can generate considerable warmth.

Public Relations

We deal with public relations messages in Chapters 8 and 9. Few organizations are spared contact with the public. There is considerable pressure these days on public agencies to operate under a "sunshine" formula, that is, to have their deliberations open for public observation, and industry is being continually pressured to explain their decisions to the people affected by them. The public is, of course, entitled to know about changes in operations that will affect them. Major expansions or cuts, chemical-waste dumping, pollution, and cuts in budgets all have consequences for the community. Thus every organization designates some people to take the responsibility of presenting public messages.

The public relations message enables the organization to strengthen its position in the community by keeping communication channels open. On the other hand, a poorly done public message can sufficiently alienate the community to imperil the organization's existence. For this reason, very careful attention must be given to public messages. Though most are delivered orally, virtually all of them are based on carefully written documents.

Professional Meetings and Technical Papers

Scientists, engineers, researchers, and university faculties are commonly required to prepare and deliver professional papers to their colleagues at various kinds of meetings. It is important that professional peers exchange current ideas. Publishing is always several months to several years behind the discovery of information, and personal contact enables professionals to question and criticize each other. Associations like the Super Market Institute, the American Medical Association, the American Psychological Association, or the American Management Association provide a variety of opportunities for sharing ideas. Normally these are presented in the form of speeches or the reading of written papers. Participation in these activities is voluntary; however, most professionals and executives recognize that they can recharge themselves by contact with new ideas and by subjecting their own ideas to competent criticism. The preparation of a professional or technical paper is usually the culmination of an extended period of investigation or research. It is a task as painstaking as writing scholarly articles. The advantage of oral presentation is that response can be obtained.

For people who desire more training, you may be interested in participating in national organizations with the purpose of studying communication or providing experiences in communication. Toastmasters International has branches in most cities. Toastmasters provides experience in speaking in a situation which encourages improvement through criticism. The International Platform Association is an organization of professional speakers who share information about trends and conditions in their particular business. The International Communication Association is composed of people who do experimental and behavioral research in communication. The Speech Communication Association of 5105 Backlick Road, #e, Annandale, VA 22003 is an organization of teachers, professional speakers, industrial communicators and research scholars. For information about their activities, write the executive secretary. They can also provide you with information about regional and state organizations of communication professionals.

Orientation and Instructions

Orientation is perhaps the simplest form of oral presentation. Mass training sessions are required when a group of new employees enter the company or when major changes are made that affect large numbers of people. Orientations are generally not as detailed as instruction sessions or briefings. They are conducted for larger groups and are often accompanied by carefully prepared visuals. Many organizations, for example, prepare packaged presentations about employee rights and benefits, with visuals, for presentation at orientation meetings. Many in-house training programs begin with a formal orientation session about the organization's goals for training and the opportunities available. Such diverse events as a high school career day and the guide to the community that the chamber of commerce prepares for newcomers to a town can be considered orientation sessions. Furthermore, with the cutbacks in funding for government in-service training, more and more public agencies are relying on their own personnel to provide training, usually in the form of an orientation and instruction session.

Other Presentational Situations

There are a great many times when formal presentations are necessary. Labor negotiations, for example, provide both sides with a number of opportunities for formal presentations. Even the process of exchanging ideas at the bargaining table can be considered a formal situation, as opening statements, at least, are carefully prepared and presented. Management presentations to employees about the company side of the issue is a particularly ticklish issue, as there are a number of laws regarding unfair labor practices that regulate what can and cannot be said in such a situation.

Executives and professionals are often required to present testimoney about their area of speciality or about organization operations. Often these presentations are given before government committees seeking information to guide in the writing of new legislation. Sometimes these committees conduct investigations into problems. Sometimes you may need to appear to lobby for your point of view. Any presentation before a government body involves careful preparation, which should include rehearsal of both the text of the presentation and answers to the questions that are likely to be asked about it. We will discuss techniques of handling question periods in Chapter 5.

A sales presentation of any kind may be considered a speech, even though the audience consists of only one person. Representing a product or service well requires careful preparation of a presentation using the forensic pattern. The salesperson must overcome resistance by showing the potential customer that there is a problem that can be solved most effectively by the product or service the salesperson represents. Even though there is considerable dialogue between a salesperson and the potential customer, control of the content of the situation rests with the salesperson, the extent of whose preparation often determines the success of the outcome.

At times, you will find yourself opposed to some idea or proposal and will need to prepare a skillful rebuttal. A rebuttal is a formal presentation, although the time you have to prepare is often negligible. Attention to the possible patterns you can use for rebuttal will help you make the rapid preparations you need. We discuss rebuttals in Chapter 5.

YOUR STAKE IN PRESENTATION

• *Every time you speak in public, your reputation is at stake.* Speech is very different from writing. When you write, you have the opportunity to edit and revise, to get it right. When you speak, you must do it right the first time. Any error or foolishness that comes out of your mouth can be used to embarrass you. Once you have said something, it becomes part of the public record. Even if it is not written down or tape-recorded, it is stored in your listeners' memories. That means that you must learn to control what you say.

Speakers in college classrooms are often advised to prepared themselves to deliver extemporaneous speeches. That is, they are told to prepare careful notes and use them as a guide to speech, rather than to write manuscripts or commit a speech to memory. In general, this is good advice. The extemporaneous mode of speaking has the advantage of careful preparation as well as the advantage of facilitating direct contact with the audience. An extemporaneous speaker is not bound to a manuscript or a lectern and consequently can respond and revise based on audience responses.

Extemporaneous speaking should not be confused with impromptu speaking. Impromptu speaking is spontaneous, "off the top of the head," and is generally unorganized and disconnected. Impromptu speaking can be witty, but it is mostly digressive. When well done, it can call attention to the speaker's versatility. Most of the time, however, it is merely distracting and time-wasting. If you are called on to make an impromptu statement, keep in mind the following principles. First, make sure that you confine yourself to the point on which you have been asked to comment. Try not to introduce new ideas. Second, be as brief as you possibly can. Third, don't try to present complicated information. It is possible that what you say will be inaccurate and you will be embarrassed by it later on. Finally, try to keep organized. In the next chapter we will present several modes of organization. Select one and keep it in mind while you make your impromptu remarks. It will help keep you on the track. Try not to be humorous in your impromptu remarks. Attempts at spontaneous humor often fall flat. Some people misinterpret them and take them seriously. Others will tend to de-value your other remarks if your humor fails. Impromptu speaking is usually always risky. Wherever and whenever possible, try to gain the time you need to prepare yourself before you speak.

The kind of preparation done to prepare a manuscript is identical to that required for a good persuasive speech. Unless you are a relatively skilled performer, however, reading a manuscript is essentially boring. Furthermore it denies you the opportunity to be responsive to your audience. Audiences tend to believe that the person who reads to them really doesn't care much about them.

When something very important is at stake or when you must have a completely accurate permanent record of what you have said, then you cannot rely on extemporization. You will need to sacrifice the opportunity to make direct contact with your audience and write out a manuscript and read it. In order to read a manuscript effectively, you must use your voice and body to sustain interest in your message. Even if you lack this skill, when major issues are at stake or when there is an opposition waiting for you to make an error you must use the manuscript in order to control precisely what you say. In Appendix A we will provide you with instructions on how to read a manuscript effectively.

There is a trend in industry and government toward the use of ghost writers for executives and supervisors responsible for a great deal of public speaking. The ghost writer has the difficult task of composing remarks compatible with the executives beliefs, phrased in a style that she or he can handle comfortably. For this reason, a great many companies are now adding speech coaches to their staffs to provide training in effective delivery for those who use ghost-written material.

Presentational skill is necessary whether you read or extemporize. You can acquire that skill through practice. You must, first, be sure that your idea is valuable, and that your presentation is well organized and fully documented. When you phrase your speech, try to do so in harmony with the kind of language you normally use. People sound awkward when they try to use a speech delivery with which they are unfamiliar. A distinguished speech scholar once said that public speaking is really little more than enlarged conversation. In the case of a presentation, try to make conversation with dignity, addressed as directly as you can to your listeners.

● *Each public appearance gives you an opportunity to build good-will, loyalty, credibility, and cooperation.* Public presentation is a two-edged sword. We have already discussed what you can lose. Actually you stand to gain a good deal more than you lose.

People in supervisory or executive positions must be seen by the people they supervise. It is too difficult to contact people one at a time. Furthermore one-to-one contact sometimes traps you into topics and situations that you would rather avoid. Public appearances are not only efficient ways to see your employees, but they enable you to control your appearance so that you can do your best. There need not be any accidents when you present your speech. By combining public appearances with a carefully controlled policy of individual contacts, you can gain a reputation for high leadership skills.

Audiences tend to respond positively to effective public performances. Politicians and evangelists know the impact of good public speaking. There seems to be a contagion effect. If you do well with a portion of the audience, their enthusiasm will be shared by others. Your supporters in the audience can influence those who are neutral commit themselves to your ideas. We do not mean to imply that if you present a speech in an organization, you need to make promises the way a politician does and threaten hellfire and brimstone the way an evangelist does. We are merely saying that there is a style of public talk that influences people to become compatible with organizational goals with a degree of enthusiasm that is very difficult to gain from private conferences. Effective presentational speaking is crisp and terse, direct and simple, designed to give the maximum of information in a minimum of time. People who can do this appear to be credible and reliable, worthy of being leaders.

• *In many organizations, the ability to communicate effectively plays an important role in your advancement.* There are some people who seek careers in which they need not make public contact with others. Anyone who aspires to an executive or supervisory role cannot expect to avoid making speeches. Once you have been designated as an executive of an organization, you become a public figure.

What the supervisor or executive does is important to those who work for her or him. It is important that official leaders be able to display their concern for their employees in public and, furthermore, be able to manage the required planning and committee work, be able to give information and instructions when necessary, and be able to engage in effective human relations with colleagues, employees, and their own supervisors. They must be able to counsel and calm, console, advise, inspire, instruct, and bargain.

Speaking skills appropriate to intimate settings are based on public skills. If public speech is enlarged conversation, conversation is private public speech. The responsibility of being well organized and of supporting your points is as relevant to private as to public contact. In both public and private contact, you are required to control what you say so that it supports organization of goals and objectives. There is very little opportunity in the course of a workday to engage in casual social chitchat. Every public and private move you make will be evaluated in terms of its relationship to the operations of the organization you represent. As an executive, you will have little private life inside the organization. Chance remarks, unplanned humor, or bursts of temper will all work against you. Thus, if you can manage your verbal output, even in situations where you do not normally think about managing it, you will cultivate the kind of style needed to lead an organization. Leadership involves the ability to control responsive communication of the kind characteristic of committee meetings (discussed in Chapter 7), private conferences with personnel (discussed in Chapter 6), and the handling of emergencies (discussed in Chapter 8). Executives tend to observe their employees carefully to discover those with a command of both oral and written communication. Those who appear responsible, accurate, considerate, and cogent in all conditions are the ones selected for advancement.

Even more important than the role communication plays in organizational advancement is the role it can play in developing your own opinion of yourself. One of the hardest things for people to do is to admit errors and correct them. Skill in communication will help you discover what to say and how to act when you discover you have made a mistake and want to correct it. A skillful communicator can be humble. Arrogance is generally a sign of lack of confidence. People tend to evaluate you by what you say. They cannot read your mind, but they watch to see if your words match your actions.

• *"The Good Man Who Speaks Well."* The Roman educator Quintilian wrote several books about the "art" of oratory, that is, about the "good man who speaks well." Public effectiveness, he said, demanded that a person be good, advocate the good, and advocate effectively. Organizational speaking reveals your personal characteristics. Duplicity and deceit sometimes work, but generally the double-dealer is discovered. There is no way to maintain power in an organization without the confidence of the people who work for you. Confidence cannot be bought for money. Any competitor can outbid you. It is personal qualities revealed through the way you talk with others that make the difference in your ability to lead. It is not the purpose of this book to teach you how to become a "good person." However, we can advise you that the decisions made about you by the people you supervise will be crucial to your advancement. If you are not credible to them, you will not be able to lead them. When followers lack confidence in you, they can cut you down. They can fail you and thus make you fail. It is not possible to succeed in an organization by yourself (unless you are the mad genius in the laboratory discovering the secrets of the universe for the company to patent and sell; unfortunately, there is only one of those per company—or less). You need the support of your employees and your peers, and you need to be believable to those above you, who hold the power to move you ahead.

One of the saddest errors made by people who aspire to success is believing that their internal qualities and qualifications will somehow communicate themselves. However, no one that can declare who he or she is without giving evidence. The writer must produce what she has written, the painter must display his work, the composer must have her music played. Sometimes these kinds of works are so powerful in their own right that they earn acclaim. Still, the writer, the artist, and the composer must depend on others to implement their work. The writer must have a publisher, the artist a gallery, the composer an orchestra. Success in an organization is a kind of orchestration of your personality and character displayed through the way you talk with others. If you can win genuine approval, you can achieve relatively permanent success. Aristotle believed that good and true things would triumph over their opposites if they received an equal hearing. Your task is to speak well enough to give yourself and your ideas an equal hearing. With that skill, you can defeat the frauds and build a career that will let you grow to the limits of your ability.

BASIC ISSUES IN THE PREPARATION OF A PRESENTATIONAL SPEECH

Propriety

What you say must be appropriate to your own personality and to the people who will be listening to you. Therefore you must examine your position as a speaker and analyze the audience so that you understand their abilities and needs. Thus you will avoid wasting time. If you speak unnecessarily for fifteen minutes to an audience of one hundred, you have wasted twenty-five work hours. You may be brilliant, but if there is no benefit for your listeners in what you say, you have wasted considerable money. Thus you must establish in your own mind that you are the appropriate person to speak and that the audience will benefit from listening to you.

By *propriety*, we mean that people should speak only on issues and ideas on which they are qualified (or can become qualified).

The decision to speak should grow out of some problem you see related to the job and the needs of the people associated with it. There must be some condition—lack of knowledge, inappropriate attitude, errors in the way things are being done—that can be corrected by speaking. It is not useful to take company time to share your comments about conditions in the world, unless those conditions affect the company and you are going to make a recommendation about what to do about them. Furthermore, if you speak on ideas that are better addressed by other people in the organization, you can make enemies. Leaders in organizations are particularly concerned about their scope of authority, and they resent it when someone intrudes on their prerogatives. Furthermore, if you speak on matters outside your competency, you are likely to make errors and cause more trouble than existed before you spoke.

Anytime you speak on matters that are not legitimate for you, you cast doubt on your competency. There are four questions you must answer before you decide to speak.

1. Is there a situation that public speech will help correct?
2. Do you have the authority to say what needs to be said?
3. Do you have the knowledge and ability to say it?
4. Can you give your listeners a good reason for paying attention to you when you say it?

The decision about when to speak is based on your analysis of whether you must provide information, modify attitudes, or change behavior. If you decide that there is a problem arising from lack of information (for example, the possible effects of the rise in interest rates on the company's inventory), you must present relevant information (for example, alert the salespeople to the fact that they may have more back orders because of reduced inventories). If you decide that there is a problem that comes from an improper attitude or belief (for example, employees are not fastening safety belts before they use the machinery), you may have to urge them to change their attitude (for example, by telling them about the rising number of accidents or about the possibility of losing their jobs). If there is something that must be done to correct a situation (for example, filling out requisition forms incorrectly), then you must give instructions and directives (for example, holding a workshop session on how to fill out the requisitions).

Not all decisions to speak arise out of crises or emergencies. Effective speaking can be done anytime it will help the situation.

Public speaking should not be done at the whim of the speaker. You do not speak when you want to, you speak when you have to: to address a particular situation as we pointed out above, or when you are required to do so by your job assignment (that is, to present periodic reports, to speak at meetings, or to present briefings on your operations).

The organization chart is a guide to your justification to speak. The chart tells you the scope of your authority and shows you where you might interfere with the authority of others. The job descriptions associated with the organization chart advise you of the topics on which you are supposed to be competent to speak. Together, chart and job descriptions should guide you to an understanding about how things ought to be going, so that you can make proper decisions about when a condition is serious enough to warrant speaking. In most cases, you will be able to check your decision to speak with someone who has authority over you. If there is ever any doubt in your mind about whether you have the authority to speak, you must check with a supervisor. If you have doubts about your competency, then you must either prepare yourself or find someone who can

handle the job for you. If you have doubts about whether the situation warrants a speech, you must seek competent advice about the reasonableness of your projection of what a speech can accomplish.

Sometimes situations arise in which no one has clear authority but in which many people are involved. These are the kinds of situations that stir up conflict and that test the patience and human relations skills of leaders. One principle of organizational life is that "nature hates a vacuum." Anytime there are circumstances over which no one appears to have authority, several people will claim it. If you choose to involve yourself in such a situation, you will need to prepare arguments on behalf of your right to be involved. Eventually conflict situations are resolved by a higher authority, and those who appear to be involved merely to seek expansion of power are usually reduced in authority as a result of their illegitimate claims. It is sometimes better to stay out of unclear situations than to risk appearing to be a power seeker.

Finally, the decision about whom to speak to will depend on the reasons you can find for people to listen to you. You must be able to make some kind of clear statement about how the people who listen to you will benefit as a result of hearing you. If the situation cannot be remedied by speaking, it is best not to speak. If there is a more efficient way to handle the situation, you should use it. Only when you can establish that speaking is the most appropriate way to solve the problem should you undertake to speak in public. It may, however, not be clear to your listeners how they will benefit from hearing you. One of your most important tasks in argument, as discussed in Chapter 5, is to establish the ways your audience will benefit from being present.

Audience Analysis

To discover how the audience will benefit from listening to you, you must analyze the audience. The first step in the preparation of any speech is to discover the reason that the audience is to find it important. Even when you are "required" to speak by your supervisors or by the regular schedule of your job, you must still seek a reason for the audience to listen. It is not a sufficient reason to say, "I was told to speak: therefore I will speak." When you are told to speak, you must assume there was a reason, and that this reason has something to do with how your audience will benefit from listening.

Speeches that refer to how the company is growing or to how it is becoming a "household word" are usually "inspirational," but time-wasting. Audiences for these kinds of speeches usually listen for a while, until they are sure there is nothing practical for them to listen to, and then they drift off. One characteristic of employees is that they know how to appear polite when a person in authority is speaking to them. There is a vast difference between looking polite and actually listening. People will listen only to speeches that give them information they need or instructions they must have, and in general that tell them what trouble they will have if they don't listen.

The general good is rarely important. In 1979, however, the employees of Chrysler were very interested in the general good. Although the real action was going in Washington, whether the company got the loan guarantees was very important in preserving the jobs of a great many people. In situations like this, people are highly motivated to listen. They want all the information they can get. There is certainly reason to believe that some companies have "gone under" because they did not give their employees enough information. On the other hand, keep in mind that in recent years speeches to employees have generally meant bad news. It is often useful to schedule an occasional "good news" meeting, for no other reason than to demonstrate that you are sufficiently concerned with

the welfare of the people you supervise to want them to feel happy or optimistic when they can.

By and large, if you can find a way to assure your listeners that what you say will improve their income, improve their working conditions, provide them with more benefits, or protect them from unemployment, you will find intensely interested listeners. If you plan to warn them of impending disaster, it is useful to have two or three suggestions about what they can do to break their fall. If you are talking about very complicated ideas, try to provide some method for them to ask questions or to get detailed information. If you are talking about technical matters, be sure you define terms and develop a common language before you get too far into the speech. In general, you analyze your audience to find out

1. How they will benefit from listening to you.
2. What they know about the topic.
3. What they believe about the topic.

The following questions will help you get enough data so that you can make these decisions:

1. What does the audience think of you? Are you the boss, a technical authority, a person in whom they have confidence? Who are you in relation to them? What experiences have they had with you in the past? Think of the best and worst job you ever did in speaking to them, and try to distinguish between the two so that you know what to go on doing and what to avoid. If you are new in the position, try to find out something about what your predecessor did. By reviewing history, you can avoid errors.
2. What rewards and punishments do you have to pass out? What have the audience got from you in the past? Do you have a reputation for being openhanded? Has your past pattern been to bring bad news? It is not strategic to use a situation in which rewards are commonly given out to present bad news, and vice versa. Try to stay alert to the nature of the situation in which you will speak.
3. What changes do you need to make in this group? What reason do you have to believe that the change will do any good? In this situation, you are developing a hypothesis that some infor-

mation, attitude change, or set of directions will improve things. Be sure to have some idea of how you will know a good outcome if it happens. Until you can specify your goal, you will not be able to work effectively toward achieving it. You will find a little book by Robert Mager (*Goal Analysis.* Belmont, Calif.: Fearon Publishing Company, 1972) very useful to you. This book will help you specify your speech goals in behavioral terms so that you will be able to evaluate the degree to which you succeeded with your audience. It will also help you distinguish between what is desirable but impossible and what is do-able.

4. What does the audience know about your topic? The answer to this question will guide you in deciding how simple or technical you must be. You want to avoid talking down to your audience. By the same token, if you use concepts they do not understand, you will seriously confuse them and thus make yourself ineffective. Therefore it is better to be too simple than too complex. You must also check on where they got their knowledge of your topic. If it is likely to be biased, or the result of gossip and rumor, you will have to make the necessary corrections. The analysis you make will not necessarily apply to all your listeners. You should, however, gear your speech to the middle range and slightly below it. The competent, well-informed people may be bored, but they will listen. That is the reason they are competent and well informed.

5. What is the audience's attitude toward what you plan to say? One company recently added the employee benefit of a plasma service without taking into consideration that a number of their employees belonged to a religious sect for whom having a blood transfusion is a sin. Obviously this is a rare circumstance, but people do have attitudes, and however silly you may think their attitudes, you must deal with them, particularly when their attitudes will determine whether they will agree with you or not. The results of your analysis in the last two steps should result in a list of equals to accomplish and obstacles to overcome.

6. What are the realistic limits on your goals? You cannot do everything with one speech. Therefore you must answer the questions: What is the best I can hope for? The worst? The most likely? This kind of profit–loss analysis will help you set

realistic goals. Once you begin to analyze what you can accomplish with a speech, you can also consider alternative methods of accomplishing your goal. The relative advantages of speaking and writing can be considered, and you can decide how best to coordinate your speaking and writing so as to have the maximum effect.

7. After you have done all this, you must also pay attention to the circumstances in which you will speak. Where and when will you speak? What setup will be required to make the room comfortable enough for your audiences? Will you need voice amplification? Will you need visuals that must be prepared in advance? Will you need projection equipment or recorders? Are written materials to be prepared and passed out at the meeting? Who will do all of this? Are there special references to persons or occasions that ought to be made in your speech.

In Chapter 4, we provide you with a number of patterns you can use to organize your presentations. Use what you know of your audience to help you specify the kind of pattern that is most appropriate and to guide you in the evaluation of the information you will place in the spaces on that pattern.

EFFECTIVE LISTENING

Listening is the counterpart of speaking. Not all speakers are effective, yet they may say something that is important for you to know. Thus you must learn ways to keep yourself attentive. Listening is a process of looking for order in what you hear. You can organize what you hear by asking some questions about the speech.

• *What does the speaker want you to learn?* Be sure you are clear on what you need to know as a result of listening to the speech before you decide you already know it. There is a constant temptation for listeners to think they know what the speaker is going to talk about and to turn off as a result. Look for the way the speaker puts the information together as a guide to its detail. The speaker may want you to know the details of something you already know or perhaps, how some new information alters it. For this reason, the speaker may talk first about what is familiar to you. Compare what the speaker tells you with what you already know and look for similarities and differences.

If you miss details, don't worry about it. Listening to capture precise details is wasteful because you cannot listen as fast as a speaker can speak. If you try to take verbatim notes, you will lose the meaning the speaker wants you to have. It is important, however, for you to find out where you can get the details if you need them. If the information is not directly relevant to what you do, then all you will need to know are the main points.

• *What does the speaker want you to believe?* Speakers often seek to change your attitudes or beliefs. They do this because they believe that if your attitude changes, something else will change. No one has the right to try to change your beliefs for the sake of trying to change them. In organizational speaking, attempts to change beliefs are usually directed at convincing you that something is worth knowing or that something is worth doing. You may be lackadaisical about complying with some regulation that is very important to the company. Before you can be convinced that you need to be more attentive to it, you must be convinced that it is important. Interestingly enough, all it might take to modify your attitude is to convince you that your job will be in jeopardy if you do not do it right. The speaker need not make you believe what the company believes in order to attain the desired outcome.

You have the right to inquire why a speaker wants you to change what you believe. Does he or she offer evidence? Does he or she explain the consequences of changing your belief? If he or she asks you to believe something that you oppose vigorously, examine the reasons carefully, but remember that you have a right to what goes on in your own mind. The big question is whether you can do what is required without changing your belief. If not, then you will confront a crisis between your beliefs and your desire to stay in this job.

We each have our own style of listening. Some of us listen best when we watch the speaker carefully. Others may need to close their eyes. Some may find their concentration improved by doodling or taking notes, and still others will actively try to signal the speaker about whether they approve or disapprove by smiling, frowning and nodding. Your first task as a listener, however, is to get the information as accurately as possible, without evaluating it. Listeners often seriously distort information when they permit themselves to react prematurely to what the speaker says.

Once you have the information, you can ask whether it is useful or whether you agree or disagree. If you discover that the information is useful and you approve of the point of view, you may want to ask questions to amplify your understanding (if you are given that opportunity).

There are two ways to take notes. One is to try to outline the information as it is presented, using one of the organization styles we will present in the next chapter. The other method of note-taking is to jot down questions that will motivate the speaker to provide needed information. Each person should cultivate his or her own style.

There are a number of gimmick listening techniques offered to you. Sometimes they are useful. If you have trouble sitting still and concentrating when listening to a speaker, you may find it useful to obtain some training in effective listening.

DISCOVERY OF YOUR STAKE

Your main task in listening is to find out precisely what is expected of you and what will happen if you do or do not do what is expected. If you decide that the request is reasonable or important, your next step is figuring out precisely what you must do. The speech will not give you all the information you need, no matter how hard you listen. The best a speaker can hope to accomplish is to convince listeners that the change she or he requests is legitimate. From there, the listeners must conduct their own inquiry into what they must do. That is why verbal instructions are so frequently misinterpreted. If the speaker does not provide you with a way to get the details, be sure to ask.

Be careful of your own biases. People tend, naturally, to be against making changes. The speaker has the obligation to overcome their resistance. Chances are you will be tempted to find reasons to ignore what the speaker is saying to you. But if the change is important to your job, you will need to overcome your own resistance. At any event, withhold your opposition until the speaker gives the reasons for making the change. Do not impose your own reasons or look for hidden motives. Listen carefully to what is said to see if it makes sense. There may be hidden motives. Clearly any speaker stands to gain something if you do what she or he wants. The point is, will you both gain?

Speakers are fallible. They can be incoherent, illogical, and sometimes wrong. For this reason, you must listen carefully to the evidence offered. Distractions may cost you money. If you are responsible for implementing a change requested by a speaker, it is particularly important that you know what is happening so that if there are errors or omissions, you will be able to get enough information to fill in the details.

A SUMMARY EXAMPLE

Before going on to the next chapter, in which we discuss the basic techniques of speech preparation, let us consider an example of an executive making a decision to speak.

The City Planner and the Shopping Center

Dan Siddi has been the regional planner for Ranal Swamp Borough for thirty years. His job has consisted primarily of reviewing requests for building permits to see if they conform to the codes and advising local magistrates of his decisions. Recently a company purchased a block of land in the north end of the borough, along the creek from which Ranal Swamp gets its water. There was a problem with the creek five years ago when a woodworking company dumped waste into it. Although there was no evidence of actual pollution, citizen pressure had made the plant move. The subsequent unemployment caused a serious problem for the local merchants. Thus the plan announced by the company to build a shopping center on the tract has excited the community. The company has applied for the necessary permits. The area needs the jobs and the tax revenues, and present shopping facilities are a bit bedraggled. Everyone stands to profit, and any person who opposes the development will be as popular as the man who shot Santa Claus.

The city planner believes it is his responsibility to report to the community about the potential effect of the shopping center on the water supply. First, there is the possibility of contamination. Second, and more important, it is clear that the development would use more water than the community can spare. Third, there is reason to believe that the auxiliary wells are dropping in production. There is no other viable source of water other than the creek and the wells. There was a plan for a large runoff reservoir that is partially complete, but work was abandoned three years ago because the council did not believe the need warranted the expenditure of the funds. With the runoff reservoir, water could be trapped before waste from the shopping center ran into it. However, communities down the creek would be irritated by waste dumping in their water supply. There are a number of problems here, and Dan Siddi feels as if he is playing the lead in a true-to-life production of Ibsen's *Enemy of the People.*

Having made the decision that he wants to speak, Mr. Siddi must discover whether he has the status and authority to speak on this issue. As planner, he feels he has no choice. Whether the community listens or not, he has the obligation to warn them about what the development might do to the quality of their lives. The problem is to pick the proper audience to address.

He has regular access to the zoning board, which meets in private and has little press coverage. The borough council, however, gets regular press coverage. Dan has the authority to address the council when necessary. He has not used this authority in the past few years, but he feels there would be no way anyone could or would stop him if he scheduled himself to speak. If he speaks to the council, he is guaranteed an audience, including the council members, whatever citizens are present, and whoever is reached by the press. It is the later audience he really wants to reach, and therefore he must present a speech that has one or two newsworthy statements that he can be sure will be printed.

As he analyzes his data, it is clear that he cannot increase the people's income, reduce their hours, or improve their benefits, but he can make their living conditions more pleasant or, at least, keep them from becoming worse by preventing the overuse of their water supply. He is, however, the bearer of bad news. In the olden days, he knows, emperors executed the bearers of bad news, and Dan recognizes that in many ways his job is at stake. He has been a relatively quiet member of the administrative team. He has cooperated, and people expect him to continue to cooperate. On the other hand, he reasons, if he did not warn the people and the water ran out, he could be fired for incompetency because he did not warn them.

It occurs to him that he doesn't have to take the rap alone. Environmental impact studies are required by the state before any major development can be approved. As the shopping center would be on a waterway used by more than one community, the whole thing will have to be studied. Research indicates to Dan that both the community and the developer are being premature, counting their money before there has been an analysis of the effect of the development on common waterways. He decides that he will not state the bad news directly but will simply remind the council that the studies must be made and that nothing can be done until then. If he is asked, he will offer his opinion that the studies will result in disapproval of the project. Dan is now ready to answer the preparation questions (see "Audience Analysis" above) on his topic: "The Shopping Center may Only Be a Dream Because of Its Environmental Impact."

He will speak in person to the borough council and through the press to the entire community. Here is how he answers the questions:

1. I am a trusted public official. They know I have never lied to them. They may not like what I have to say, but they will believe it because of the record of credibility I have built up in the past.

2. The only reward I have for them is to change their expectations so they will not be disappointed. It's not much, but it is better than having them invest and then discover they have lost their money, or than having their water supply ruined in the unlikely event that the project will be approved.

3. The change I need to bring about is to get them thinking about alternative locations that will have less environmental impact or, better yet, to think about improvement of the commercial areas they now have. I will know they have changed their minds when the press stops reporting news about plans for the project and when people stop talking about how taxes can be reduced when the project has been completed. In fact, when they start talking about "if" the development goes through as opposed to "when" the development goes through, it will be a major victory.

4. They don't know much about my topic. I am the expert. They have a lot of unsupported figures given by the developer, but there haven't been any official figures released yet. Their misconceptions about the effect of the development on taxation were planted by the developer to rally community support. They do not know how much money it will take to develop

alternate water supplies in the event their present supply is polluted. Most likely when I tell them, they will wonder who is bribing me to oppose the development.

5. I am dealing with explosive political attitudes, but the council has a record for behaving responsibly, and I suspect that after griping a bit, they will work to calm down the community.

6. I must do the following: I must inform them about the standards that the builder must meet before he can start, including the state environmental impact regulations; and I must inform them about major details of their local water supply so they can understand the possibility of pollution. The best I can hope for is fair coverage in the paper and perhaps some verbal support from a few members of the council. The worst would be that I will be ignored entirely. The most likely is that I will take a lot of abuse for a while, until they begin to understand.

7. I will have to fit my speech into roughly twenty minutes, and I will have to prepare some simple slides diagraming the water situation, and perhaps a handout for the press about the details of the environmental impact statement. I must schedule my remarks ahead with the president of council.

Mr. Siddi presents his speech and his prediction is correct. He is attacked by the developer, by various members of the council, and by some local business interests. The downtown merchants give him marginal support. However, one week after the speech the local paper came out with a strong editorial on his behalf. Two weeks later the environmental specialists appear. Their report is never released because the developer withdraws his application about ten days after the specialists' appearance.

SUMMARY

Preparation is the key to success in presentational speaking. Before you decide to speak you must be sure that you have a worthwhile idea and the information you need to support it. Once you have your material you must organize it so that your audience can understand it. You must be careful to speak in language familiar to your audience and to deliver your speech interestingly enough to hold your audience's attention.

Speeches are delivered to give information and instructions, to inspire people, to present and advocate ideas and proposals, and to provide information for people too busy to seek it for themselves. They are also given for ceremonial purposes and to represent the organization to the public.

Your reputation is at stake when you speak publicly. You have a great deal to gain or lose. If you fail, you can appear incompetent or indecisive and lose your influence. If you succeed, you can appear credible and intelligent and gain influence and prestige. If you do not speak at all, you must resign yourself to having little or no influence on the events around you and probably to not advancing in the company. Because you can acquire communication competence, it is worth the risk to attempt to speak out. The ability to speak well in public is so important that many companies use it as a major criterion for advancement. Your effectiveness is based on the content of your speech as well as on your delivery.

Here are the steps you must take to prepare a public presentation.

1. You must be sure that you have something to say that warrants the use of your audience's time.
2. You must be sure that you have the authority to say what you plan to say.
3. You must understand your audience well enough so that you can convince them that they will not waste their time listening to you, as well as to overcome whatever objections they may have to your point of view.
4. You must carefully adapt your presentation to your audience's level of understanding and technical sophistication.
5. You must be sure that everything in the speech supports your goal.
6. Once you have done all this, ask yourself whether an oral presentation is the most effective way to get the information to your audience, or whether a written message might not be more effective.

If you have finally decided on the oral message, and you know what you want to say, when and to whom, you can proceed to structure your speech. In the next chapter we will present to you specific instructions for organizing your speech and getting it ready for presentation.

READINGS

Some good books on how formal communication is used in organizations are Richard K. Allen, *Organizational Management through Communication.* New York: Harper & Row, 1977 (which provides an in-depth discussion of the role of communication in organizations, particularly in management, and managers' use of communication to bring about change, to motivate, to lead, and to inform the public); Randall Capps, Carley H. Dodd, and Larry James Winn, *Communication for the Business and Professional Speaker.* New York: Macmillan, 1981 (which offers a discussion of communication in a variety of settings in organizations and emphasizes formal experiences like public speaking); and Arnold E. Schnider, William C. Donaghy, and Pamela Jane Newman, *Organizational Communication.* New York: McGraw-Hill, 1975 (which provides a good overview of the forms and functions of oral and written communication in organizations).

A simple source of advice about public speaking in organizations is Roger P. Wilcox, *Oral Reporting in Business and Industry.* Englewood Cliffs, N.J.: Prentice-Hall, 1967 which provides a thorough set of instructions on how to prepare and organize an oral report, with emphasis on presentations using visual aids.

A good source of material on listening is William I. Gorden, *Communication: Personal and Public.* Sherman Oaks, Calif.: Alfred Publishing Co., 1977, pp. 103–134. The process of listening is described along with a review of problems listeners have and how to overcome them. Capps, Dodd, and James (pp. 235–259), cited above, includes a discussion of five areas in which people can improve their listening.

Chapter 4

The Preparation
of the Speech

PRESENTATIONAL OBLIGATIONS

Every public presentation you make should be persuasive. No matter what your topic, you must offer reasons for your listeners to regard what you say as important. Whether you want them to learn something, believe something, or do something, you are obligated to make your request meet their needs and concerns. Effective speakers offer reasons that make sense to listeners. Ineffective speakers offer reasons that make sense only to themselves. Arrogant speakers offer no reasons at all.

Even the most important executive must justify his statements. In the 1980 presidential debates, both Jimmy Carter and Ronald Reagan sought the support of their fellow citizens by speaking about how problems in the society would be solved, how people would have a better life if they were elected. It is characteristic of democratic societies that we expect our leaders to serve us. It doesn't matter what the purpose of the organization is; the executive officer is there to meet the needs of the people involved, the stockholders, the employees, and the community at large.

Persuasion is most evident in employment interviews. Your task as an interviewee is to convince the interviewer that you are the person to be hired. Your interviewer will not look for reasons to support you; you must provide them in response to her or his questions. In formal presentations, you must anticipate the listeners' questions and provide answers before they are asked. By concentrating on what is important to your audience, you avoid preoccupation with reasons and justifications that relate only to yourself. The most persuasive presentation, of course, is one in which your needs and those of the audience mesh.

You do not have to modify your ideas to suit the audience. Quite the contrary, you must persuade the audience to modify their ideas to suit you. Changing your ideas merely to win audience approval is dishonest. As a speaker, the position you have in relation to an audience should be clear and honest. You have a point to make that you regard as important to the audience. If you can gain the agreement of the audience with the reasons you offer, then you will be successful. If you cannot convince the audience that they would be better off if they agreed with you, then you will fail. Here are some of the "good reasons" you can offer an audience.

1. What you ask them to know, believe, or do will make their job easier.
2. What you ask them to know, believe, or do will clarify some confusion.
3. What you ask them to know, believe, or do will mean more money, advancement on the job, security, or employee benefits for them.
4. What you ask them to know, believe, or do will make their life more pleasant.
5. What you ask them to know, believe, or do will help them defend themselves against forces that would hurt them.

In addition to offering the audience a good reason to agree with you, your speech must be interesting. You can get their interest in some of the following ways.

1. If you want them to believe what you ask them to believe, show them how their present beliefs result in unproductive actions, jeopardize their physical and emotional security, or confuse them, and how your beliefs would do just the opposite.
2. If you want them to learn something, show them how the effort will be pleasant and enlightening, and how it will facilitate what they are currently doing.

3. If you want them to do something, show them how simple it is and how it will help them be safe, use less energy, do better work, or find pleasure.

In the 1950s, it was common practice for employers to include leaflets with inspirational messages in the pay envelopes. Studies showed that the employees did not read the leaflets, no matter how interesting the layout. On the other hand, announcements about changes in benefits were read 90 percent of the time. Normally you should not make a request of an audience unless it is very important. People find it uncomfortable to change what they believe or the way they do things, and learning new material takes time and effort. There must be some clear harm that will come if they do not do what you ask, and some clear benefit if they do. A great many speakers take the audience's time to discuss trivial matters related to their own personal convenience. They usually get a polite hearing because most of us are trained to display politeness, even when we do not listen at all.

Your responsibility to address your audience's concerns is referred to as your *burden of proof.* To understand this concept, think of the physical force of inertia. An object keeps doing what it is doing until some force is applied to change it. People also tend to behave this way. They are comfortable in what they know, believe, and do and will not voluntarily change unless they discover a good reason. You must first give them reason to doubt by providing arguments about weaknesses in what they know, believe, and do. Then you must show them that what you propose will make things better.

Goal Setting

The first step in preparing a presentation is to set goals. Your goal statement is about what the audience is to know, to believe, or to do as a result of your speech, for example,

1. I want my audience to know that there are new regulations for reporting accidents.
2. I want my audience to believe that it is important to reduce accidents.
3. I want my audience to be able to fill out the new accident-report forms.

or

1. I want my audience to know how much sales have been declining over the last ten years.
2. I want my audience to believe that a decline in sales means that the company is in trouble.
3. I want my audience to do what I tell them to do to help get more sales.

or

1. I want my audience to understand the technical reason for the increased breakdown rate of our product.
2. I want my audience to believe that we will lose business if these breakdowns continue.
3. I want my audience to take the following new steps in production in order to prevent breakdown of the product.

The second step in preparation is to make some kind of statement that will tell you how you will know you have attained your goal, for example,

1. One evidence of success will be some good questions asked by people in the audience when I have finished my presentation.
2. One evidence of success will be people's giving their own examples of why they believe what I have suggested to them.
3. One evidence of success will be people's doing the task correctly.

Teachers measure success by scores on examinations. As a speaker, it is your task to devise some simple examination to give yourself that will convince you that you have accomplished what you set out to do. Combining a specific goal with a statement explaining how accomplishment can be recognized enables you to focus on what ought to be included in the speech.

Your third step is to discover one good reason that the audience will be hurt if they do not accept your idea and one good reason that they will be helped if they do accept it, for example,

1. They will be hurt because if they do not fill out the forms correctly, they will not be compensated for their expenses; they will be helped if they are compensated.
2. They will be hurt if they lose their jobs because sales keep dropping; they will be helped if they earn bonuses because sales went up.
3. They will be hurt because continued defects may close down the production line; they will be helped because correct performance could result in increased production schedules.

It is not difficult to do these three steps so long as you keep your statements very simple. You will be able to accomplish only one goal per speech. Furthermore, as it is virtually impossible to discover whether you have really changed someone's attitude, you might focus your attention on what the audience is to know and to do. You can assume that if they know it and do it, a change in their attitude was an intermediate step.

You can find out whether someone has learned something by asking her or him about it, and you can find out whether someone has changed behavior by watching her or him.

PREPARATION CHECKLIST

To help you prepare, fill out the following checklist and keep it handy to guide you in the development of your presentation.

1. What is your goal for the audience in this presentation?
   a. They are to know. . . . .
   b. They are to do. . . . .

2. How will you know if you have accomplished this goal?
   a. If they say. . . . . , I will know they know it.
   b. If they do. . . . . I will know they have done it.
3. Who are "they"? Who are the people to whom you will speak?
   a. Friends? Neighbors? Employees? Work colleagues? The community? Your boss? Anyone else?
4. What reason will you give them for coming to listen to you?
   a. They ought to take time out of their busy lives because. . . . .
5. How will they be helped by doing what you ask them to do?
6. How will they be hurt by not doing what you ask them to do?

Once you have made your goal clear by filling out this form, you will find it easy to select a proper organization pattern for your presentation.

ORGANIZATION OF IDEAS

The most efficient way to prepare your message is to reduce it to a single sentence. Think of what you would like the audience to remember, if they forget 95 percent of what you say. What would you want to stick in their heads?

1. A great many people, including their friends and relatives, got sick last year because of industrial wastes in the water supply.
2. It is morally wrong for a company to cause the sickness of human beings.
3. They had better shut off all waste valves at the completion of a flushing project.
- If they remember these three things, they will probably support the company's antipollution campaign.

or

1. I want them to know sales dropped 37 percent from this time last year.
2. I want them to believe that the lost sales have put us on the edge of bankruptcy.
3. I want each of them to get on the phone and call ten new prospects today and try to get an appointment tomorrow.
- If they remember these three things, they may do something that will boost sales in the weeks ahead.

Each of these examples contains a message for listeners. In the first, there is an appeal to guilt caused by the possibility of doing harm to others, as well as fear of losing a job if regulations are not followed. In the second case, there is a strong suggestion that jobs may be lost if the company goes under because of lost sales.

Here are some more examples.

1. The last city council defeated the proposed zoning ordinance by one vote.
2. But the zoning ordinance would make the audience's neighborhoods cleaner and safer.
3. They had better put pressure on their council members to vote for the change the next time it comes up.

1. We lost $142,000 last month because of logistics errors.
2. Preventing those kinds of errors is the responsibility of the division head.
3. If we get a new division head, we will cut our losses.

1. If we save 15 percent of our fuel oil, we can cut our dependence on foreign oil to a minimum.

2. Anything that reduces dependence on foreign oil is good.
3. Buying and installing our oil-use–reducing devices would help make that saving.

1. I have the training and experience for this job.
2. People with my kind of background are indispensable to this company.
3. I should be hired.

REPETITION AND REDUNDANCY AND SAYING IT AGAIN

Once you have discovered the idea you wish to leave with your audience, the next *logical* step is to select the *logical* pattern for organizing your *logic,* so that it will appear *logical* to the listener. The organizational pattern that is most *logical* will emerge from your idea statement. One component of a *logical* presentation is to be redundant, so that the *logic* is clear to the listener.

If you got the impression that being *logical* was the next step in preparation, you arrived at a *logical* conclusion. The first task, to give the audience a reason for paying attention, appeals essentially to their emotions. Fear of losing their job, satisfaction in doing something well, and security in knowing the facts are essentially emotional. Once you have established the emotional notion, you must demonstrate that it is reasonable to accept your ideas because they can be supported with proof. Your *logical* presentation is redundant with your emotional presentation.

Redundant means "repetitious." It means that you say the same thing over and over in various ways. You paraphrase your ideas and put them in different contexts in order to make sure people remember them. After you have given an emotional reason for their paying attention to you, you provide a logical reason. Your logical reason can include a statement from an authority that agrees with you, an example of how doing it your way is effective, some numbers that demonstrate the consistent benefit from doing it your way, and a definition of how to do it your way. Each time you can say your main idea and continue to make it interesting to your audience, you increase the changes that they will remember it after you have finished. Thus you do not simply repeat yourself crudely (as we are doing here); you stylize your redundancy by trying to find ways to repeat yourself that are interesting and different.

1. Sometimes you repeat by defining what you say, for example, telling them that redundancy is repetition, telling them that redundancy can be accomplished in a variety of ways, and detailing the ways by which redundancy can be accomplished.
2. Sometimes you repeat by offering examples, such as how one orator was redundant by ending all of his speeches by saying, "thus Carthage must be destroyed." Then you can show them how the old salesman used to spin off cracker-barrel yarns, each one supporting his main point. You might even want to show them how the parables in the Bible taught by repeating in different ways examples of the power of the Lord.
3. Sometimes you repeat by citing authoritative quotations supporting your position, for example, Phillips and Zolten, in their book *Structuring Speech* (New York: Bobbs, Merrill, 1976), advocate stylized redundancy as a way of reinforcing your point.
4. Sometimes you repeat by offering statistical evidence, for example the English language is about 50 percent redundant because being 50 percent redundant enables people to fill in gaps where they may not have heard accurately.

We rest our case on redundancy.

ORGANIZATION PATTERNS

Using an effective organization pattern helps you stylize your redundancy so that your listeners have a good chance of remembering what you want them to remember. When we talk of *organization patterns,* we refer to what you may have learned was an outline. The term *outline* is somewhat misleading because an outline is nothing more that a set of statements or words related to each other through the use of numbers, letters, and indentations. For example,

I. Seriousness of the problem.
   A. Cost
   B. Danger

If we were to make a pattern, however, it might look like this:

Here are the components of the problem.	
It costs a lot, because ·	It is dangerous, because ·

The use of a pattern shows you what kind of material has to be inserted and where it should be put. Each of the dotted lines under "It costs a lot" can be filled in with examples of costs or statistics about the cost. Each of the dotted lines under "It is dangerous" can be filled with examples of accidents or statistics about the number of accidents. Each set of supports can be backed up by the statement of an expert.

When we talk about a pattern of organization, we mean a *rule* about a logical way to connect your ideas. Building a pattern is like setting up a file. When you examine the evidence, you have to see whether it fits on the pattern. If it does not fit, you can set it aside because it might be misleading. If it fits, you will be guided to the precise point where it should be inserted. No matter how important your information is to the audience, they will not understand it or be able to do what you request unless you make it clear to them what they are to understand or do. There is a difference between agreeing that they ought to understand and do and actually understanding and being able to do. The emotional content of your speech makes them willing to understand and do, and the logical component shows them exactly what they are to understand and do. In order to complete Aristotle's recommendation about the three components of persuasion, we must add that none of the emotion and logic work unless the audience is willing to accept you as a legitimate authority and a trustworthy human being. Aristotle once said that the three components of persuasion were *ethos* (the personal character and reputation of the speaker), *pathos* (the emotional appeals made by the speaker), and *logos* (the logic of the presentation).

Human minds are orderly. It is, however, hard to impose order on disorderly input, and so members of the audience look for reasonable and logical ways to put what they hear in order. It is much more efficient for you, the speaker, to impose the order on what you say than to rely on the audience to put it together the right way. As we will show you later on, there are a great number of ways in which people can misunderstand each other. You can help minimize misunderstanding by imposing a logical pattern on what you say. Sometimes making yourself clear stirs up both questions and disagreement. Don't let this throw you. It is far better for someone to disagree with what you actually said than to agree with something he or she thinks you said, which you really did not say. (Did that sentence make sense? If not, take a look at how an orderly diagram can clarify it.)

There are two alternatives for listeners:			
I. They can agree.		II. They can disagree.	
They can agree with what you said. A	They can agree with what they think you said. B	They can disagree with what you said. C	They can disagree with what they think you said. D

We can now fill in each box with information about the consequences of each situation:

A	They can agree with what you said.	
	They will learn what you want them to learn.	1
	They will do what you want them to do.	2

B	They can agree with what they think you said.	
	They will learn what you did not want them to learn.	1
	They will do what you did not want them to do.	2

C	They can disagree with what you said.	
	You can try again to convince them.	1
	You can understand the differences between you.	2

	They can disagree with what they think you said.	
D	They may actually agree, but you will never discover this because you cannot spot your errors.	1
	There will be considerable confusion in what they think they know or what they try to do.	2

You can now fill each cell with appropriate supporting information. Think of each cell (A1, A2, B1, B2, C1, C2, D1, D2) as storage bins. The sentence inside the cell provides instructions about what goes into it. You can now look at the information you have gathered and place it in the proper place. If you find that you do not have an example, a quotation, or a statistical statement to go into a particular cell, you can go and look for one. You may have a great many supporting ideas to place into a particular cell. If this is the case, you may choose the most effective one. When you finish, you may have information left over. If so, it means that you simply do not need it for this presentation. The purpose of drawing the diagrams and identifying the cells is to help you discover precisely the information you need and to help you decide which information would not be useful in your presentation.

Patterns are organized on a redundancy principle so that each cell supports your main idea, and so that what you put in each cell supports the statement that supports your main idea. It should now be clear how you can generate an outline from the pattern, if outlining suits you, or how you can develop notecards, each one representing a cell. If you plan to write a manuscript, each notecard can represent a paragraph in your presentation. The pattern serves as a kind of sieve, which retains important material and allows trivia and unrelated material to be removed.

The various types of patterns arise logically from your goal. There are only a few ways in which the mind can understand. The mind can understand relationships of:

Chronology: the order in which events come or the steps in a process.
Description: the distinctive features of something.
Structure: how something is put together, how a process is organized.

Set: the components of a thing, a condition, an event, or an idea.

Comparisons: how two things, events, or conditions are alike (even if they are not obviously alike.

Contrasts: how two things, events or conditions are different, even if they appear to be similiar.

Criteria: the standards of comparison used to judge or evaluate things, events or conditions.

Associations: how things, events or conditions are connected so that predictions or causal relationships can be discovered.

Forensics: arguments made on behalf of solutions to particular problems.

Deliberations: quests for solutions for particular problems.

By putting your goal statement into one of these patterns, you raise your chances of being understood. Check each of the following outline patterns carefully each time you set out to prepare a speech. One of them will be best suited to your goal.

Chronology

A chronological pattern works best if you are trying to present a narration of events or if you are trying to give a set of instructions. The main points of your presentation are connected in an orderly sequence, in which each unit must precede the unit that follows it; otherwise nothing would make sense. For example, if you are trying to explain how to fill out a report form, you could say,

> Fill in the date. Then put down the statistical data in the right spaces. You get the statistical data from the tool room superintendent. Oh yes, the forms are in the drawer in the table in my outer office. And so on.

You might get it right after two or three tries, but most people would simply despair of trying to follow your instructions. If, however, you concentrated on what must be done before each step can be accomplished, you might get a sequence like this:

1. Take Form 15B from the table drawer file in my outer office.
2. Gather the information you will need for the report: get the

statistical data from the tool room superintendent; get the stock numbers from Catalog 77Y; and get the exceptions information from the production superintendent.

3. Fill in the heading (your name, the topic, today's date).
4. Fill in the statistical data as follows, 1 . . . 2 . . . 3 and so on.

Chronological patterns are based on a technique called PERT/CPM (program evaluation and review technique/critical path method). This is a software system used by the government and many large manufacturers to make sure that the steps in production are done in order and that errors are avoided. The system has been adapted to the administration of agencies and divisions. Essentially you can set up such a system by asking people to write down everything that must be done on cards and then thinking through the process so that the cards can be put in order. The process of putting the cards in order requires decisions about what must come first in order for the next step to happen. The process also reveals missing steps. The whole thing can be tested, if you care to test it, by a mathematical and logical system, and an estimate can be made of how likely things are to come out right. Of course, you need not go through this process in your own work. What is important is to recognize that when *time* is the governing principle by which your ideas are to be connected, you can write down on cards all of the things that happened (in the narration) or all of the things that must happen (in instructions) and then think through the order in which they ought to come and search for missing steps. The basic pattern looks like this:

1	This is the *first* thing that happened/should happen (describe, explain, give examples, whatever you need).
2	This is the *second* thing that happened/should happen (describe, explain, give examples, whatever you need).

Etc.

Each box becomes a minor goal statement that dictates its own pattern. You can see how the process of patterning can take you right down to the paragraph or sentence level. As we present each of the possible patterns, we will show you how putting together a presentation is nothing more than a process of completing the requirements of the components of your pattern.

Description

A descriptive pattern identifies the main features of some object, person, or place sufficiently clearly so that someone else will recognize it if they see it. A descriptive pattern requires you to identify the features that distinguish your thing, person or place from all others. Trivial details are not helpful in building a satisfactory description.

A descriptive pattern is really a form of the definition. In it, you must isolate the characteristics without which the thing would not be what it is. It is relatively easy to describe (define) an object. All you have to do is look at it and say what you see, for example,

1. The main characteristic is that it is a blend of three geometric shapes: circles; squares; and triangles.
2. Each of the shapes is lightly tinted: circles/pink; squares/pale blue; and triangles/yellow.
3. When light is focused on the object, it has the following effects:

    . . . .
    . . . .
    . . . .

It may be necessary, at this point, to demonstrate the object. The descriptive pattern suggests the use of visuals to make the ideas clear. A map, for example, could be used to show a location. The location could further be described by its landmarks, geographical features, the people present, and so on.

It is sometimes necessary to describe (define) an abstract concept. In these cases, you may need to use examples, to *illustrate* what you mean. Notice that the word *illustrate* has a visual connotation. The use of an example to describe or define implies that you are using words in order to give your listener a visual (concrete) image of what you are talking about. Try this concept:

Morale refers to the mood of the workers:
1. When they are in a good mood we can see them (now add the illustrative examples).
2. When they are in a bad mood we can see them (now add the illustrative examples).

Sometimes illustrations can be made more coherent if you turn them into structures.

Structure

A structual pattern is a diagram of components showing their proper relationship. It is more precise than a description because in addition to identifying the main features by which the object can be distinguished, it also shows how they are connected, how they relate to one another, and, in many cases, what the consequences of separating them might be. The organization chart of a company, for example, can take the abstract idea *administration* and make it more concrete by showing how the company is run then make it even more concrete by showing who is in charge of whom doing what.

You can further identify each of the components by illustrating their structure or by referring to the next organization pattern, set.

Visual space can also be diagrammed by a structural pattern. For example, if you want to describe what goes on in a particular unit of a company, you could present a map like this:

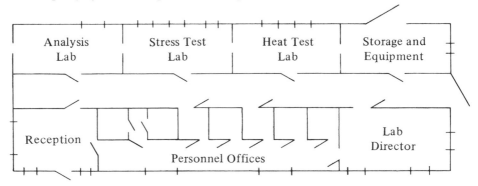

You could then "guide" your listeners from room to room on your map, detailing what goes on in each of the locations. You could use a chronological pattern to describe the tests that are performed on in each lab, discuss the duties of each of the technicians and scientists who occupy the personnel offices, and provide an overview of the whole operation by describing the duties of the lab director.

Set

Set is the most frequently used pattern. When you use it, you say the following:

1. I have decided that the topic I am talking about consists of these (list them) components, and nothing else.

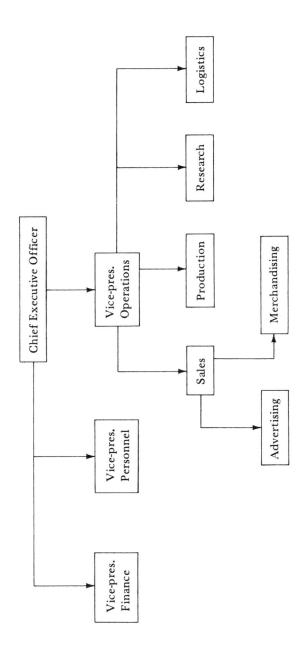

2. I have decided that the best way to explain something is to explain what it is composed of.

The reason this is called the *set pattern* is that it is based on the mathematical principle of set and subset. By using this pattern, the speaker can specify what is important, what is included, and the amount of detail she or he wishes to use in talking about it.

Each of the patterns mentioned above could be expanded by use of the set pattern. For example, in the organization chart, each component of the company could be explained in terms of its duties, for example,

In Research and Development the following duties are performed:			
New-Product Tests	Quality Control	Endurance Tests	Guarantee Estimates

Each component could be further patterned in essentially the same way, by means of whatever pattern is most useful. "New-Product Tests" could be discussed according to a chronological pattern:

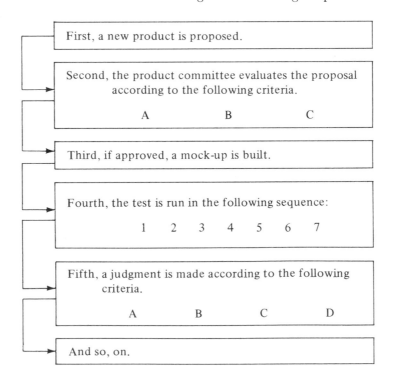

Notice how the speaker uses a heading for each component box to help make the decision about what sort of pattern is best suited for the contents of the box. In the third step, a structure could have been used to illustrate mock-up building. In the first step, the procedure for proposing a new product could have been explained by means of a chronological pattern. The speaker continues to subdivide the topic until she or he has reached the level of detail desired in each component.

Notice that the set pattern does not require any particular order of presentation. The preceding three patterns all specified an order. In the chronological pattern, ideas are necessarily connected in chronological order. In structure and description, ideas are connected by contiguity. In a set pattern, you can decide on the order you wish to use and can arrange the components from most to least important or from minor to major (if you want to achieve some kind of climactic effect). Furthermore you can control the amount of detail so that if you wish to give an overview, you can do so merely by mentioning each of the components. Then, by providing subpatterns in the component you wish to discuss in detail, you can provide both emphasis and information.

Job description are commonly developed according to a set pattern. For example, in the structural diagram, the duties of the "laboratory supervisor" could be detailed, if necessary:

Receives materials to analyze from authorized personnel.
Assigns analysis procedures to appropriate personnel on the following forms.
Fills out and transmits periodic reports on the following schedule.
Fills out laboratory operation reports for each test according to the following schedule.
Keeps inventories and records of materials and equipment.
Submits purchase requisitions.
Selects laboratory personnel according to company procedures.
Prepares and submits personnel and program evaluations.
And so on.

Each component of the job description could be further detailed according to the needs of the holder of the job, his or her evaluator, or management.

The set pattern is based on mathematical set theory. It guarantees that items that relate to each other are presented together. It provides rigid control on the divisions of a topic, following these rules:

1. Every item in a box must relate to the title of that box.
2. Divisions of a box must be relatively equal. They can vary in the amount of information contained in each division.
3. Boxes cannot overlap. This is particularly important. For example, you can discuss "Work Performed" in a division, but you cannot introduce information about personnel, because personnel would overlap all of the components. For example, "Here's what goes on at our college. We have undergraduate programs, graduate programs, and continuing-education programs." If you wanted to talk about how strong the English program is you would have to revise the pattern because there could be an English program in each of the three components you have named. To give an overview of the entire program, however, you could develop a matrix, as follows:

	Graduate	Undergraduate	Continuing Ed
English			
Math			
For. Lang.			
Science			
Other			

In such a pattern, you can choose whether to speak from row to row or column to column and build your outline accordingly. For example,

> I will discuss what goes on in our college by talking about our four major subject programs and how they are developed on the graduate, undergraduate, and continuing education levels.

I. English
   A. Graduate
   B. Undergraduate
   C. Continuing Education
II. Math
   A. Graduate
   B. Undergraduate
   C. Continuing Education
And so on.

or

I will discuss the three levels on which we conduct programs and show how our major subjects are handled in each.

I. Graduate
   A. English
   B. Math
II. Undergraduate
   A. English
   B. Math

Notice that this pattern provides a "table of contents" statement that you can give your listener. By using similar headings each organized in a similar fashion, you can help your listener to catch some of the detail of your presentation. You can also diagram it simply, if you are using visuals or a handout. Most importantly, you can improve your own organization and preparation by using the pattern as a guide to where you will put information.

Chronological, descriptive, and *structural* patterns are also *sets.* We have distinguished them here because each of the three dictates how material is to be presented. When you organize an idea according to time units, each unit is a component of the set and can be subdivided according to a common principle. It is not always possible or desirable to subdivide each component the same way. However, if you are trying to make comparisons, it is absolutely imperative that the subdivisions be the same in the two things you are comparing. We will illustrate this as we talk about the more complicated patterns. What makes a complicated pattern complicated is that it uses more than one set, that is, to do what you intend to do, you must use at least two patterns connected to each other.

Comparison

Sometimes it is useful to compare two ideas to show that they are similar. It is possible to make a complicated idea easier for the audience to understand by showing how much it is like something with which they are already familiar. When you use this pattern, you simply take two sets with similiar components and lay them side by side. For example, here is an explanation of a company's orientation procedure made simple:

Orienting a new employee is like welcoming a weekend guest.	
Welcoming a Guest Consists of	Orienting an Employee Consists of
Greeting the guest, like this . . .	Greeting the employee, like this . . .
Familiarizing the guests with the surroundings.	Familiarizing the employees with the surroundings.
Explaining the basic rules of the house (meals, washing, storage, and so on).	Explaining the basic rules of the house (punching in, checking out tools, and so on).
Asking questions and relaxing	Asking questions and relaxing

The main pattern shows the similarities between the two processes. As a matter of fact, there are some differences in each of the steps. These can be explained by means of the next pattern.

Contrast

Contrast is the reverse of comparison. It is used when you wish to show that there are differences between two things that appear to be the same. Consider the box headed "Explaining the basic rules of the house" in the previous diagram. While guests and new employees must be told the basic rules, the rules themselves differ. This can be explained as follows:

Here are some of the rules a guest must be told	The rules for the new employee are in the employee handbook.

Hang your clothes in the closet.	Put your clothes in your locker.
Use the second-floor washroom.	Use the washroom in the main corridor.
Mealtimes are . . .	Lunchtime and breaks are . . .
Learn some of our habits.	These are your rules: Checking out tools Setting up jobs Inspection of machinery

You can see how the two patterns can be blended to show the similarities between things that appear to be different (welcoming guests/ orienting employees) and to show the differences between things that seem to be similar (rules of the house).

These two structures can be blended to show some refined differences when you must argue for a particular point of view that you can best defend by explaining or defining subtle differences. For example, suppose a division head and a personnel manager are trying to work out the wording for an advertisement for personnel. The personnel manager wants to advertise for "chemists," but the division head insists on "chemical engineers." The personnel manager is not clear about the distinction. The division head establishes a set called *distinguishing features* and declares that chemists and chemical engineers differ on the following features:

1. Basic training.
2. Types of research.
3. Degree earned.
4. Orientation toward work.

By establishing these four elements, the division head guarantees that the two will be compared and contrasted on the same points. (He may wish to defend his reason for regarding these four elements as important. We will examine this procedure with the next pattern.) He can now make the distinction he wishes to make by setting up a matrix:

	Chemists	Chemical Engineers
Basic Training		
Type of Research		
Degree Earned		
Orientation		

The following distinctions are made:

Basic Training	Chemists are trained in theory.	Chemical engineers are trained in techniques.
Type of research	Chemists examine fundamental theoretical questions.	Chemical engineers solve practical problems.
Degree earned	PH.D.	Professional degree.
Orientation	Theoretical and abstract.	Practical.

Because the job requires work on specific problems and the discovery of practical solutions, the division head argues that a chemical engineer is most appropriate for the job. This kind of procedure is the basis of the next pattern, *criteria*, used to evaluate and choose between alternatives.

Criteria

It is very difficult to make clear the reasons for choosing one course of action or thing over another. It is not enough, in most cases, simply to say, "I prefer this one." Particularly because of affirmative action, for example, it is imperative that supervisors be able to explain why they chose to promote one employee instead of another. Criticism is the basis for these kinds of decisions. By criticism, we mean comparing two or more of anything to show which is superior. Comparisons are always with a set of standards, or criteria. Thus criticism consists of the following steps (chronological pattern):

1. Establishing the basis for the criticism (criteria).
2. Showing why the criteria are important or useful.
3. Comparing each thing (person, idea, art object) with the criteria.
4. Declaring which one best meets the standards (or which deviates the least).

In a speech, the pattern would look like this:

I have selected Smith over Brown for the position, because		
There are three important abilities require by the position.	Smith has done the following.	Brown has done the following.
Technical skill		
Ability to work with people		
Creativity and imagination		

The speaker has the privilege of deciding whether to go across the rows, "Here is how Smith and Brown compare on the quality of technical skill"; "Here is how they compare on ability to work with people"; "Here is how they compare on creativity and imagination." Or "Here are Smith's qualities" and "Here are Brown's qualities." If it is necessary to defend or justify the criteria, the job description could be used as a basis:

Technical skill is important because:
The job requires this kind of production.
The job has these kinds of emergencies,
and so on.

Every company requires evaluation. The basis of evaluation is information, which must be organized in such a way that valid comparisons can be made. The criteria pattern guides you in organizing your information. Suppose you are required to present a statement evaluating the laboratory supervisor. You start with the job description and specify what "standard," "substandard," and "exemplary" performance would look like;

The supervisor is expected to	Here is what normal performance looks like	Performance is inadequate when	Exemplary performance is identified by

By adding two more columns, labeled, "The supervisor actually did . . ." and "Here is what it most resembled," You can draw a conclusion and justify the evaluation. Here is how the whole pattern would look:

Expectation	Normal	Inade-quate	Exem-plary	Done	Conclusion
Assign analysis					
Receive materials					
Fill out reports					
And so on					

Each bit of information would be placed in the proper box. By organizing information this way, the supervisor would be guided to the information she or he needs before a valid evaluation can be made. The evaluation could be extended if the company has some standards by which they evaluate such intangibles as "interpersonal relations," "cooperation," "creativity," or anything else they feel to be important. Of course, attendance would be the easiest to evaluate, because a simple numerical standard is available. This kind of pattern can be used to evaluate anything that requires a choice or a formal evaluation.

Association

The most complicated of all the patterns is the pattern of association. Association is a scientifically based pattern used when connections must be made between circumstances or events and outcomes. There are three main types of associations:

1. *Projections* are used when it is necessary to make an educated guess about the future, to anticipate events, so that decisions can be made about how much to buy, what to produce, how large an inventory is needed, how much money must be borrowed, and so on. Insurance companies must predict with reasonable accuracy how many of what kind of people will die of what, or how much automobile prices are likely to rise.
2. *Hypotheses* are statements about how one event may cause another.
3. *Functions* are statements about how two events are connected in some regular way.

These patterns are generally based on statistical computations. If you are not trained in statistical reasoning, you might find it useful to take introductory training, at least enough so that you can understand presentations based on these kinds of patterns. For example, any program recommendation is based on some hypotheses, like

> If present conditions continue, we can expect the following . . .
> If we get what we expect, it will have the following results . . .
> Results like these represent a serious condition (criteria pattern) . . .
> But, if we adopt the proposal, we will either prevent the outcome, change the pattern of relationship, or solve our problems.

One of the most difficult things to do is to explain in relatively simple terms the mode of reasoning involved in making these "guesses." Audiences generally are not sophisticated in statistical reasoning. And as a matter of fact, statistics are not an infallible means of arguing. They are often misused and are frequently misleading; yet they represent the best we have. The guiding premise in making predictions about the future is

> In the past, when events like this occurred, we got the following result; therefore, if events continue, we can expect a similar result. (You can see how this is a variation on the criteria pattern). The speaker must offer reasons for (1) why he believes this situation is similar to the past situation (comparison, contrast); and

(2) why he believes that nothing will change the situation (using a set in which various possible influences are examined).

The guiding premise in making statements in which one event is declared to be the cause of another is

> Every time this happened, we got a similar result, and no other set of events seems to produce this set of results. (Use a set of times when "this" happened and a subpattern narration or chronological pattern. Then compare the narrations to show that they are similar. You can also contrast different occurrences to show that what "caused" them differed in each case.)

The guiding premise for statements showing that events fluctuate in a regular way is the same as for cause and effect, except that instead of a 1:1 correspondence, a more complicated formula for relationship is used.

Here are some examples of the complicated patterns that result:

Calculations indicate that orders for Product S seem to be tied to the prime interest rate.			
1976, rate up	1978, rate up	1979, rate down	1980, rate up
Sales drop	Sales drop	Sales increase	Sales drop

Notice that you are actually using two sets. The reason that statistical computation is necessary is to determine whether the relationship between the examples is an accident. The best that statistical computation can get for you is an estimate of how likely it is that any connection you observe is not an accidental connection. Therefore statistics do not result in infallible conclusions. Medical and other scientific experimenters understand this and take it into account in their conclusions, although in many ways, people who use statistics to study social events and conditions in society are much more rigid in their reliance on numbers. Our advice to you is to get enough information so that you can evaluate statistical conclusions as arguments. (We elaborate on this point in Chapter 5). It is also useful if you can find a specialist that you trust, who can help you understand a statistical table.

Let us continue to explore the connection between Product S and the decline and rise of the prime interest rate. In 1980 there was a rapid fluctuation of the "prime," and it was accompanied by the following events in regard to Product S:

	Rate	Sales
Jan.	Up	Down
March	Down	Up
April	Up	Down
June	Down	Up
July	Up	Up*

*This unexpected occurrence is accounted for by the shipping of back orders for June.

The speaker must fill in the details briefly and note the exceptions. The conclusion is obvious: the product's sales are very closely connected with the rise and fall of the prime interest rate. The next step is to discover if there is any good reason for this.

It is fairly simple to explain the connection if Product S is a kind of building nail used in the construction of housing frames. Because housing starts are connected to the rise and fall of the prime interest rate, we can expect the sales of Product S to go up as housing starts to go up. Now our whole argument sounds reasonable, and we can argue as follows:

> We ought to find out which of our products are used primarily in housing starts and base our decisions about production, inventory, and promotion on our projections of what will happen to the prime interest rate.

We now have a proposal for a course of action to solve a problem. The proposal is based on the causal and functional connection we have found between two events and our prediction of what might happen if it continues into the future. The proposal itself is a hypothesis, an educated guess, about which we can argue. Let us examine another example.

When you are presenting a proposal, the first step is to use a set pattern to explain the problem the proposal is supposed to solve.

There is a problem in shipping merchandise which consists of the following difficulties:
Shipments into Region B are arriving two weeks late.
Customers in Region K complain about back orders.
Customers in Region W complain about damage.
Cost control says it costs too much to ship to Region M.

Each component of the problem can be detailed by means of another set pattern. By using the word *because* at the end of each sentence, you can be guided to specific statements that will make your main point clear.

Shipments into Region B are delayed because:
Our freight line trans-ships all shipments to a central warehouse and holds them until they can take a full load into the region.

We have too many back orders in Region K
                            because:
Shipping delays fragile items until they can get together an air freight shipment

We have instances of damage in Region W
                            because:
Our shipper in that region is careless and has the largest number of damage claims of any shipper in the country.

Costs are high in Region M
                            because:
We ship there exclusively by parcel post

Notice that your set consists of a causal statement that explains each component of the problem. You can obtain the information about these causal statements by conducting your own investigation or by using the advice of an expert.

Now you can prepare a plan consisting of four components, each component addressed to a particular problem. You can hypothesize that if your plan is adopted, it will eliminate late shipments into Region B, stop the back ordering of merchandise for Region K, reduce damage to shipments in Region W, and reduce the costs of shipments into Region M. If the plan does not create some other problem, and if you can demonstrate that your plan can be reasonably put into action, you have a winning proposal.

Forensics

The forensic pattern is used to "argue" a case, either for or against some idea, proposal, general policy, or resolution. It is based on the classical principles of argument, which require the person who proposes some change to assume the *burden of proof* for it by stating the following:

1. There is a problem that must be solved.
2. Here is a plan that will solve the problem.

3. It is reasonable to believe that the plan can be put into action.
4. The plan will not bring any greater problems with it.

The person who argues against a proposal can base her or his argument on any *one* of the four issues in the burden of proof. She or he can claim that there is no problem, that the plan is not directed to the problem, that the plan is impractical, or that the plan is undesirable because it will bring along conditions even worse than those it is supposed to solve.

The original proposal must identify an *impairment.* An impairment is

1. Something that is happening that should not be happening, the results of which are causing injury to the organization, or
2. Something that is not happening that should be happening, the results of which are causing injury to the organization.

The proposal seeks to eliminate the impairment. The speaker uses a set to present the details of the impairment, an association to show how the components of the plan will eliminate the components of the impairment, and perhaps a chronological pattern to show how the plan would work and that it is practical. As we point out in Chapter 5, the speaker may not mention possible negative consequences at all but must simply be prepared to argue that there won't be any, if someone else charges that there will. In the next chapter we will offer detailed instructions on how to argue your case.

Deliberation

There is a final pattern for the organization of a talk that we refer to as *deliberation.* This is a process of examining conditions in order to discover whether they represent a problem and if so, what the possibilities are for solving it. We mention it here although it is the substance of Chapter 7.

Deliberation is commonly conducted by a group of people who have been requested to develop solutions. It is actually the step that precedes argument. It is the source of proposals. In the democratic process, it is found in the committees of legislatures, where proposed bills are put together by researchers, investigators, and committees of specialists. The group problem-solving that characterizes the deliberation pattern is a major component of organizational life and requires special communications training. We will discuss the deliberation process in detail in Chapter 7.

ORAL STYLE

Your presentation should be prepared so that it can be delivered in *oral style*. Whether you use the extemporaneous mode or work from a manuscript, you must recognize that there are some major differences between speaking and writing, which you must consider in your preparation. People cannot listen well to material that is prepared exclusively to be read. Some kinds of literature can be interpreted orally, but if your intention is to speak to a group, you do best if you prepare yourself in the best oral style.

Written style can be both complicated and subtle. In general, writers expect some effort from the reader. They make every effort, of course, to hold the reader's attention, but as it is often necessary for writers to present complicated detail, they must assume that the reader will take all the time he or she needs to work through the material until it is understood. Readers have the advantages of being able to stop when they are confused, to look up the meaning of a word, or to review what they have read. Furthermore they may proceed at their own pace in whatever blocks of time they choose to devote to reading.

Oral style, on the other hand, is concise, direct, and more dramatic than written style. It must take advantage of the fact that the listeners are gathered in one place all at one time so that the speaker can reach them all at once. There is little doubt about your opportunity as a speaker compared with your opportunity as a writer. As a speaker, you have the audience, and it is up to you to use them well. You have only once chance. Thus your message must be completed in the proper time, and it must be complete by the time you finish. You must speak at a pace that listeners can adjust to. You must use language they can understand and be clear enough so they can follow you. Readers can pick up the material and put it down as they choose. Listeners must follow a thread through an entire presentation. If they lose the connection once, they lose the entire message. There is, obviously, a high risk in presenting oral messages, but there is also the possible gain that you will get the message to everyone who ought to have it.

Speech is more immediate than writing. Listeners react as they hear the speaker. They may not shout out approval or disapproval, but a skilled speaker can tell by how they look at her or him, whether or not they fidget or yawn, and how they are taking notes whether or not they are getting what is being presented. Whether extemporizing or reading a manuscript, a skilled speaker can adapt to the audience by changing his or her vocal presentation. Furthermore, in an extemporaneous presentation, the speaker can include and delete material depending on how he or she interprets the behavior of the audience. A writer does not have this luxury. Once a writer has finished the final draft, there is absolutely nothing she or he can do to motivate possible readers, clarify points for them, or explain to them why they ought to read on. If she or he loses them, that's the end of it.

A great many people regard speaking as spontaneous. They cannot figure out where good speakers get their words and how the ideas come so fluently. They do not understand that public performance (and a good deal of private performance) is preceded by careful thought. In fact, some people object to training in oral performance on the grounds that it is "manipulative" and would take unfair advantage of a listener. What you must consider is this: as a speaker, you are taking the time of a great number of people. It is your obligation not to waste that time. When we work with others to deliberate about possible solutions to problems, everyone recognizes that a good deal of time will be wasted as we struggle to say things clearly. A formal presentation, however, requires, above all, that the speaker be clear. Anyone who tries to listen to the message ought to understand it. This clarity takes considerable preparation.

Writers can have as many tries as they care to take in preparing their material. Hardly anyone transmits a first draft. Writers can clean and polish, add new information, get editorial advice, and correct themselves until they believe that what they have written is ready for the eyes of a reader. A speaker must do all this preparation in imagination, *before* getting up to speak. By keeping in mind some simple points, a speaker can guide his or her preparation so that it is most productive.

- *Avoid rash, overdramatic, or irrelevant statements.* Be sure that your presentation is about one idea related to audience concerns and is presented in a fashion they can understand. You may be filled with other exciting and interesting ideas, but they must be reserved for other speeches. Listeners cannot accommodate to much detail. The simpler and more direct you are, the more likely it is that your audience will listen to you and understand you. This means that you should not push too hard to be humorous. A great many speakers try to be funny. Their problem is that their humor is often strained and off the point. Thus they may get the audience to laugh at the expense of losing their attention on the main point of the speech. Humor is useful only if it relates directly to the topic of your speech. Sometimes, in response to an audience, you may be able to come up with a spontaneous bit of humor that your audience really appreciates. When this happens, be grateful, but don't expect that you will do it every time.

• *Use your preparation to compose a careful outline, a manuscript, or a useful set of notes.* You must assure yourself that you will say everything you plan to say. In order to do this, you need to develop some kind of format for deciding what goes in and what stays out and what goes where. We have already introduced you to the various patterns of organizing your speech. Here is how a simple pattern can be turned into an outline:

Topic: There are four main components of the new federal regulations that will affect your job.	
Changes	How They Will Affect Your Job
All chemicals used must be logged.	Here are the new forms you will need to log the chemicals.
Reports must be submitted weekly to the regional office.	Here are the reports that you must complete and transmit accordingly to the following procedure.
All wastes must be measured and accounted for.	Here are the changes we will make in the labs to handle the wastes.
All wastes must be stored in safe areas.	Here is what will happen to the wastes after you have accounted for them.

The speaker gathers together the specific details and groups them in the proper cells. The speaking outline might look something like this:

I. Regulation 16.01 says, "All chemicals listed must be accounted for at time of receiving and all processes involving the aforesaid chemicals must be accounted for."
   A. We will have the following process when the chemicals are received.
      1. Simpson at receiving will check the shipping manifest and check all boxes.
         a. He will weigh or count each unit of the chemicals.
         b. He will transmit a computer card with his count to Smedley at inventory control.
      2. Smedley will enter the cards into the master inventory.
   B. The procedures we have for you will enable Smedley to keep his inventory current.
      1. Here is Requisition Form X. It is filled out as follows (put display slide on screen).
         a. Step one.
         b. Step two.
      2. Here is Form Y. It is your record of having made a requisition. It is filled out as follows (put display slide on screen).
         a. Step one.
         b. Step two.

And so on, until all of the details are covered. The outline can then be used to guide the listeners to an understanding of what they must do and why they must do it.

Notice that the four requirements of the regulations are organized in a set pattern. The instructions for filling out forms are organized as a chronological pattern. There are no complications here. The speaker is trying to keep the message as simple as possible. (To be sure everyone gets it correctly, of course, the speaker has prepared a written manual of instructions to be passed out at the conclusion of the speech.)

● *Leave nothing unsupported.* Chapter 5 will show you how to support your ideas. When you give a presentational speech, you must support everything. You must

1. Establish yourself as the legitimate person to speak.
2. Show the audience what they have at stake by listening.
3. Present a clear message.

Avoid using your personal experience if you possibly can.

Supports should not be overwhelming. Some speakers try to use everything they have. The reason we advised you to analyze your audience, however, is to discover precisely what kind of support would be most effective for them. When you write the document on which your speech may be based, you can use the bulk of your documentation.

• *Keep a record of what you have said.* When you read a manuscript, you have a permanent record in advance, if you succeed in sticking to the manuscript. When you deliver an extemporaneous speech, you cannot be sure after the speech is over what you have said. Because people will sometimes try to hold you accountable for something you did not say, it is helpful to have some kind of record of your actual statements. This means that a tape recording of the speech is necessary in most cases. By keeping such records, you can check on yourself to be sure that you did not leave out important ideas and that you gave correct instructions. If you are challenged, you can demonstrate what you have said. Finally, you can use your

speeches to refer to when you prepare subsequent speeches. If one was particularly successful, you can check it for guidance on what to do again. When you did not do so well, you can check to see what to avoid.

   • *Be ready for questions.* Most of the speeches you deliver in your organization in connection with your job will probably have question periods associated with them. It is wise to schedule a question period whenever possible, as the kinds of questions your audience asks will help you evaluate how well you did. Even when a question period is not scheduled, there is nothing to prevent a zealous member of the audience from shouting out a question. Although the platform, technically, "belongs" to the speaker, you can be embarrassed if you fail to respond when a valid question is asked. You can legitimately ask people to hold their questions until you are finished, but it is not effective to try to prevent people from asking questions. Strategically, it is most effective to handle good questions when they arise, because if one person asks a question, it is reasonable to assume that many other people in the audience thought of it but did not want to face the public attention that asking a question brings.

   When you encourage questions, you appear to be confident and concerned about audience needs. You also have the opportunity to make a number of important corrections to meet the specific needs of members of the audience. Direct, responsive answers improve your credibility. In the rare cases where it is not possible to have a formal question period, be sure to tell the audience where they can get more information if they need it. To be effective in handling questions, keep the following in mind:

1. If someone wants to argue with you or make a statement, feel free to interrupt and ask for his or her question.
2. Insist on short questions. When someone takes too much time asking a question, the people around that person will usually pressure him or her to speed up. If they do not, you can attempt to help simplify the question.
3. Sometimes people will attempt to ask a string of questions. To be fair to the other members of the audience, you must cut them off. On the other hand, if a question springs logically from the previous answer, you should answer it as well.
4. Be sure to repeat the question, briefly, for the benefit of the audience. Where there is no sound system, it is very difficult

for all of the audience to catch questions. In fact, you yourself may find it difficult to hear, and you may have to ask the questioner to repeat for you. Be sure you have the question correctly before trying to answer it.

5. Be brief in your answers. Don't use the question period as an opportunity to give several more speeches.

6. Take turns in recognizing questioners. Even if someone is signaling frantically, it is customary to recognize those who wish to ask a first question before recognizing someone for a second question. It is helpful to announce the procedure you will use to recognize questioners. For example, "I'll start at the back and work toward the front" or "I'll call on you in the order in which I see your hands."

7. You can limit the number of questions you will handle by announcing, "We have ten minutes for questions," or "We have time for three or four questions." When we want to cut off the questions you can say, "We'll take that lady over there, and the gentleman in the back, and that's all." Be sure to remind people where they can get more information.

8. When the question period is over, don't just leave the podium abruptly. Give a one- or two-minute summary of what happened in the question period. You can use the time to remind people where more information is available. Thank the person who has chaired the meeting and turn the program back to her or him, or announce that the program is over and thank the audience for coming.

Occasionally someone may try to heckle you during your speech. If this happens, try to avoid combat. Nightclub comics get a lot of mileage out of insulting hecklers. However, in a presentational speech, you can be drawn off the track and lose the purpose of the situation if you permit yourself to be heckled. Your best defense is simply to request that questions be held until the end of speech. If the individual seems to want to continue, request that he or she schedule a formal private session with you, if possible, or suggest a time and place to meet for discussion.

• *Stay within the time limits.* It is a good idea to let the audience know roughly how long they will be there. Sometimes you can do this by announcing that the speech will fit into a specified time period. Even so, it is useful to say, "I'll speak to you for about half an hour, and then we'll have fifteen minutes for questions." The idea is to try to set the expectations of the audience so that they will not be dismayed halfway through your speech and start wondering when you will be done. If you take time out of a workday to speak to people, most of them will have their minds on the work waiting for them. They will appreciate it if you are brief and if they know how long they will be listening. If you do announce how long your speech will take, try to stop two minutes early. If you finish before the time limit, you make friends. If you go ten seconds beyond, however important the ideas are, you make enemies. Staying within reasonable time limits demonstrates your respect for listeners' valuable time.

• *Observe ceremonial obligations.* Speakers are often invited to address meetings on special occasions. In such cases, as the speaker, you have an obligation to find out the circumstances of the meeting at which you are to speak, if you were not responsible for setting up the meeting yourself. It is customary to acknowledge the occasion by mentioning the name of the organization or indicating that you respect the honor being bestowed. Excessive time in introductions is distracting, however. Telling too many jokes or reciting little anecdotes about people you know in common wastes time and adds little to your presentation. In Chapter 5, we explain what properly goes into the introduction and conclusion of a presentational speech.

• *Make it clear that there is more information than you have presented.* It is very important that the audience know that they do not know everything they may need to know as a result of listening to your speech. Unless you are delivering a brief speech outside the organization, there is usually considerable information that you could not include that might be important to some members of the audience. Be sure that you remind the audience of this material and tell them how they can obtain it if they need it.

SIMPLE PRESENTATIONS

The simplest forms of presentation are instructions and ceremonial presentations. Longer and more complicated presentations should be prepared according to the advice offered in Chapter 5.

Instructions

When you give instructions, remember that your success is not measured by how interesting you are as a speaker but by whether or not your listeners can follow the instructions you give them. If they can do the task properly after listening to you, you can congratulate yourself on doing a good job. However, it is very hard to follow oral instructions unless there is some "feedback" arrangement. If you are trying to give instructions to a large number of people, you will need to make arrangements to check their work shortly afterward. You will also have to make time available to deal with a wide variety of questions. If the task in which you are instructing them is important to their regular daily duties, they will be very urgent about feeling that they know how to do it, and it is your responsibility to make sure that their anxieties are calmed. The following advice will be helpful. (We also recommend checking the final chapter of this book for instructions on how to write instructions. Much of what we advise there can be applied to oral instruction-giving.)

1. Check your presentation carefully against a chronological pattern to make sure you have left out no *necessary* steps and that the steps are in the proper order. PERT/CPM criteria will help you to be sure that your instructions can be followed, but it will also be useful to experiment with your instructions and to try them on one or two intelligent but uninformed people so that you can spot and correct major errors.
2. Remember that your listeners may not have a technical vocabulary. Make sure that you define any technical words you use. You can tell your audience that you recognize that many of them know what the words mean but that to be sure that everyone does, you will provide definitions. Be prepared with visuals with which to support your definitions.
3. Permit listeners to interrrupt with questions. It is useful if you built checkpoints into your presentation. "By this time, your form should look like this . . ." or "Let me walk down the aisle and check what some of you are doing." Do not single out anyone for correction. Keep talking while you are walking, but keep your eyes open for recurrent problems that you can refer to when you are back at the podium.

4. Use visuals as much as possible. Try to coordinate the visual illustrating each step with the words you are saying about it. The visuals will clarify the instructions and also help to hold your audience's attention.

Briefings

A briefing is a digest of information. When you are assigned to "brief" someone, your task is to select the main information from a complicated or extensive body of information and present it clearly to the person who requested the briefing. Briefings are sometimes about what is going on and are sometimes abstracts of written documents.

1. Briefings should use the main headings of the document as an outline. Try to stay with the chapter headings, if possible. If you are not working on a document, use the set pattern to set up the main headings for your briefing.
2. Briefings must be "brief." They are used when the person requesting the information has very little time. The information will probably be used very quickly, so accuracy is important. Be able to tell the person requesting the briefing where more information is available if it is needed.
3. The best briefing is simple enough so that the listener does not feel the need to ask any questions.
4. Briefings should be accompanied by a one-page synopsis, including references to the source of the briefing.

Ceremonial Presentations

Executives and supervisors are often required to preside at ceremonial functions. At such times, there is a temptation for them to talk too much. Masters of ceremonies, however, generally see themselves as funnier than they really are. The important point about ceremonial occasions is that they are potentially boring unless everyone concerned does her or his business efficiently. Keep the following suggestions in mind:

1. Introductions of speakers should be brief. When introducing a famous person, there is a temptation to say too much about

her or his credentials. One or two major points that qualify her or him especially on the topic on which she or he is to speak are generally sufficient. No introduction should take more than one minute.

2. In giving honors, emphasize the main reason for the honor: "Fred Smith sold more grevitzes than any man in the company this year," "It is a pleasure to salute Mary Dugan on the occasion of her retirement," or "May I present the man you selected as 'man of the year.' " If you receive an honor, it is not necessary to act like a bit player who won an unexpected Academy Award. A simple "thank you" is usually sufficient, unless giving a formal speech is the price you have been asked to pay for the award.

3. If you give an annual report, avoid overwhelming your audience with detail. As the report is probably printed, it is usually enough to take seven to ten minutes to note major differences and to help the audience to understand the report when they get it.

PERFORMANCE

Presentational speaking is a performance. It is important that you know how to use your voice and body to make yourself effective. The best preparation can be wiped out by poor presentation. You cannot learn to use your voice and body by reading about it in a book; vocal training requires the services of a skilled instructor. We can, however, offer you some cautions and ideas that might be helpful in your presentations:

1. It is jarring to an audience to hear words mispronounced. Do not assume that you know more than you do. Any word that is the least bit unfamiliar should be checked for pronunciation. You should check your knowledge of proper pronunciation by rehearsing your speech and asking the person listening to you to advise you of mispronounced words. Also use your dictionary to check on proper pronunciation.

2. Be careful of straining your voice. It is important to avoid vocal strain because untrained speakers frequently suffer from nodes on the vocal cords, which often require surgery. If you feel the least bit of strain, use an audio system to amplify your voice. A

cordless microphone and a decent stereo system can be of great help. However, if you are using an audio system, make sure that it works well and does not have static. A defective audio system has destroyed many a good speech.

3. Avoid sloppy diction and regionalisms. Blurred consonants and distorted vowels signal that you are less competent than you are. There is a tendency in contemporary society to use a loose, conversational style when speaking. The "laid-back" style may work at social gatherings, but it does not hold the attention of audiences. Try as far as you possibly can to speak General American English, the pronunciation radio announcers use. This format of pronunciation works with most audiences. This comment should not be construed as a criticism of ethnic accents or dialects, merely as a practical suggestion to improve intelligibility.

4. Try to avoid phrases like "y'know" and "and, uh." Vocalized pauses distract your listeners and suggest that you are lackadaisical and not concerned about them. Sloppy performance is often interpreted as evidence of sloppy thinking. One of the advantages of a written manuscript is that reading it tends to prevent vocalized pauses.

5. Try to be reasonably direct. Most public speaking books advise making "eye contact" with your audiences. This is a difficult bit of advice to interpret. The best interpretation is that the audience should believe that you are talking to *them*. You can accomplish this by looking up periodically, by looking at different parts of the room, and by taking time periodically to meet the eyes of whoever happens to be looking at you at the time. Once you have given a few speeches, you will discover you can get fairly free of your notes or manuscript and thus free yourself to make direct contact with the audience. The important thing about looking at the audience is getting a sense of how well they are understanding you.

6. Don't jump to conclusions about the meaning of nonverbal behavior in the audience. It is hard to tell what various expressions mean. The person whose eyes are closed may be dozing or concentrating. The person who is nodding may be agreeing with you or may have trained herself in the technique of nodding. Keep in mind that there is no code of meaning for nonverbal behavior. Once you get to know a person, you might be able to

interpret it, but when you observe behavior in an audience, all you can do is react to what you think it means. Obviously, if the audience is very restless, you will need to do something about it, and if they interrupt you with periodic applause, you can permit yourself to believe that they approve of what you are saying.

7. Emphasis and intonation are important. You tell the audience what is important in your speech by the way you say it. When you speak to an audience, modify your voice, making it louder and softer, speaking more slowly or more rapidly to tell your audience how attentive they should be. You can suggest that an idea is important by raising the pitch of your voice. You can slow down for very important points. The act of modification itself tells the audience about your interpretation of what is important.

8. Use your body in a dignified way to support your ideas. Many speakers feel very tense when they first take the platform. They may learn to overcome tension in their voice, but sometimes their faces and bodies give away their nervousness. Don't worry about this. You can start out holding on to the podium if it makes you feel more comfortable. It is important to remember that audiences are sympathetic with you. They understand that you probably feel tense. Years of research have demonstrated that the best way to manage tension is to learn skillful performance. If you are well organized and know your material, your nervousness will tend to disappear, and your face and body will start working to help you.

VISUAL SUPPORTS

Designing visuals and integrating them into oral presentations constitute an art for which special training is required. In your organization, you will probably find someone who specializes in designing visuals to support speeches. It is your responsibility to figure out exactly what you will need and where it fits into your speech.

Speeches do not succeed merely because they are accompanied by expertly designed visuals. In fact, visuals sometimes distract from the content of the speech. Slide shows and multimedia presentations do not necessarily convey information efficiently. In fact, if you use visuals sparingly, mostly to help define obscure ideas and to identify unfamiliar things, you will get their maximum effect. Visuals can also be used to illustrate steps in the process in which you are instructing your audience.

Visuals are another form of documentation. In Chapter 5, we discuss various kinds of support for the points you are trying to make, and we show you which kinds of support are best coordinated with visuals. Visuals, in general, should be used when words alone are not enough. They should not be used by themselves; they should always be accompanied by some explanation. Visuals should conform to the following criteria:

1. They should be attractive and easily seen by everyone in the audience.
2. They should not be an end in themselves. Do not give a speech simply because you have some visuals available.
3. They should be simple enough to make the point you are trying to make.
4. They should always be accompanied by a verbal explanation. Visuals that are not explained distract the audience; people do not know what to look for in a visual unless you tell them.
5. Visuals should not be art exhibits. They should not be so interesting that they distract people from your presentation.
6. Visuals should avoid clichés. Try not to be "cute." Little "Peanuts" cartoons don't work if they are overdone.

The main purpose of the visual is to catch attention, not to hold it. You sustain attention with what you say about the visual. Visuals are to be used as examples or illustrations, not as the proofs themselves. You may choose from diagrams, charts, graphs, mock-ups, physical displays of the object itself, multimedia, film and videotapes, and the chalkboard. You should base your selection on the technology available to you, the facility with which you can get the visuals to the place where you are speaking, the amount of time available for production, the cost of the visual, its potential for use on other occasions, and the importance of the point to be illustrated. It is usually distracting to bring in a great deal of visual equipment and then use it to show one picture. If visuals are used at all, they should be spaced throughout the speech or used intensively where needed and then put away so that the audience is not anticipating the next

picture. Showing slides in a darkened room and speaking from the back of the room can put an audience to sleep. Chalkboards are awkward to use because you have to turn your back on the audience to use them, and often you have to stop speaking while you put your material on the board. Furthermore not everyone can print neatly enough on a chalkboard so that the material can be easily read. The same is true of flipcharts on which you write with crayon. It is most useful to have your visuals prepared in advance, ready to show when you need them.

SUMMARY

Presentations are arguments presented to your audience designed to get them to revise information, change their attitudes, or take some action. Each possible objective dictates obligations that must be fulfilled. You have obligations to the audience. You must give them good reasons for what you ask them to do. Fulfilling these obligations means that you have assumed your burden of proof.

Ideas must be presented redundantly, one idea to a speech. You must rephrase your message several ways so that you catch the attention of most of the people in your audience. There are ten basic patterns you can use to organize your speech:

1. *Chronology,* when you must deal with steps or events in sequence.
2. *Description,* when it is important for the audience to be able to recognize something.
3. *Structure,* when you want to explain the relationships of parts or to describe how a space or a procedure is laid out. Flowcharts for computer processing are structures.
4. *Set,* when you want to emphasize components or categories.
5. *Comparison,* when you want to show similarities between apparently different ideas.
6. *Contrast,* when you want to show differences between apparently similar things or ideas.
7. *Criteria,* when you want to evaluate something according to some standard.
8. *Association,* when you want to project the future, show how one thing causes another, or show how two things fluctuate according to some pattern.
9. *Forensics,* when you want to make a proposal and defend it.
10. *Deliberation,* when you want to explore a problem and suggest solutions.

Oral style differs from written style because of its immediacy. This means that your speech must be well prepared. You can't afford to make many mistakes or to leave much out because you get to speak only once, and the audience cannot check back on you as they could a written document. Skillful speakers can adapt to the audience, entertain questions, and get a firsthand estimate of how they are doing as they speak. Oral presentation requires assessing how important a situation is and doing the preparation required to meet the needs of the situation. This means you can decide between manuscript, outline, or notes, but you should have a record of what you actually said, regardless of which method you use.

Giving instructions, briefings, and ceremonial presentations are the simplest forms of presentation.

Presentational style requires skillful use of face, body, and voice. It is not manipulative to train yourself to perform well.

You can use visuals and other mechanical aids to support your presentation.

READINGS

Some special features of presentational speaking are described in Jean DeJen, *Visual Presentations Handbook for Business and Industry.* St. Petersburg, Fla.: Oravisual Co., 1959. The author provides an explanation of how to use a variety of visual aids, including simple flannel-board and blackboard operations. Examples are provided. Thomas E. Anastasi, Jr., *Desk Guide to Communication.* Reading, Mass.: Addison-Wesley, 1974, Chapter 12, focuses on the use of boards and charts, models, mock-ups, projectors, and tapes and on the preparation and use of handouts.

Those interested in more information on the use of the voice should check Jon Eisenson, *Voice and Diction: A Program for Improvement.* New York: Macmillan, 1979. This is a rather advanced book, but it provides basic information about vocal anatomy and describes techniques and exercises for improving loudness, pitch, duration, and quality of the voice. A simple and practical approach to the improvement of diction, including photographs of the mouth to guide in the accurate production of sounds, can be found in Walter Schumacher, *Voice Therapy and Voice Improvement.* Springfield, Ill.: Charles C. Thomas, 1974.

The standard work on vocal improvement and delivery is Dorothy Sarnoff, *Speech Can Change Your Life.* New York: Doubleday, 1970.

Virtually any public speaking textbook can review the principles of presentation for you. A particularly good one is Eugene White, *Practical Public Speaking.* New York: Macmillan, 1982 4th Ed.

Chapter 5

The Argument of the Case

THE ABSOLUTELY CRUCIAL POINT

Truth does not win out because it is truth. It wins only when it is well argued. The process of decision making in Western society has been based on the idea that if people argue their points of view in front of other people who have the responsibility of making decisions, the best ideas will win out in the end. This is the guiding principle of democracy, and it is the guiding principle in organizational life.

Think of the many times you *knew* that your ideas were better than the ones that everyone seemed to believe. It made you bitter. You wondered why you weren't discovered. The problem we all face is that no one notices us unless we ask to be noticed. People tend to listen to people who speak up. They ask advice from people who have obviously stored up important information (experts). They ask for advice from people who have the credentials to give it (doctors, lawyers). If you are not the outstanding expert in your field, if you are not a licensed advice-giver, and if you are not already a top executive, you have to earn the right to be heard by speaking well.

You must argue whenever you have an idea that someone might disagree with. You cannot assume that people will believe what you say just because you say it. Even the experts, the advice givers, and the top executives have the responsibility of arguing their point of view, of demonstrating its superiority over the alternatives. The president of the United States argues with his advisers, with Congress, with members of the opposing party.

Argument is not a popular word in our society. We have just come through a period in which it was regarded virtuous to be "laid back" and "cool," to avoid confrontation. The word *argument* conveys the idea of confrontation. This is not really the case, however. Confrontation can exist only if you believe that you can get the person who opposes your ideas to change his or her mind. This almost never happens, and it is not even useful to try. It doesn't matter how long, loudly, or effectively you argue, you will rarely convince your opponents to admit that they are wrong. If your opponents are going to change their minds, they will do it after the fact, in private, and they will probably not give you the satisfaction of knowing they have done it. Thus we do not argue to convince our opponents. The purpose of argument is to convince the person who has the power to make the decision. If a single executive is to make the decision, then you must influence her or him. If a group is to decide by majority vote, then you must influence the majority of them. If you speak to the community in general, you must get those who already support your ideas to support them more strongly, you must tip the neutrals to your side, and you must put doubt into the minds of those who doubt you.

There is no way to argue without combining your personal qualities with appeals to the emotions of your listeners in order to get them to pay attention to your reasoning. Winning an argument is like an effective job of selling. You must get the prospect to listen, you must offer something he or she finds worthwhile having, and you must provide him or her with logical reasons for accepting what you offer. This is the same advice that Aristotle offered 2,500 years ago.

Your personal reputation is an important element in argument. We have already advised you that you must have some reason to believe that speaking can make a difference before you decide to make a statement. Your position, your past record for accuracy and intelligence, and your general appeal to the people to whom you speak will determine how respectful they will be when you talk to them. If your standing is not good, then you will have to struggle to advance your case. Effective use of emotion depends on how well you assess the needs and commitments of the people to whom you speak. If you can discover what it is they need and want badly, and you can find some way to get them to believe that they can get it by accepting your point of view, you have the most effective emotional appeal.

The bulk of argument in the organization depends on your logic. Decision makers in the corporate world cannot afford to let themselves be committed by their passions. They have achieved their positions largely on their ability to separate their personal feelings from their understanding of the corporate good. Thus, if you can get them to listen at all, you are most effective when you present a well-supported and logical case, delivered, of course, in a way that will not bore them.

Skillful presentation showcases your logic. Totally logical presentations require the kind of careful attention only a committed reader can give. Speakers cannot assume that their audience will give that kind of attention. Furthermore, even if the audience listens attentively, they will miss many of the fine details and risk being lost in the complicated pathways. Thus the argumentative presentation must feature the main issues and use a limited number of highly effective proofs to support the ideas. Like all the other oral presentations in organizational life, there is usually a written document to which those interested in details can refer.

THE CONCEPT OF IMPAIRMENT

You argue because you believe something is wrong and you have something to say that, if accepted, will make things right. When you present a point of view and ask for its acceptance, you declare that you are willing to accept responsibility for the outcome. You are willing to "take the rap" if you are wrong and look forward to taking the credit if you are right.

The urgency to argue grows out of

1. Your perception that something is wrong.
2. Your recognition that what is wrong can be changed.
3. Your belief that you can propose a course of action that will bring about that change.
4. Your belief in your ability to make it clear to an audience that there is something happening that should not be happening or something not happening that should be happening.
5. The assessment that the audience to which you speak regards you as enough of an authority to justify listening to you.

For example,

1. Production is dropping. People in the plant do not seem "happy." The production supervisor is singing, "We need a little Christmas."
2. You recall that just a year ago production workers were pleasant to be with and apparently dedicated to accomplishing company goals. You believe they can be that way again.
3. You remember that on your last job there was real difficulty in the plant when the production supervisor was so involved with problems at home that he was not rewarding good work. You think your ability to analyze situations will help you find out what is wrong.
4. You examine the situation and discover that the production supervisor has two assistants, both of whom are competing for power. One is male and one female, and each wants to be the number-one assistant. The supervisor is so distracted by the feud that he has lost touch with his workers. You have discovered an impairment: something is happening that should not be happening, and it is obviously interfering with something important.
5. You decide to speak to the production supervisor and his two assistants, the vice-president for production, and the trouble-shooting task force to present your ideas on the matter. You feel secure in doing this because you have spoken to the task force several times, and they have respected your position as an efficiency expert.

There are two important things to remember before assuming the responsibility of arguing:

1. You must have standing. During a football game, an infinite number of recommendations come from people in the grandstand who will not be heard because they have no standing. If you do not have standing, your first task is to achieve it, for without it, you will never get to speak to the people who can make a difference. Without standing, you are no better off than the soapbox orators in the park. Finding the appropriate audience is a matter of finding out where you have or can get the standing to speak. (Don't despair—if you are paid for doing a job, the fact that you do the job well gives you some

standing to begin with. Advancing in the company is a process
of acquiring standing.)
2. You must be able to identify an impairment. Problem-solving
   groups (see Chapter 7) have the time and the authority to work
   through conjecture and speculation. If you seek time to speak
   to others, you have to pinpoint the problem. You must be able
   to make a causal connection between a condition that is causing
   trouble, loss of money, time, personnel unrest, production difficulties, and so on, and something that is happening that
   should not be happening or something that is not happening
   that should be happening.

There are some standard places where impairments can be discovered in any organization.
   • *There can be problems with organizational goals.* Do people
understand what the organization's goals are? If people do not understand the goals, they may find it difficult to work to accomplish
them. If people do not agree that the goals are important, they may
not work hard to accomplish them. If goals are impossible to achieve,
it may be frustrating to try to accomplish them. An impairment in
goals can cause low morale, misdirected effort, confusion, and ambiguity, and, in general, it can affect the tone of the whole organization.

• *There can be problems with the goods and services provided.* Does anyone else agree that what the organization does is worthwhile? If the organization is supposed to provide services but people are not using them, then the whole organization is jeopardized. If no one is buying the goods that the organization produces, then income is reduced and people lose their jobs. Goods and services must be in demand by people who are able to take advantage of them and who are willing to pay for them. Quality and product, customer/consumer satisfaction, sensible obsolescence policies, and new product and service development are important components of organizational success and can be the source of legitimate recommendations to overcome impairments in goods and services.

• *There can be problems in the relationship of the components of the organization.* Are the divisions of the organization working well together? If there is competition between divisions for the limited attention of the executive, for funds, for credit, or just for pride, there can be an impairment. If divisions are not aware of where they fit and what other divisions do, there can be unintelligent decision-making that affects the organization. If communication links are not well maintained between organizational components, then there can be duplication of effort, confusion, and head-on combat between divisions. Improvement of communications and information flow is a proper recommendation for impairments in relationships.

• *There can be problems in the way that administrative personnel carry out their duties.* Administrators and executives do not hold power by the "divine right." They must earn their wages daily by giving appropriate orders and directions and by making effective decisions. Incompetence or major errors by a responsible person can represent an impairment. Conflicts between administrators that interfere with the smooth operation of the organization are also impairments. Inability to cope with emergencies, hostility from employees, suspicion of colleagues, and inability to communicate with the public —all represent possible locations of impairments, the appropriate recommendation for which is the dismissal or transfer of the person involved.

• *There are a number of problems with personnel that can interfere with organizational operations.* Employee morale, the competence of personnel, grievances, employee benefits, work assignments, the quality of direct supervision, gossip and rumor, excessive competition, lack of commitment to the organization, ineffective reward and punishment systems, accidents, absenteeism, and many other situations can represent impairments in personnel, for which complicated and subtle recommendations can be made.

- *Financing is a consistent source of trouble for organizations.* Impairments can be found in the sources of funds, the adequacy of the bank balance, accounts receivable and payable, disbursement methods, accounting procedures, taxation, funding and allocation, and dishonesty in handling money.

- *Logistics also presents a source of impairments.* Issues like records, computer storage and retrieval, the routing of information, shipping and receiving, warehousing and storage, filing systems, and the general ease with which components of the company work together represent a frequent source of impairments. In addition, the physical plant, the equipment, the supplies, and the ambience may also present problems.

- *Impairments can be found in external relations.* Getting along with competitors, with the press, and with the community at large is important to an organization. Impairments in these areas can have serious consequences.

Each of the above categories represent a source of data for a formal presentation. Responsible personnel in organization are alert to possibilities in all of these areas. Constant monitoring of all aspects of the organization with which you are connected will reveal a large number of problems, any of which might warrant some proposal for solution. To make an impairment clear enough to an audience so that they might be willing to act, you must provide them with answers to the following questions:

1. What is the problem? What is happening or not happening? Who or what is being hurt by it? What does it cost the organization in money, time, quality of activity, confusion, and so on? Who decided it was a problem? Has anyone requested a solution?
2. What is the cause of the problem? What were the events that led up to it? How is the audience involved?
3. What must a solution acomplish in order to solve the problem?

After demonstrating the existence of a problem and describing its nature, the speaker makes her or his proposal following the forensic pattern (see Chapter 4). In Chapter 7, we review these steps in detail and show you how problem-solving groups analyze situations in order to identify problems and construct solutions.

The concept of impairment permits you to be very precise in defining the topic of your presentation. If you can discover and explain an impairment, you will not have to waste the audience's time with a discussion of intangibles and abstractions. Here are some examples of proposal presentations made by people in various organizations, each addressed to a particular impairment.

1. A vice-president for research and development observed that many of the company's scientists had resigned and later patented a product with considerable commercial value. He decided that there was something wrong with the company's patent policy. He proposed a program of joint development so that the company could obtain the right to produce such inventions, and a stock transfer would be made to the inventor so that he or she could remain involved.

2. A supervisor of clinical personnel in a community counseling agency observed that counselors assigned to families of alcoholics had a dropping case load. She discovered an agency in the community specializing in alcoholism and proposed that alcoholism services be terminated in his agency.

3. A marketing manager received a number of complaints about defective products and proposed revisions in production procedures as well as a recall, refund, replace program in order to keep customers satisfied.

4. A representative of a labor union discovered that many of his members were upset by increasing hospital costs. He argued for an expansion of union hospital benefits to reduce this impairment in morale.

5. A vice-president for public relations argued that special funding should be provided for voluntary installation of antipollution devices and that advantage should be taken of tax write-off allowances because she believed that if the company waited for a court order, community ill will would interfere with operations at the plant.

In each of these cases, it was easy to see what the impairment was and how it affected the organization. If the impairment is clearly identified, then it is fairly simple to discover what the solution ought to be about. It may be very difficult to construct the solution, but at least you are guided in a productive direction.

BURDEN OF PROOF

In the above cases, each of the speakers advocated some change in what was going on. Once having done this, he or she had to assume the *burden of proof*.

1. The vice-president for research and development had to detail the financial loss from scientists' leaving and explain the potential gain if they were persuaded to stay.
2. The supervisor of clinical personnel had to demonstrate that cases were being handled elsewhere and that counselors would benefit from reassignment.
3. The marketing manager had to show the financial loss from defect claims and demonstrate how that loss might be made up for by production changes and compensation.
4. The labor union representative had to show that the cost of increased hospital coverage would be made up by reduced losses from low morale.
5. The vice-president for public relations had to show the consequences of community antagonism on a balance sheet against the cost of installing the recommended devices.

Your burden of proof arises directly out of your topic. It is not enough to show personal inconvenience unless the recommendation relates only to your own work. The organization's good must somehow be involved in the recommendation you make. Your defense of the recommendation has to employ evidence drawn from the organization as a whole. If you address the problem of individual discomfort or inequity, you must show how the organization is affected.

Specifically, you have the responsibility of documenting what you say with evidence. If you claim something happened, you must describe what happened and provide some proof that it really happened. If you claim that a situation is a problem, you must explain the nature of the problem and show the connection between it and the situation. If you claim that something is not up to standard, you must explain the standards, demonstrate that they are important, and make the comparison. Here are some examples:

1. A sales manager offered statistics comparing orders received and processed for the last five years to support her claim that sales were falling.
2. An agency director of a facility that transports the elderly offered examples of six catastrophes arising from calls that drivers missed to document his claim that inefficient driver scheduling was injuring the agency's operation and reputation.
3. An executive presented statistics on frequency of product failure as well as the details of two lawsuits arising from product failure to support his recommendation for major changes in the design of the product.

Once you decide what you will speak about, you must investigate to discover what you absolutely must do in order to fulfull your obligation to the defense of the idea.

THE AUDIENCE FOR ARGUMENT

Before you start to argue, you must identify the person or group that can make the decision about whether or not your idea should be accepted. When you argue, you must direct your efforts exclusively to that person or group. Your arguments should be constructed so as to have maximum appeal to your audience. It may be exciting to argue directly with an opponent, but rarely can you get your adversaries to change their minds. Rather, advocates present their cases to the person or group that has the power to decide.

American society offers many examples of arguments directed at responsible decision-makers. Our legal system, for example, works on the premise that matters of right and wrong must be resolved by a jury or a qualified judge. Attorneys are bound by formal rules of argument, and the judge has the power to penalize anyone who violates the rules. Proposals are also made to legislative bodies, city councils, the U.S. Senate and House of Representatives, or the board of trustees or the directors of a major organization. There is virtually no complex organization in the Western world that does not have some arrangement for arguing ideas in front of authorized decision-makers.

Argument permeates other aspects of our lives as well. Commercials argue for our attention to their products. Teachers argue that their subject matter is worth learning. Salespeople offer us direct arguments to get us to part with our cash in exchange for the product they sell. The clergy argue for our souls. Children argue for attention in the family. Pressure groups argue for attention from society. The arguments that work with us are the ones that are addressed to what we need and want.

You can prepare yourself to make decisions about what to include in your argument by specifying your audience and asking some questions about it. The answers to the questions should guide you in the selection of the material most appropriate to supporting your case.

1. Why is this the proper person or group to address? What are its powers? Can he, she, or they do what I request, or can they see that it gets done? What do they stand to gain by solving the problem I am addressing? There is no point in trying to convince your opponents or in wasting time arguing in front of a group that does not have the power to act.

2. How have the decision makers behaved on previous occasions? Have they supported or rejected proposals like yours? If they supported them, what convinced them? If they rejected them, what grounds did they give for doing so? Responses to these questions can help you to avoid errors and to discover the most persuasive arguments.

3. What do the decision makers know about the issue, and what is the source of their information? Are they biased? What axe do they have to grind? Do they have external loyalties (political, economic, religious) that might shape their opinion on your idea? Once you know what they know, you will be able to adjust your language. Once you know their possible biases, you will be able to use them on your behalf or work to overcome them.

4. What is your standing with the person or group to which you will speak? Do you have the right to speak to them? How did you go about getting the opportunity to speak to them? What do they know about you, and where did they find it out? What is your reputation for honesty, credibility, and knowledge? You should be aware of your assets and limitations when you

speak to the group. If you are credible, then you can give more of the same. If you have a handicap, then you must work to overcome it.

It is important to know who your opposition might be and whether their opposition is to your idea or to you. The notion of having opposition is frightening to most people, and a great many otherwise competent people avoid presenting their ideas because they fear they will not be able to handle public opposition. Opposition, however, is part of the decision-making process. If you feel that it is unjustifiable to oppose you, then you are excessively arrogant. No one has the wisdom and the skill to be right all the time. The smart decision-maker will listen to a number of points of view and try to select from them what makes the most sense. You must be able to select the most important issues that your opponents present and be prepared to deal with them. This does not mean you have to hate your opponents or even get involved in face-to-face combat with them. You must, however, deal with the important ideas they present.

The bulk of your opposition will be people who favor doing nothing. People are generally uncomfortable when they anticipate changes that might affect the way they live their daily lives. The first opponent of any proposal is the status quo, the tendency that people have to keep doing things the way they have always done them until they have a good reason for changing. It is certainly easier to take no action and hope for the best when you are confronted with a problem. Sadly, the best does not always happen. It does not even happen frequently. The fact that things just don't work out by themselves gives you your main justification for making a proposal.

Sometimes there are several proposals for action to solve some problem. Each proposal reflects the interests of the person who proposed it or of the group the proposer represents. Each arguer tries to establish conviction on their side. Effective decision-makers often try to pool the wisdom of the various points of view by appointing a committee or task force to deal with an issue through the process of group discussion. Formal argument takes time, and it is much more efficient to listen to a presentation that involves the ideas of several different people than to listen to those same people present their ideas individually. The fact that it is possible for people to get together on an idea even when they are inclined to disagree should encourage you. It means that argument does not necessarily have a hostile and unpleasant result. In fact, effective argument generally results in effective solutions.

It is wise to give considerable respect to your possible opposition. Try to identify the grounds on which they oppose you. Examine their arguments carefully and try to see which ones you can agree with. The most effective argument is directed at one small point. "Shotgunning" an opponent by disagreeing with everything she or he says is inefficient, and if you use this technique, you are likely to find yourself on thin ice with some of your arguments. In Chapter 7, we show you how to build a consensus out of disagreement. In the interests of your own effectiveness, you should work toward the best consensus you can find and disagree only with those parts of your opponent's case that you can prove are erroneous or dangerous.

Be aware of the decision-making style of the people you seek to convince. Some decision makers prefer confrontation between points of view. Others prefer a more tentative approach, so that they can make their own synthesis. Some will play devil's advocate and cross-examine everyone that presents ideas to them. Preventing polarization is most useful. Effective executives are interested in keeping their employees on speaking terms, and thus they cannot afford to let arguments get too serious or to get people too far out on a limb in defense of their point of view. If the executive who can get people to argue their best but is willing to cooperate with a synthetic proposal constructed out of everyone's ideas, he has the best chance of getting productive solutions to problems. But even being headed toward eventual consensus does not mean that you can afford to dilute your argument. When we advise you to "argue hard," we mean that you should select the best evidence and documentation you can find, use the most logical reasoning, and present your ideas clearly and cogently without making personal attacks on the people opposing you.

Remember that any responsible position demands that you be visible. Even if you do not enjoy arguing, you have the obligation to present your point of view. Presumably that is what you are being paid for. If you do not assume this right, you might lose your opportunity to influence outcomes. If you are in a position that requires you to exercise responsible leadership, you will, at some time, have to argue your case against opposition. It may not be written into the job description, but it is a given that advancement in an organization is directly related to the skill with which you argue, and the higher you advance, the more direct will be the confrontations you must make on important issues.

THE JAPANESE MESSAGE

There has been a sudden recognition that the Japanese have become very effective at managing communication among and between their workers. Japanese industry has advanced materially because of the way employees participate in solving the problems that confront any productive enterprise. Japanese management works actively to encourage the exchange of information and argument about how things should be done among their employees, under the assumption that the people who actually do the work should be the experts on how it should be done.

While there are some major differences between American and Japanese companies, the most important fact is that employment is permanent in most Japanese companies, American management could borrow many techniques from the Japanese. In fact, much of what the Japanese do was originated in the United States in the early days of the group dynamics movement.

One of the major features of the Japanese view is that short-term profits are not the most important goal for the company. Japanese managers encourage long range goal setting, which permits considerable imagination to be employed about the directions a company should take. Imagination results in a great many proposals for changes in goals and methods, and each of them has to be discussed and debated thoroughly. According to William Ouchi in an article "Individualism and Intimacy in an Industrial Society," *Technology Review*. Vol. 83, No. 7, July, 1981, P. 36, Japanese workers talk with each other to make their values and beliefs compatible, and to give each person the best chance to contribute important information and ideas. This system works because management is trained to accept and use the ideas presented by workers. Similar systems have not worked well in American industry because the workers had the the idea that their contributions were largely ignored by management, and that they were encouraged to speak as an indulgence, not out of respect.

The issue of the nature of argument and discussion in Japanese industry will be considered in detail in Chapter 8. It is important to understand that the way American industry is currently being run is in the process of change. The direction seems clear; there will be more oral participation by employees on all levels of production and management. Learning to present your case well will put you in the forefront of change by equipping you with the skill needed to present your important ideas.

PROOFS AND SUPPORTS

The word *proof* should not intimidate you. It merely means the things you say to support your ideas. If you offer information, you must explain it by defining your terms, giving examples or statistics, or relating detailed narratives. Those are your proofs. If you declare that one event is the cause of another, you must provide the basis for your reasoning so that the audience can understand the connections you make. Proofs are the *reasons for* understanding, believing, or doing.

There are four basic categories of proofs:

1. *Definitions* detail the characteristics by which you can identify a thing, a condition, a state of affairs, or a concept.
2. *Examples* are concrete illustrations of either definitions or generalizations, sometimes presented as narratives of events.
3. *Statistics* are generalizations built out of examples, and phrased in precise numerical form.
4. *Citations* are statements of opinion, generally drawn from people who qualify as authorities.

Speakers use these four kinds of proof to provide reasons for listeners to find what they say acceptable. No matter what your purpose, it is absolutely necessary for you to offer proofs in order to fulfull your burden of proof.

Each of the four types of proofs contains obligations for its expert use. There are simple rules to which you must conform in order to make your proof effective. Commonly speakers gather more information than they can possibly use in their presentations. By comparing each unit of information against the standards for quality, you can assure yourself that you will select the best proofs for your presentation.

Definitions

Definitions are used to clarify. When an audience hears words or ideas that it does not understand, it cannot follow your reasoning and consequently will not accept your ideas. Definitions do not apply only to individual words. Sometimes definitions refer to conditions or situations. "The nation is on the verge of a depression" is a phrase that requires a definition. "The period of transition," "the prime interest rate," "the situation in the Coshocton branch," and "the state of the relationship between the United States and Soviet Union" are all phrases that could be made more clear by the use of a definition.

The dictionary definition is nothing more than a group of words about words. The dictionary is a historical record of the meanings that have been assigned to words. Definitions of concrete entities like battleships, aardvarks, or elm trees can be taken from the dictionary, although certain words become colloquial like *gay* or *bad,* or change meaning like *electron.* If you select a dictionary definition, make sure that it is currently in use, for if you use a word and assign it a meaning that does not agree with the meaning commonly in vogue, the audience may be misled the next time they encounter the word. If the dictionary offers alternative definitions, be sure to specify the one you choose for your word.

For example, the dictionary offers two meanings for the word *consensus:* (1) ". . . general agreement or concord: harmony," or (2) "majority decision." The two are very different in meaning. A "majority decision" can be made without "general agreement," and "harmony" is not necessarily part of it. If you ask a group to come to a consensus, you need to specify whether you want them to approximate a unanimous decision, as implied in a "general agreement," or whether a simple majority vote to decide the issue will do.

A scientific or technical definition provides the details of a process. For example, "by permitting each person to state his or her ideas regardless of how much they disagree, and then by looking for things you can all agree on, you will eventually be able to synthesize an agreement. You can do this best by (1) not permitting anyone to offer a complete solution; (2) taking care to record areas of agreement; or (3) attempting to resolve conflict between ideas by subsuming them under broader ideas." The preceding would function as a technical definition of *consensus.* Technical definitions are commonly used in scientific reports or program plans.

An operational definition is a statement that restricts the amount of confusion by specifying "how you would know one if you saw one." For example, "you can recognize a consensus when a group agrees that for better or worse, this is the report they will give, and there is no minority report."

Often it is necessary to present pictures and diagrams to provide an adequate definition. Technical operations can often be specified by mathematical formulas or blueprints. Even simple objects, however, often need something more than a dictionary definition. If you wanted to talk about armadillos to people who never saw one, the definition on page 73 of the *Random House Collegiate Dictionary* is not very helpful.

> *armadillo* . . . any of several burrowing, chiefly nocturnal edentate mammals of the family *Dasypodidae,* ranging from the Southern U.S. through South America, having strong claws and a jointed protective covering of bony plates.

This definition may tell you a good deal more about armadillos than you care to know without enabling you to identify one if it came crawling out from under your hedge. For that reason, a picture is included. The picture does not explain what *edentate* means (you can look that up in the dictionary), but it does give you an idea of what the creature looks like. The problem is that neither definition nor picture specifies size, and so you would not know whether the armadillo is likely to wreck your garage or nip your knuckles.

Occasionally speakers use definitions to amplify ideas. They may offer a special definition that they have made up: "Consensus is a situation where members of a committee are too frightened to go off on their own, so they stick together even though they may not want to, you know, like Benjamin Franklin's comment, 'We must all hang together or we will all hang separately.'" This kind of definition is useful in gaining and holding attention, but its metaphoric quality makes it too slippery to be useful in providing a clear explanation to the audience. Personal definitions should be used only when the speaker is sure the audience knows the dictionary, technical, or operational definition.

Examples

A report, a narrative, or a detailed account of one thing used to clarify a general statement about a number of similar things is called an *example*. The picture of the armadillo is actually an example, because it shows one armadillo from which all other armadillos can be recognized. The Cleaver family (remember Beaver and Wally?) was an example of the "ideal family" according to one critic. The discovery of the double helix is an example of "scientific method." A personal statement about what happened when you traveled to France is an example of what foreign travel might be like. There are a number of different forms of examples:

1. An individual can be present at an event and describe it as he or she saw it. This is called an *eyewitness account*. It is a fragile kind of example because it is not really clear that the person who saw the event saw it as it was or even as other people saw it. The main idea of an example is the get one to represent many.

2. An individual experience can be declared typical of all other experiences. When a number of things, ideas, events, circumstances, or objects are grouped together and included in a general statement, the one that best approximates the general statement can be used as an example. The elements found in it, theoretically, can also be found in any other case included in the generalization. Thus one object in a class can *illustrate* all the other objects in the class. It can be used to demonstrate what the components are that distinguish the class. For example, "This is a chair. One can sit on it here. This one has arms, but arms are not necessary in a chair. This one has legs. Legs are necessary because one quality of a chair is that it allows you to sit above the floor."

3. An example can be constructed from a statistical generalization. For example, "The typical American family has 3.7 members and an annual income of $17,000. Consider the case of the Smiths and the Browns, who live next to each other on Pine Street. The Smith family consists of Mother Smith, Father Smith, and little Timmy Smith. The Browns, Susan and Alexander, have two children, Billy and Myrtle." The narrative can be extended so that the listener gets an idea of the various elements that were included in the study that led to the generalization. This kind of fictional statement is called a *hypothetical example*.

Examples are the substance of generalizations, and they can be used to clarify generalizations. Keep in mind that a definition is really a generalization about the qualities of all the things included in the class that the definition represents. Here is an "illustration" of how the most typical object in the group can be used as an example.

> A citizen in a community discovers that the paint on his house is pock-marked. He reports it to the local health department. [There is one example.] Several other citizens report similar circumstances. [Now we have several examples.] The local health officer concludes as a result of his examination of the examples that there is an "epidemic" of paint pocking in the town. He checks each case and discovers in each example evidence of a particular chemical. He draws the conclusion from examination of the several examples that the particular chemical is the cause of the pocking. He then paints several boards and applies the chemical. In each case, pockmarks appear. He examines paint that is not pockmarked (in the next community) and discovers that there is no evidence of the chemical. His conclusion is that the chemical is the cause of the pockmarks. [He has built a causal statement out of the examination of several examples. In the process, he has applied several sophisticated statistical techniques, which we will not discuss here.]

In each case, the examples were used to construct a generalization, and each of the examples could be used to clarify the generalization. Generalizations can be made only if the examples are sufficiently alike to justify the conclusion. Thus examples must be selected very carefully. When the health officer painted the boards and treated each one with the chemical, he was doing an experiment, which is nothing more than constructing examples under conditions where control can be exerted over extraneous and confusing factors in order to check whether a possible connection can really be made.

Generalizations are often phrased as numbers (averages, medians, modes, special ratios), and thus it is virtually impossible to find a typical example. It may then be necessary to build one. In fact, the hypothesis in a scientific experiment, like treating the paint with the chemical, is actually a hypothetical example. For example, if the health officer discovers traces of the chemical in question in the air in the community where pockmarking occurs but does not find it in the air in the community where there is no pockmarking, he might hypothesize that somewhere there is a factory that is putting the chemical in the air. The factory is fictional. He must seek it, to see if it exists. He can then examine each factory in the area, take air samples, and analyze them to see if he can discover the chemical. If he finds the chemical associated with a single factory, he can develop another hypothetical example, that is, a factory that does not put the chemical in the air. Once again, he can test by getting the factory to stop production. If there are no further cases of pockmarking, he can allege that the factory was the cause. (Once again, he must use very sophisticated statistical operations to justify this conclusion.) To explain the conclusion to an audience, however, he need only provide a narration of "how I stopped pockmarking at the Johnson household."

When you use examples in your presentation, it is necessary to make sure that they conform to the following rules:

1. Make sure that the generalization your example is to illustrate is carefully stated.
2. Select the absolutely essential characteristics or elements in the generalization.
3. Make sure your example fits into the generalization.
4. Make sure your example contains the absolutely essential characteristics you want to make clear to the audience.
5. When you offer your example, don't expect it to do all the work. Be sure to explain what it is an example of, what the characteristics are that are contained in the generalization, and how they operate in the example.

Statistics

Any kind of quantitative statement can be considered a statistic: "This is bigger than that"; "Sales are increasing"; "We have 22% less waste this year"; "Chi square equals 14.06 significant at an alpha level of point zero five." Each of the preceding sentences is an example of a statistic. Quantitative statements are generalizations. They are not the objects themselves but are abstractions about the objects. Once a generalization has been translated into numbers, it proceeds to operate according to the rules of numbers, not according to the things from which the numbers were derived. What this means is that statistics are accurate to the extent that the things they represent behave enough like numbers to justify the use of the numbers.

Speakers must be very careful in their use of statistics. For one thing, it takes considerable training to be able to use statistics well. Furthermore, even if you understand the science of statistics, it is very hard to translate numeric relationships into words. (If words were sufficient to express the relationships, probably no one would use the numbers to begin with). Professional statisticians are often very suspicious of the way numbers are used to support arguments. For this reason, if you want to use statistical data to support some of your ideas, you may, if you are not trained yourself, want to call on the services of a professional statistician to help you make an accurate translation of the numbers into words. There are some simple questons you can use to help you examine the statistical generalizations you may encounter as you look for supports, as well as to help you phrase that information so that it can be used convincingly and honestly with an audience.

1. Are the cases about which the statistical generalization is drawn clearly identified? This is particularly important in projections of the future. Life insurance companies must have a clear idea of the source of information on which their rates are based. They will eventually have to bet on individual cases (examples), and thus they must be very clear on what the examples are typical of. (That is the basis for excluding certain kinds of medical conditions or making the rates higher for particular conditions.) Although pure statisticians will advise you not to try to apply statistical generalizations to particular cases, life insurance companies must do so. Corporate decision-makers must also make decisions about quality control, when to re-place machinery, how to revise production, and many other particular cases, based on statistical generalizations. Thus clarity in the nature of the generalization is very important.

2. Are the cases included in the generalization typical of the body of information about which the conclusions are drawn? If you read a study that draws conclusions about how a particular method affects learning skills, you will want to know whether the people studied were college students, children under ten, a representative sample of the population at large, or what. A conclusion can be extended only to cases typical of those in-cluded in the conclusion.

3. Does the statistician who offers the conclusion comply with rules of procedure in handling his or her data? This is a very difficult question to answer. Each statistical operation is based on assumptions and requires that specific operations be per-

formed. Only if you are well trained in the field will you be able to answer this question.

4. Given that the conclusion satisfies the criteria for statistical reasoning, does its application seem to fit the way things are? It is possible to find statistical differences in minor matters that simply have nothing to do with reality. When a statistical conclusion about differences can be justified mathematically, it is called *significant.* The question for the speaker, however, is whether it is about matters that are important.

5. Does the statistician have an "axe to grind" that might lead him or her to bias the findings? For example, the statisticians that worked for the tobacco companies might be suspected of shaping the data to make cigarettes look less dangerous. The criteria for evaluation of any authority (which we will present shortly) can be used to evaluate the statistician. It is always important to find out who is paying for what when you evaluate statistical information.

Statistical conclusions can take various forms.

1. *Demographic statistics* describe proportions of occurrences in whole populations. Income ranges, housing types, jobs performed by people in a community, number of marriages in a community, and size of family are all examples of demographic statistics.

2. *Actuarial statistics* are predictions and trends. They operate on an "all other things being equal" basis; that is, things will remain the same if events remain the same. If there are intervening events, new calculations must be made.

3. *Inferential statistics* are really statements of the *odds* that events and/or conditions are *not* connected by accident. Medical research, for example, is based on a process of gathering information under carefully controlled conditions so that accurate statements can be made about the causes or treatments of particular diseases.

The basis for statistical reasoning is the physical sciences, the movement of atoms and molecules. The application of statistical generalizations to human events and conditions is sometimes risky. Statistics applied to gambling can sometimes be bankrupting. Before relying on statistical evidence in your presentation, be sure that you know enough to be properly critical of it.

Citations

Speakers often have to rely on the opinions provided by authorities. An authority is someone in a position to know, with sufficient sense and wisdom to offer a reasonable opinion. Fame does not automatically confer authority. The testimonial device is a standard technique in advertising and propaganda. The football hero's endorsement of pantyhose, the musician's endorsement of a political candidate, even a recommendation by your father or your teacher do not qualify as authoritative opinion. The "librarian" who endorses a laxative to her TV neighbor and the ex-TV doctor who supports decaffeinated coffee are used to "con," not to support argument. *Con* may stand for *con*vince, but it may also stand for *con*fuse.

Authorities must be selected with care. There are as many opinions about things as there are people who are willing to open their mouths. Thus you must take precautions when you decide to use someone's opinion to support your argument.

Legitimacy. To establish legitimacy, you have to demonstrate that the person expressing the opinion knows something more about the matter in question than an ordinary, intelligent layperson. People are entitled to express opinions as they choose. However, in order for that opinion to qualify as a support, it must be *competent*. To be competent, the authority should have

1. Considerable experience with the object of the opinion.
2. Knowledge beyond that of the ordinary layperson.
3. A considered opinion, including an awareness of the consesequences of that opinion before it is expressed.
4. An ability to present the substantive evidence on which the opinion is based.

If the opinion is about an event, the authority should have been there or should be in a position to evaluate other people's firsthand accounts as well as circumstantial evidence about the event. If the authority is offering a generalization, she or he should have had a hand in gathering the examples on which the generalization is based.

If the generalization is in statistical form, there should be some evidence that the authority is competent in the statistical method. If the authority expresses an opinion that differs from that of other authorities, he or she should be willing to assume the burden of proof about the opinion and demonstrate how the opinion makes up for the flaws in the opinions he or she criticizes.

Selecting authorities for use in a presentation is *not* a matter of simply selecting opinions that agree with yours. Often you will find it necessary to sacrifice an opinion that might be persuasive to that of a lesser-known but more cogent authority. A famous person may be an authority, but she or he is not an authority because of being famous. An authority may agree with you, but that alone does not qualify his or her opinion as useful. An authority may have considerable appeal to the audience, but unless his or her opinion can qualify as competent, it should not be used as support.

Independence. Insofar as possible, the most useful authoritative opinion is unbiased. Obviously everyone is biased in some way. Even the most austere scientific investigations express some bias, if only in what they select to study. Furthermore each question a scientist asks may bias her or him against answering other questions. However, this is not the kind of bias we are talking about here.

Authorities must be free of religious, political, and economic bias, or the bias should be made obvious so that you can consider how it might have shaped their ideas. A devout Christian may express ideas about the teaching of evolution in the schools and be sincere, but a religious bias may distort the reasoning that underlies the opinion. Political radicals and political conservatives can differ drastically in their opinions about social programs even though both have the same set of facts. The predictions of a person with an economic interest in an outcome may be colored by his or her desires or expectations. When the surgeon general declared that tobacco was injurious to health, the tobacco industry hired scientists to conduct investigations on their own. There is no need to question the quality of the investigation; the fact that the scientists were paid by the tobacco companies tends to invalidate their findings.

The most influential authoritative opinion is that expressed against a known bias. Thus, if the tobacco scientists had discovered that smoking was injurious to health, their findings would have been very powerful as persuasion. When a member of the administration criti-

cizes administration policies, she can be very persuasive. If a division supervisor suggests a cut in his own budget, his opinion is powerful.

Be careful of what you find in print. Just because something is printed does not make it authoritative. Publications have their own biases and often select their articles to support their points of view. The *New Republic* will offer one type of idea, the *National Review* another. A great many publications are nothing more than public forums for the views of organizations. Check the journals and magazines you use to see who publishes them and what the general editorial policies of the pubisher are.

Book publishers keep an eye on the market. They select material they think will motivate people to buy. There are a few publishing houses that specialize in obscure material with limited market appeal. These houses are usually associated with a more commercial publisher. There are also publishers that print anything they are paid to print. Be particularly careful about opinions expressed by people who must pay someone to publish them.

Common sense is often your best guide to the selection of an authority. Think of what you might answer if someone in the audience asked, "Why did you select that person's opinion?" If you can think of a good answer, then you are probably justified in using the authority.

THE DEPLOYMENT OF PROOFS

Once you have gathered the information that you can use in supporting your case, you must fit it into the cells of your pattern. This is a very simple process. For example,
You have a *set.* Now you must arrange your proofs to show why you

There are the conditions at the Coshocton branch:			
Sales are dropping.	Morale is low.	Turnover is high.	Costs are excessive.

believe each of the headings in your four boxes. By adding the words *because* or *for example* to the end of the sentence, you can arrange your materials sensibly.

Sales are dropping, because
Statistics show that sales figures for each month of 1981 are lower than for the comparative month in 1980.
Statistic: Sales dropped 8 percent in January and decreased lower each month to a low of 22 percent in October.
Example: Let me tell you about Smedley and Hockenbein and how their sales dropped.
Citation: The sales manager said, "In the twenty years I have been with the company, I have never seen a worse drop in sales."

In each box, you insert the information that you think would have the most appeal to your audience. Your selection is based on what you know about the audience and the amount of time you have. By inserting small units of proof, one at a time, you have the opportunity to discover how long it will take to say each one, so that you can be sure that your speech will fit within the time limits. Let's look at each of the other boxes.

Morale is low, because
Definition: By morale, we mean (offer your operational definition).
Example: The district manager reports the following complaints about her personnel.
Statistic: Here is the absentee record. Note the high number of absences on Mondays and Fridays.
Citation. Business psychologist Fred Freebish says Monday/Friday absenteeism is a sign of frustration and low morale.
Example: When I visited the branch, here is what I saw.

Turnover is high, because
Statistic: Resignations are 1% per month higher than normal. (Note the use of criteria pattern here.)

Costs are excessive, because
Definition: Excessive means 5 percent above the company average.
Statistic: The branch shows 11 percent above normal.
Citation: The accountant says that continuation of this situation could bankrupt the company. (His proofs could also be used.)

Notice how the supports are blended. Definitions are used where necessary. Examples and statistics are blended. Citations are presented, sometimes with their proofs. This process should be repeated with each component in whatever pattern you use. In a chronological pattern, for example, you would use a narrative as an example in a box headed, "This is what happened in 1950." In a structural pattern, you would use examples and definitions to explain each component of the structure.

If the statements do not fit logically after the words *for example* or *because,* you may have to reword them or discard them entirely. It is very hard for beginning speakers to cast information aside. It is hard to get information, and it seems reasonable that once you have it, you should use it. However, you have gone through a very difficult and complicated process of selecting your ideas and analyzing your audience. To maintain the quality of your presentation, your proofs must be carefully evaluated against the criteria for each and should be used only if they help carry your ideas to your particular audience. Presentations must be *edited* so that they are most appropriate to the audience and so that they fit within the time limit. Deploying proofs in this fashion will reduce possible confusion and help you achieve the maximum appeal to your audience in a thoroughly honest way.

QUESTIONS AND OPPOSITION

Information

Most questions addressed to speakers seek information. Because people often cannot listen as fast as the speaker speaks, they miss details. If there is a question period, you can expect to be asked to repeat material from your presentation, or to provide examples related to the personal needs of the questioner. Such questions are relatively easy to handle. If you have the information, you can provide it quickly. If you do not have it, you can tell the questioner where to get it. Your obligation is to be as accurate as possible.

Requests for information are useful to your purpose because they give you an opportunity to be redundant in a constructive way. Each of the proofs you insert into your pattern supports redundancy, because each focuses on the main statement you wish the audience to remember. Each question will do the same. The answer enables you to add one more support to your proof.

Sometimes, however, questioners ask too much. The question is either too detailed or too personal. A public arena cannot be used to talk about the personal problems of any individual. A public speech cannot be used to discuss the technical details of a complicated process. If a questioner seems to be getting too personal, you can suggest that she or he see you after the meeting. If a questioner seems to be getting too technical, you can point out where the details can be found and, if necessary, have him or her see you after the meeting to obtain a bibiliography.

Confrontational Questioning

When someone tries to use the question period to offer a rebuttal, you must deal with it so that you do not give credibility to the opposing point of view. If you make too much of an objection, you emphasize it. Sometimes speakers will offer you long quotes and ask whether you agree or disagree. You need not express an opinion. In fact, it is better to say, "I cannot offer an opinion until I have read the entire quotation. Please provide me with the documents, and I'll drop you a note." That is a courteous way of making a public matter private without appearing to evade. When someone simply says, "I have no question but I want to disagree about . . ." it is perfectly legitimate to let him or her speak for a minute and then cut him or her off with "Thank you for your opinion. There are some questions, however." Recognize someone else and move on. If he or she interrupts another questioner, he or she will defeat his or her own cause. People with opposing points of view usually have legitimate channels through which to present them. The question period for your speech is not a legitimate channel.

OPPOSITION TO OTHERS

Sometimes you will want to object to someone else's proposal. Your first obligation is to find a legitmate channel for objection. Sometimes the best you can do is file a memorandum or ask for an appointment with the authority so that you can raise your objections. It is courteous and sensible to inform your opponent that you plan to raise objections. From the audience's (decision makers') point of view, it is most helpful if opposing views can be considered together. A good face-to-face debate between the proponents of opposite points of view is an excellent way for the decision makers to get the information essential to their final decision.

As an opponent, you need not assume the full burden of proof. You must select one or more issues in the opponent's burden of proof and attack them.

1. You can argue that the conditions alleged to be a problem do not exist.
2. You can argue that the conditions alleged to be a problem exist but do not represent an impairment.
3. You can argue that an impairment exists but that it is a personal impairment not an impairment in the organization.

4. You can agree that an impairment exists but that the proposal will not remove it.
5. You can argue that an impairment exists but that the proposal offered will carry with it a worse impairment.
6. You can argue that you have a proposal that would be more effective in removing the impairment. If you do this, however, you assume burden of proof for your proposal.
7. You can argue that there are defects in the proofs offered by your opponent that reduce the credibility of his or her argument. Among the defects are imprecise definition, the testimony of incompetent observers, lack of qualification on the part of the speaker, the selection of invalid authorities, statistical errors, biased interpretations, and flaws and fallacies in reasoning.

When debate clearly centers on one of these possibilities, it is legitimate. When the debaters attack each other personally, their arguments are valueless. Good debate depends on competent arguers, each seeking to convince the decision makers and paying careful attention to what the other says and adapting to it. Win or lose, the ability to handle debate competently can make you very valuable to an organization.

ERRORS AND FALLACIES

It is important to be able to spot logical errors, fallacies in proof, and propaganda devices in speeches. Sometimes you will inadvertently include information in your own speech that violates the rules of logic. You must do a competent job of editing your remarks to remove errors and fallacies. Furthermore, when you listen to someone else's presentation, you will want to be able to spot flaws in reasoning or presentation of proof so that you can evaluate the competency of the proposal, and if you wish to oppose it, you will have identified some weak points toward which you can direct your attack. The references at the end of this chapter will provide you with some sources in which you can find detailed explanations of the various flaws, fallacies, and propaganda devices. Following are some of the most common ones.

Reversed Generalizations

It is easy to reverse generalizations. For example, if you declare the engineers must be trained in statistics, it might be tempting to regard statisticians as engineers. But every generalization contains a *some* term and an *all* term. The statement "Engineers must be trained in statistics" really means "*All* engineers are *some* of the people trained in statistics." Other people are also trained in statistics. The statement "Poor people sometimes cheat on welfare" means "*Some* poor people are *some* of the people who cheat on welfare." Check generalizations carefully to make sure you know which terms imply *some* and which imply *all*.

Attacks on People

Mudslinging is dangerous because those who do it usually get dirty themselves. Issues can offen get confused between arguments about a proposal and its details and proofs and the merits of the individuals who offer the arguments. Sometimes good ideas are not considered seriously because listeners do not like the person who presented them, and sometimes poor ideas are accepted uncritically because the person who advocated them enjoys personal popularity. The individual presenting the argument must be separated from the argument itself, except in the rare case where it is necessary to question the qualification of the individual who is speaking. Even then, it is not necessary to attack the personal character of the speaker, merely to compare her or his qualifications with the standards for competency as an authority.

Mass Opinion

Advertisers, particularly, try to convince us to try their product just because so many other people are using it. This is not a cogent argument. There are situations in which most of the people who believe something are wrong. Consider how many people opposed the proposition that the world was round when it was first offered.

Faulty Connections

Sometimes people connect two ideas that they think are associated when they are not. For example, when a student argues that he is entitled to a good grade because he worked hard, he implies that hard work alone is sufficient to produce quality. Consider strange connections carefully. Statements like "I don't know what she sees in him, he's bald," or "What can you expect from a shop foreman" imply connections between ideas that cannot be documented. You are entitled to ask the speaker who uses this kind of statement to demonstrate for you how the ideas are connected.

Presumption Beyond the Proof

It is not reasonable to believe that other people will believe exactly as you do. Therefore, if you assume anything at all about what they believe, they are likely to disappoint you. You must take care to offer proofs wherever possible so that you do not tread on someone else's assumptions. If you argue that something should be done because it is in harmony with the "free-enterprise system," you ought to be able to offer some documentation that the free-enterprise system is worth being in harmony with. If you claim that a particular proposal is creative and innovative, you are resuming that everyone believes that being creative and innovative is good. This is not necessarily so, and you should be prepared to support the contentions that innovation is good for its own sake and that creativity is good for its own sake.

Appeals to Pity

If you feel someone is entitled to a charitable act, it is perfectly legitimate to say so. If, however, you try to argue the general worth of an idea because of the hardship of some of the people affected by it, you engage in a serious fallacy. If you argue that a branch office should remain open, the hardship of the people who would lose their jobs if it closed is not a proof. It is a consideration that you may want to point out; in this case, it requires another proposition, that it would be good to keep these people from being put out of work. In fact, you can make it a part of your proposal, rather than a proof of it.

Extortion

Threatening people with dire consequences if they do not support your point of view is unfair. There is a difference between predicting dire consequences if something is not done about a condition and declaring that the audience will be injured if they do not agree.

Defective Generalizations

We have already pointed out that it is very difficult to build good generalizations. People make three main errors with generalizations:

1. They look at a small or unrepresentative sample and try to draw a broad conclusion from it. For example, if the first four people to submit their expense accounts were engineers, it is not reasonable to declare that engineers are "money-hungry" or "broke." If a study is conducted on people in Ottumwa, Iowa, you cannot necessarily assume that the conclusions are valid for New York City, and vice versa.
2. They try to connect two events that appear together without logical proof. The classic example of this error is the man who drank whiskey and soda on Sunday and had a hangover on Monday. On Monday he drank rum and soda, and on Tuesday he had a hangover. Tuesday night he tried gin and soda and had a hangover on Wednesday. He decided that he had better give up soda. If a person with hay fever sneezes, it does not mean that the goldenrod is blooming, and if a company goes bankrupt shortly after Smith takes over, it does not necessarily mean that Smith caused the bankruptcy.
3. They try to draw generalizations based on random accidents and coincidences. If the last three people to dent your fender were men, you cannot conclude that men are worse drivers than women. If you find a bone in your hamburger in a fast-

food restaurant, you cannot claim that bones in hamburger are characteristic of fast-food shops or even of that particular fast-food shop.

Poor Comparisons

Speakers and writers enjoy using metaphors because they make presentations more interesting. A poor selection of metaphors or invalid analogies can confuse your listeners. Simple comparisons are sometimes invalid. For example, you cannot argue that socialized medicine would work in the United States because it works in Sweden because there are some vast differences in the two countries; by the same token, you cannot argue that socialized medicine would not work in the United States because it does not work in the Soviet Union. If you argue that management and labor "have to pull together like the members of a mule team," someone could declare that was all right, as long as they are pulling in the right direction.

Emotional Use of Words

Words themselves can do strange things to listeners. Her "modish" dress may be the same color and pattern as her "garish" dress. Shades of difference in meaning can prejudice your listeners. You want to

use interesting language in your presentations, but you cannot sacrifice accuracy to word selection.

There are some other voodoo tricks that speakers do with words. For example, to say that the average American smokes 7.472 cigarettes a day seems to imply that every American smokes. The statement that the average family has 3.78 members is misleading, as few families consist of a husband, one child, and a wife who is 6.3 months pregnant.

Take care to clean your presentation of errors. As you do more and more speaking, you will find it advantageous to get a good book on errors and fallacies so that you can do a more refined job of removing them from your speeches. When you discover errors and fallacies in the speeches of others, you can point to them in order to raise questions about the credibility of the proof. You should not use them to embarrass the other speaker, nor should you attempt to base your opposition entirely on flaws and fallacies.

BEGINNINGS AND ENDINGS

The final touches on your presentation are the introduction and the conclusion. Do not write either until you are absolutely sure what you are introducing and precisely what conclusion you want to draw. Novice speakers who write introductions first sometimes find themselves locked into propositions they do not wish to defend, and worse, they may find that their introduction is to some other speech. The introduction and the conclusion are properly prepared when you have done all the necessary revisions on your presentation.

The main purpose of an introduction is to gain attention and to prepare the listener for what is to come. Avoid cuteness. Some speakers struggle to make their introductions funny. This is all right if you are really funny, but often, when overdone, it distracts from the presentation. If a speaker presents a funny introduction, the audience will expect the fun to continue throughout the speech, and this expectation sometimes represents an intolerable burden on the speaker, particularly if the presentation is on a serious topic.

A good introduction accomplishes the following:

1. It states the main idea that the speaker is presenting clearly and briefly: "I will present a proposal on how to expand our mem-

bership"; "I will give some reasons for adopting the 1982 research-and-development proposal"; "I will analyze the three main difficulties we are having in the shipping department."

2. It gives the listener one good reason (at least) for listening to the presentation: "Increasing membership will reduce the amount of extra time each member will have to devote to the organization"; "The R&D proposal will generate new products, new jobs, and security for those of us already in the company"; "We must understand what is happening in the shipping department, for it is our responsibility to solve their problem."

3. It provides the audience with a *listening rule,* actually a table of contents so that they will know how to listen to the speech. The listening rule refers to the main headings of the largest boxes in your pattern. Once the listeners understand that these are the main heads, you can help them follow the speech by referring to these heads when you start each main point and when you finish. Thus you have effective redundancy built into the speech, for example, "I will propose recruitment activities for our members, for the officers, and for the trustees"; "I will discuss the three main components of the R&D proposal; product improvement plans, resource utilization plans, and long-range product-development plans"; "I will discuss increased shipping costs, packaging problems, and problems of transportation scheduling."

Introductions should not dominate the speech. No more than 5 percent of your speech should be devoted to the introduction, including your greetings to your audience and any acknowledgment of the special nature of the speaking situation.

Conclusions should be equally simple and even more brief than the introduction. They should contain a review of what you have said and a restatement of the main reason that what you have said is important to your listeners:

1. "You should now be familiar with the reasons that our shipping costs are going up, with our packaging problems, and with the difficulties we are having with scheduling, so that you can turn your attention to some possible solutions."

2. "You may be asked to assist R&D with their work in product improvement and resource utilization, and your ideas for future

product development will be welcome. Your help will benefit all of us."

Conclusions should be about one paragraph long. They should not contain extended exhortations, inspirational messages, or any material that you have not presented in the speech. Some speakers try to use their conclusions to go beyond what they have already demonstrated. It is not fair to demand action from an audience in the conclusion to the speech if you have not given them a good reason for it in the speech itself.

SUMMARY

Argument is addressed to a decision maker, individual or group. You do not use it to try to change the minds of the people who argue against you. Your task is to influence those people who have some stake in the matter and who have the power to act. To accomplish this, you must be perfectly clear about your message and what it means to your listeners. Your effectiveness is determined by your personal reputation, the extent to which you can make your message important to your listeners, and the logic and proof in your presentation.

An argument begins with the demonstration that something is wrong that requires action, for to fail to act would be costly, inconvenient, or dangerous. There are standard areas in which problems occur: organizational goals, goods and services, clients and customers, the articulation of organizational components, leadership, personnel, finance, logistics and communication, physical plan, and liaison and public relations.

If you propose any kind of change, you assume the burden of proof. You can fulfill your burden of proof by showing that the information you offer is valuable to the listener, that the attitude change you suggest will result in benefits for the listener, or that the action you recommend is important to the listener's well-being. You must offer proofs to support your ideas.

Your proofs should be selected so that they are best suited to your particular audience. They should address the audience's level of knowledge as well as their possible biases. You should also take into account your own standing with the audience, and if you have to make up for deficiencies in your reputation, you should utilize your proofs to help you.

The main tools in proof are definitions, examples, statistics, and citations. Definitions are used to achieve clarity and should be unambiguous. Sometimes you may have to construct an operational definition for your particular message. Examples must be precise and typical. They are used to clarify definitions and to explain statistical generalizations. Statistics frequently require the help of an expert before they can be used as proof. Speakers should be careful not to mislead the audience through a defective use of statistics. Statistics can be used demographically, actuarially, and inferentially. Citations are statements from authorities. The authorities must be competent and unbiased. Speakers misuse authorities when they believe that expertise in one area qualifies an authority to speak in another area.

The effects of a good presentation can be mullified if a question period is not well handled. Most questioners seek information. The speaker must either provide the information or tell the questioner how to get it. Opposition can be handled by direct refutation, but when a questioner uses his or her time to oppose the speaker, the speaker should avoid overreaction. When you oppose someone else's presentation, focus on one aspect of the burden of proof: need, the proposal itself, the problems that would accompany the proposal, or the qualifications of the speaker.

You should take care to edit your presentation to remove fallacies and errors. Your final editing task is to prepare an introduction, which catches attention, states the main idea, and gives the listener a reason for paying attention. An introduction should provide the listener with a table of contents for the speech. Conclusions are usually very brief. They simply review the main headings of the speech and remind the listener of why it was important.

READINGS

The process of outlining can be reviewed in Judy L. Haynes, *Organizing a Speech: A Programmed Guide*. Englewood Cliffs, N.J.: Prentice-Hall, 1973. This is a self-instructional programmed book with examples designed to teach you how to organize and outline a speech. The technique of using formats described in this book is presented in detail, with examples, in Gerald M. Phillips and J. Jerome Zolten, *Structuring Speech*. New York: Bobbs-Merrill, 1976.

The techniques of argument are clearly described in Erwin P. Bettinghaus, *The Nature of Proof.* New York: Bobbs-Merrill, 1909; and in Abne M. Eisenberg and Joseph A. Ilardo, *Argument: An Alternative to Violence.* Englewood Cliffs, N.J.: Prentice-Hall, 1972.

The use of supports in speaking are discussed in Phillips and Zolten, where the authors present a discussion of how and when to use definitions, examples, narrations, testimony, and statistics. Ernest G. Bormann and Nancy C. Bormann offer simple explanations of how to use various forms of support in Chapter 10 of *Speech Communication: A Comprehensive Approach.* New York: Harper & Row, 1972.

The standard work in logical reasoning, the use of supports, and the avoidance of fallacies is Monroe C. Beardsley, *Thinking Straight.* Englewood Cliffs, N.J.: Prentice-Hall, 1975. Those who are interested in a simple, nontechnical explanation of statistical procedures should see Abraham Franzblau, *A Primer of Statistics for Non-Statisticians.* New York: Harcourt, Brace and World, 1958.

Chapter 6

Personal Communication in the Organization

We have already discussed formal situations like interviewing and presentational speaking. Both are characterized by clear-cut objectives for both speakers and listeners, as well as by the opportunity to prepare for the experience. In presentational speaking, the speaker comes with a carefully constructed message adapted to her or his listeners, who know why they are present at the speech. In an interview, the questioner has an opportunity to prepare a protocol in advance, while the respondent at least knows the area that will be covered and can think it through. Job seekers can prepare themselves by writing careful résumés and rehearsing answers to the questions most likely to be asked.

In this chapter, we examine face-to-face contact between participants. Because these situations are characterized by an exchange of talk, it is hard to predict their outcome or to know how to prepare for them. However, even in informal and intimate situations, people still have goals, and they can use strategies to try to accomplish them. Mastery of personal communication demands on awareness of possibilities and opportunities, as well as an organized storehouse of information that can be retrieved quickly and used when needed.

ORIENTATION

Workers usually learn their jobs from a manual or from an individual given the responsibility to orient them. General training sessions are usually followed by an exchange of information between the new employee and a veteran, who tries to indoctrinate the newcomer with the spirit of the organization and a sense of the way things are done.

Basic job instructions, particularly in production-line positions, are usually prepared by engineers competent in designing efficient programs of instruction. They seek to minimize ambiguity and to maximize accuracy. This kind of instruction giving requires careful preparation and presentation. There are, however, aspects of every job that cannot be learned from a formal manual or a training session. Supervisory, technical, and professional personnel in particular must learn their jobs from the people around them. After a formal orientation in the company and their role in it, they must seek information from peers, subordinates, and their own supervisors in order to get a sense of the intangibles that operate in every organization.

What a new employee needs most is elaboration of the job description. The job description specifies what must be done, but the new employee must learn the various ways to do it. Supervisors, in particular, have their own unique styles. Going by the book can be dangerous, but employees are used to one pattern of instruction, and they tend to get uneasy when the newcomer tries to direct their work in a style with which they are unfamiliar. Furthermore new employees must learn about emergencies and special needs, and these cannot be included in any kind of formal manual.

In effect, orientation is a dialogue between a new employee and anyone willing to talk to him or her about the organization chart, the job description, and particular people in the organization. The newcomer must know what is expected, not only by the "brass," but also by the people she or he supervises and her or his peers. Thus it is the newcomer who seeks the information.

Formal orientation specifies what the final product is to look like. The newcomer must seek to know the precise role played by the people around him or her in generating that final product. He or she must get information about how the product fits the organization's mission, how it affects the sale of products or the dissemination of services, and how important it is to the people in power.

Specific duties are detailed in the job description, but the newcomer must discover how to make requests, where to get information, how to give criticism, and how to relate on a daily basis to the people around him or her. The duties presented in the job description are simple compared with the human relations problems encountered in trying to get them done.

It is also important to discover how evaluation proceeds. Once again, the words in the manual do not give adequate guidance to the particular techniques of evaluations. The newcomer must understand what is punished and what is rewarded, and what constitutes acceptable work. The newcomer will have to sort through gossip, rumor, myth, and legend about past incumbents of the position and about the people around him or her. Getting a sense of history of the organization and the people in it is important, although it can be very confusing to learn a great many personal details about colleagues, subordinates, and supervisors.

The person who tries to orient a newcomer can be of the most service by permitting the newcomer to ask questions. The problem with simply plunging in and offering information, no matter how accurate and important it is, is that the newcomer doesn't know whose information is credible. In the first few days on the job, she or he will acquire an incredible amount of conflicting information and needs the time to decide on whom she or he can depend. The best way to appear to be dependable is to be available and sociable but not to appear to want to take over.

The university is a good example of how the exchange of wisdom in the early days operates. Universities commonly define the tasks that a professor must perform as "teaching, research, and service to the university and the community." What those words mean, exactly, is rarely made clear. Thus the new professor must examine the department's history, see who got promoted and what they did, and discover what affects job evaluation. Universities cannot formally specify how they evaluate good teaching, for example, yet they must do it when considering a person for a promotion or tenure. The same holds true for companies. Cost effectiveness is commonly used as a basis for evaluation. It is very difficult, however, to relate intangible acts of human decency to money saved, yet very often, it is the way a supervisor deals privately with his or her employees that makes the difference in how they perform. An important component of effective orientation is the discovery of how evaluation takes place.

The major part of orientation is reducing the new employee's feelings of tension on coming into a new situation. An important component for the people already there is the discovery of what will motivate the new employee to do his or her best work. The initial exploration of a new employee largely concerns how she or he will fit in to the social patterns of the department. Colleagues will make various tentative moves to socialize and to explore the personality of the newcomer. Supervisors often make similar moves, designed to discover what the newcomer values. These findings may shape the way the supervisor deals with the new employee in subsequent encounters.

Both the formal and the informal components of orientation are supposed to bring about a smooth transition. Actually organizations are quite accommodating to newcomers, as long as the newcomer does not seriously upset existing patterns of behavior. When the newcomer is billed as a "new broom" who is supposed to make major changes, there is often considerable suspicion and even hostility. In any case, there is considerable talk whenever a new employee enters the scene. On the production line, this represents no great problem because performance quality is fixed. The new employee can hold the job whether or not she or he "makes it" socially with her or his colleagues. Professional and supervisory positions, however, are objects of considerable talk and confusion. Formal instruction in duties, privileges, and obligations provides an arena for informal and social talk about the nature of the position.

QUESTIONS AND RESPONSES

It is not safe to assume that you will understand all of the directions and orders you are given on the job. The people that instruct and assign you will sometimes make errors, sometimes not say enough, and sometimes use language you do not understand. Therefore it is important to learn to ask and answer questions.

Asking questions is not a completely spontaneous activity. Before you ask a question, it is important to get a precise definition of what you do not know. Most people ask nonproductive questions like "What do you mean?" or they will say, "I didn't understand that; will you explain it again?" Such questions are not helpful because the best the person asked can do is repeat what has just been said. Furthermore there is usually only a limited time for questions. Thus repetition alone is not enough, particularly if it does not improve on the original message. A person who can ask good questions generally gets good answers. A good question is identified by its ability to evoke the needed information from the person asked.

You can discover good questions in the patterns you learned in Chapter 4. A question is nothing more than a one-sentence speech designed to motivate an audience (of one) to provide a useful piece of information. If you think through the patterns, you can word your question precisely to get the information you need. For example,

Chronology: What is the next step?
　　　　　　How do I prepare for the meeting?
Description: How does it look?
　　　　　　Show me one?
　Structure: How is it put together?
　　　　Set: What is it made of?
　　　　　　What are the important elements?
Comparison: Is it like the X process?
　Contrast: How does it differ from the old system?
　Criteria: How can I identify a good one?
　　　　　　How will I know if it is substandard?
Association: What happens if my work falls below standard?
　　　　　　What effect does temperature have on the machinery?
　　　　　　What will happen if we don't do it?
　Forensics: How can I use it?
　　　　　　Why is it a problem?
　　　　　　Where does the money come from to buy it?
Deliberation: What should be done about it? By whom?

There are also a set of definitional questions related to specific task assignments:

Who does it?
Why does he or she do it?
How does he or she do it?
With what does he or she do it?
Where and when does he or she do it?
Who pays for it?

You can fill in any name (including your own) for *who* and any task for *it*.

Good answers are provided in the same mode as the question. Questions about sequence should be answered by descriptions of events or steps. Questions about description should be answered with details and pictures. Respondents can decide on a good answer merely by discovering the mode in which the question was phrased. A good answer is one that responds to the question. The respondent cannot read the questioner's mind and can therefore respond only to what the questioner asks. Consider the following dialogue:

Q. What is the procedure for filling out Form B?
A. Get the data from Fred in accounting, record the date and the time, fill out the blanks, and have Peabody initial it.
Q. After Peabody signs his name, what then?
A. Put it in an interoffice envelope addressed to "Production" and leave it in the interoffice box.
Q. How can I tell if it is the right form?
A. It's the blue one, 8466, with three copies. Look, I'll show you.

Q. How is the duplicating room laid out?
A. There is a desk as you come in where the receptionist checks in your job ticket and checks your instructions. Behind him is the quick duplicator, which you can use to make one copy. Let's take a look.
Q. What do they do in duplicating?
A. They handle four basic kinds of work: quick duplication instead of carbons, handouts for general distribution, the processing of visuals and display materials, and the printed stuff like the house organ and the stockholders' report.

Q. Do we fill out 8466 and 8477 the same way?
A. Yes, in both you get the information from accounting.
Q. Then what's the difference between them?
A. Form 8466 goes back to production, so you have to fill in information about the types of defects; 8477 goes back to accounting, so you need to figure the costs of defects.

Q. How do the layout people know when to start production?
A. They start when the duplication technician tells them their material is reproducible.
Q. What are defective copies?
A. There shouldn't be any folds in the paper or smudges, and the ink shouldn't be too heavy.
Q. What if I spot a defect?
A. Get back to the duplicating supervisor and report it.
Q. What causes the defects?
A. Sometimes problems in the machine; sometimes poor typing or poor art; sometimes feeding it too fast.

Q. What about temperature?

A. They don't use the machines when it is cold. They use an intensity meter to tell when the room and the machine are warm enough to use.

Q. How can I find out how to do these operations?

A. Here is an instruction manual. Read it, and if you have any questions, see Edna Johnson the duplicating supervisor.

Q. What does it cost if we make an error?

A. The cost of the materials and the clerical time to redo the job, plus the standard cost of the duplicating operation.

Q. How do we make up the costs?

A. There's a reasonable cushion, but if you go too far over, you'll be in trouble. Try doing it right the first time.

Notice how the questions used all of the patterns. Go back over the questions and see if you can identify which pattern was used for each one. The order of questioning it to (1) decide what you need to know? (2) find the pattern most suited to that topic; (3) ask your question; and (4) check to answer to see if it gives you the information you need. If it does not, keep asking.

EVALUATION: GOOD NEWS AND BAD NEWS

A great deal of talk in organizations has to do with evaluations. Supervisors are constantly required to tell employees that they are not doing well enough. They are also responsible for giving occasional rewards to employees who do very well. Supervisors must carry the word about layoffs and dismissals, raises and promotions. Both good news and bad news require careful communication.

It is "folk wisdom" that compliments should be given in public and criticism in private. The world is not that simple, however. If a supervisor publicly commends an employee for doing a job well, other employees may be resentful. They may wonder why they were not also complimented. On the other hand, an employee who does good work prefers a public commendation, and if the reward is given in private, he or she may wonder whether the compliment is genuine.

In his book *Social Behavior: Its Elementary Forms* (New York: Harcourt Brace Jovanovich, 1975), George Homans refers to "distributive justice." This means that as long as all employees share the same benefits and miseries, morale will remain high, but if there appears to be a disparity in rewards, discontentment sets in. Amitai

Etzioni in *Active Society* (New York: Free Press, 1968) talks of "inauthenticity." This means that if people do not get what they are promised, they may become apathetic and unproductive or they may rebel against the organization. Good news and bad news signal benefits and miseries. They are also the bits of news that tell employees whether promises are being kept.

If people believe that they are not getting the rewards they earned, they can disrupt production. Thus, when telling an employee how well she or he is doing, the supervisor must also explain the details in a way that is clear to everyone else. If an employee is publicly rewarded, the other employees must know the reason for the reward, and they must also understand why they were not similarly rewarded. By the same token, they must also believe that if they do what the person rewarded has done, they too will earn a reward. This means that the supervisor must clearly communicate to all employees what is praiseworthy and must be alert to praiseworthy acts so that she or he does not miss someone who deserves to be praised.

The conditions that generate rewards and punishments are often not clearly defined, although it is easier to spot bad work than good. For the most part, however, good work and bad are judgments by the supervisor. There is no problem in dealing with the obvious, but it is important to spot bad work that is concealed, and it is important to identify good work that is not obvious.

One way to handle both is to maintain regular contact with employees. There should be times set aside periodically to talk to each person you supervise (although this may be impossible if you have hundreds of employees under you; in that case, you must permit regular access, that is, be available at regular intervals to anyone who wishes to see you). During regular interviews, you can discuss what is happening on the job and communicate relevant good news and bad news. Because everyone will know that both rewards and punishments are delivered during private talks, there need be no excessive concern about who gets what. If the person rewarded wishes to talk about it in public, that is his or her business, and the person punished has the privilege of taking his or her lumps in private. Talk periods can also include discussions about the performance of others, and the supervisor can use them to find out who else is doing well. They should not be used to get negative information about other employees as this will trigger considerable anxiety.

Union contracts tend to ensure uniformity in the presentation of both punishments and rewards. Furthermore most unions maintain a grievance procedure, so that an employee who feels that she or he has been criticized unfairly will be given a hearing. Where there is no formal grievance procedure, supervisors must be particularly attentive to the justification of both their rewards and their punishments.

Most organizations maintain tight security over salary information except for hourly-rated jobs. They know that if employees discover that someone doing the same job is getting more money, they become very discontented. Money is regarded as the most effective reward. You can maintain confidentiality in giving raises simply by notifying employees by letter or by including a note in the pay envelope. Still, the giving of a raise is an opportunity for a productive contact between the employee and the supervisor. News of raises can be given during regular contact periods, but employees should know approximately when raises are being given, as mystery leads to apprehension. Supervisors must understand that they have no control over what employees say to each other. However, if salaries are not posted, one employee can ascribe a higher salary reported by another to exaggeration and thus save face.

Saving face is an important element in the giving of bad news. During evaluation periods, retribution piles up, often for periods as long as a year. Those that have not done well can be convinced to do even worse if they are humiliated before their peers. When employees must be dismissed, every effort must be made to provide them with a way to make a gracious exit, including permitting them to tell whatever story they like about the reason for their departure.

You can prepare yourself to talk about evaluations by considering a reward or a punishment as the solution to a problem. The reward is a solution to the problem of how to motivate the employee to continue doing good work, and the punishment, presumably, is supposed to motivate the employee to do better work. Consider these matters in both a criteria and a forensic pattern. You use the criteria pattern to compare the actual behavior of the employee to the standards set for performance. The residual (better or worse) becomes an impairment, or the reverse in the case of an employee who does well. The reward is offered as incentive to do more of the same (and you can explain what the "same" means merely by showing the employee the difference between the standard level and his or her level). The punishment must be referred to the deficit, the gap between the standard performance level and the performance level of the employee. By having specific data, you can divert the suspicion of personal motives.

Reactions to bad news are unpredictable. When employees are informed that they are about to lose a job, they may take it with dignity and make a gracious departure. They may come unglued and demand help from you. They may argue and protest about it. They may brood and attempt to sow dissension among the other employees. Many companies develop an exit procedure designed to reduce the bad effects of dismissing an employee, but when there are general layoffs, it is very hard to soften the blow. However, in the case of a general layoff, at least, the "misery-loves-company" situation prevails, and the employees can provide a little comfort for each other. Supervisors often feel guilty about giving bad news. It is very hard to avoid being responsible when you have to look into the eyes of the person whose livelihood you are taking away. On the other hand, if you are merely transmitting a decision made by someone else, you can protect yourself by conveying the person's reasons. If you have made the decision, you can ease your own tension a bit by having specific reasons to give for your action.

What is most important to avoid is giving personal advice to employees. There is a temptation to try to help people who have received bad news. When a person is passed over for promotion, he or she will want to know why, and it is reasonable to offer suggestions related to task performance. Matters like attitude, "getting things together at home," and learning how to do better in managing money should be avoided. The problem with giving advice is that people sometimes take it, and then they hold you responsible if it doesn't work. In job-related matters, you can take that responsibility, and if you explain how an employee can do better, you have a basis for a reward if you see tangible evidence that your advice was taken. You do not have enough information to predict what will happen in the employee's personal life, however, and so it is important to avoid any suggestion of meddling.

The following suggestions will be useful to you in giving good news and bad news:

● *Be direct.* The employee should know immediately whether she or he is receiving good news or bad news. Ambiguity stirs up tension. A good-news or bad-news interview is not the time to be cute.

● *Be prepared to give reasons.* We have already told you how to find the reasons. Once you have given the news, quickly offer the reasons for it. Allow a few minutes for questions, and terminate the interview. A person receiving bad news should be permitted to leave quickly, and a person receiving good news should not think that you are rejoicing with him or her.

● *Have a public statement ready.* Whenever a person is rewarded or punished, it becomes grist for the gossip mill. You have no control over what the employee says to his or her fellows, but you should have some brief statement to offer the person who asks why he or she did not get a raise or when his or her promotion will come through.

● *Have a party line.* You should be able to tell employees how the procedures operate, how they are evaluated, how decisions are made to reward and punish, and how the decisions are communicated. You may have to do this several times. When you are asked about individual cases, you can refer to the general statement and simply inform the person that you will watch carefully during the next evaluation period to see how well she or he is doing.

● *Be sure of your data.* Try to avoid punishing on the basis of intangibles. Telling the employee that her or his "attitude isn't good" gives no information. If you can point to irritating situations, fights, confusions, or suspicions, you at least give concrete reasons for your acts. If an employee has made a mistake, be sure that you can explain what happened, why it was a mistake, and what the consequences were. Be sure that the mistake you point to really was the employee's fault.

● *Don't ignore the gossip and rumor circuit.* When cutbacks are imminent, there are usually a great many stories circulating about what is going on and what is likely to happen. When someone is dismissed, a number of unpleasant stories are often generated. If there are no official data, people will ease their uncertainty by making some up. The information you release may not be credible to some of the employees, but an official statement tends to reduce the quantity of rumors and the virulence of gossip.

• *Avoid personal comparisons.* When you talk to employees about why they did well or poorly, avoid comparing them with anyone else. It is best if you do not even mention other people during the interview. Point only to the tangible information on which you based your decision. If they bring up anyone else's name, refuse to discuss it. Do not give information about how anyone else is doing. Do not point the finger of suspicion at anyone else. Merely mentioning another employee's name during an evaluation interview can set off unpleasant rumors. All the employee you talked to has to say is "We discussed you during the interview," and the fat is in the fire.

PERSONAL RELATIONSHIPS ON THE JOB

Employees tend to expect more from their supervisors than the supervisors can actually give. Psychoanalysts have pointed out that people sometimes regard supervisors as "fatherlike" and try to get them to take control in their personal lives. Requests for personal advice should be deflected. It is flattering to believe that someone else regards you as an authority, but it is easy to get trapped into a position for which you are not qualified, that of father, big brother, or confessor.

Generally talk with colleagues is best when neutral. Counselors often advise people to look for close friends outside the company; a number of problems can arise if you work alongside close friends. When one of you gets promoted, for example, the other will be hurt, and it will be necessary to put social distance between you. It is difficult to maintain a special friendship with someone you supervise without planting suspicions of favoritism in the minds of other employees.

Supervisors and executives have a difficult time maintaining social contacts with people above and below them. It is never absolutely clear to a supervisor why an employee seeks her or his friendship; it may be a matter of simple courtesy, it may be that the employee really likes the supervisor, and it may be that, consciously or unconsciously, the employee is seeking special favors. Thus smart supervisors keep a reasonable distance from both their employees and their bosses. When socialization takes place, it is most effective when everyone is included.

There are always political considerations in any organization. Production workers can generally take care of their political urgencies through their union. Those without unions, however, try to form political alliances with the people with whom they work. A skilled management consultant once remarked that a touch of suspicion is useful for anyone in a company. It is also sensible to wonder a little why someone else is seeking your attention. What favors can you do for them, and what do they offer in return? If you find yourself giving favors for which you receive no return, you might find it productive to move away from the contact to avoid being "used."

Organizational life is also characterized by arguments over issues. Ideas are proposed for the good of the organization, but each one will have consequences for each individual job. It may be hard to figure out why people support or oppose your ideas. They may support them because they, too, believe that the company will benefit, or because they believe that they will get some personal gain. They may be opposed because they feel that your idea will inconvenience them or because they think it will hurt the company. They may support you because they like you or oppose you because they dislike you. If you have a reputation for good ideas, you will have supporters, but it one of your suggestions should fail to work out, you will find people moving away and looking for someone else to follow. People like winners and fame is fickle. Thus you should take support from your colleagues with the proverbial grain of salt. Remember that socialization with colleagues often has political purposes, and stay open to the possibility that a friendly talk during the lunch hour may have some ulterior motive, like finding out the details of some proposal or discovering who is supporting whom in some political conflict.

Few organizations are truly democratic. Decisions are almost never made by majority vote. Most people have the suspicion that the person who has the boss's ear is the one whose ideas are accepted. This may be so, but usually it is the person who has consistently offered good ideas who gets the boss's ear.

It is also important to remember that bedfellows make strange politics. There is a tendency in organizations for ambitious men to try to make contacts with women who have access to confidential information or who exert influence over important officials. There are also cases of women using sex to advance their personal cause. Although this kind of association can sometimes be effective, it is also frail. A connection easily made can be easily broken, and if you become truly dependent on a sex partner, it is a monumental betrayal when the partner transfers affection to someone else for political reasons. Staying reasonably discrete is a good policy. Advancing on merit is more substantial than trying to advance on a social connection or a sexual relationship.

YOUR INFLUENCE ON DECISIONS MADE ABOUT YOU

You can help advance your own cause in the organization by successfully convincing your supervisors of your own competency. Except in cases controlled by civil service, most advancement in organizations is based on meritorious work that comes to the attention of those who make the decisions about advancement. Most companies try to publish criteria for advancement. In those cases, you have considerable influence over what happens to you. The evaluations that people make of you are based on published criteria. The problem is that many of the published criteria are intangible.

For example, "dependability and reliability" are often mentioned as criteria for advancement. Secretarial work, for example, cannot be evaluated on these criteria without an investigation of matters that are not obvious, like whether the secretary is willing to work overtime to get an important job done or how he or she responds to complicated corrections that were not his or her fault. In many organizations, secretaries have command of intricate organizational details beyond their job descriptions and their ability to perform may depend on their productive use of information they have. Businesses with an eye to the future have integrated skilled secretaries into their "word-processing" systems and have tried to develop evaluation procedures for the mastery of intangible organizational details. Furthermore, there is a trend toward advancement of secretaries into supervisory positions because their command of details makes them particularly competent at administration.

Whatever your job, your skill in communicating to others about it will be important to your advancement. Somehow you have to let people know how well you are doing without appearing to be sounding your own trumpet, buttering up the boss, or bragging. The work you do on your own behalf must be subtle and accurate. Supervisors will observe, for example, how you deal with the people you supervise. They will expect to see skilled interpersonal relations. When you are asked questions by a supervisor, a succinct, informed answer will call attention to your competence. The reports that you are required to make, the way you speak at committee meetings, your willingness to take charge in times of emergency or to do a little extra work when required, and the kinds of questions you ask will all be influential in your advancement. The following checklist is composed of items suggested by various executives. They represent criteria for advancement. Those marked with asterisks (*) are criteria in which ability to communicate effectively plays an important role. Check yourself to see how competent you feel on each item. If you feel you meet the standards, give yourself a +. Give yourself two +'s (++) on starred items. If you score 25 or more pluses, you are a legitimate candidate for an executive position.

Task Accomplishment
_____   1. Performs the tasks specified on the job description without error.
_____   2. Performs the tasks specified on the job description on time.
_____   3. *Calls the attention of the supervisor to legitimate problems in task performance.
_____   4. *Calls attention to problems in the work of others in such a way that unobtrusive corrections are possible.
_____   5. Avoids talking about personal problems with supervisors.
_____   6. Suggests ways to improve his or her job as described in the job description.
_____   7. *Convinces supervisors of ways to save money or speed up work.
_____   8. Avoids conflict with associates over tasks.
_____   9. *Is able to settle disputes between colleagues.
_____ 10. *Collaborates with others to solve problems.

Personal Style
_____   1. Dresses appropriately for the job.
_____   2. Does not advertise sexuality.
_____   3. *Does not conduct personal business on the premises.

_____ 4. Speaks well of colleagues.
_____ 5. Does not gossip.
_____ 6. Does not spread rumors.
_____ 7. Does not belong to a political faction.
_____ 8. Associates generally with the people around him or her.
_____ 9. Does not socialize intensely with colleagues.
_____ 10. Supports ancillary organizational efforts like charity drives.

Vocational Communication Ability
_____ 1. Asks useful questions.
_____ 2. Answers questions clearly and concisely.
_____ 3. Transmits information accurately.
_____ 4. *Works effectively in small-group problem-solving.
_____ 5. *Defends opinions with evidence.
_____ 6. *Makes effective public presentations.
_____ 7. Encourages others to work effectively.
_____ 8. Demonstrates an understanding of organizational goals.
_____ 9. Does not patronize, indulge, or insult others.
_____ 10. Makes complaints that are justified.

PROBLEMS IN SOCIAL COMMUNICATION

Whatever is true of social communication in society in general is also true in organizations. However, people in organizations see so much of each other and are required to maintain such harmonious relations that inability to socialize well can jeopardize your ability to work well. Following is a guide to some of the important types of social talk required in organizations.

Small Talk

There are many occasions for small talk. Coffee breaks, lunch hours, and regular social occasions like the Christmas party or the company picnic all provide opportunities to talk to your colleagues about matters other than company business. To avoid the temptation to get involved in personal talk, cultivate skill in small talk.

Small talk is generally neutral. It does not identify your personal commitments or problems. Topics like religion, politics, or major social concerns should be avoided. It is not that these matters are unimportant, but controversy about them can get in the way of working well with others. Small talk is constructive, for it can help you to find out something about the communication style of your fellow workers as well as to identify some nonthreatening subjects about which you can talk together. Small talk sometimes includes joking, although sometimes jokes are excessively prurient and sometimes they insult minority groups. Thus even joking can have threatening consequences. Discussions of local sports, movies and theater, books, current fads and fashions, and local news events can all make legitimate small talk.

Small talk can be opened with a discussion of hometowns, the nature of your work in the company, and comments on the local scene (like problems with the bus line you use to get to work). Small talk does not last long. People tend to move about, get refreshments, greet other people, or just drift off to listen to someone else. That is the main benefit of small talk. It is pleasant, but it does not involve you in any intense discussion.

Competition

Even though cooperation is vital to the success of the organization, its members often compete to attain personal goals. Management motivates competition by limiting rewards. There is no way to prevent competition in the organization, and, in fact, when it arises fairly in legitimate organization business, it can be very helpful. The theory is that if rewards are limited people will be motivated to work hard in competition to achieve them.

Virtually every competent act you do in an organization can be regarded as competitive. This does not mean that you have to work with your "back to the wall and your eye over your shoulder to see who is gaining on you." Corporate competitiveness, although rigorous, is usually fair. In rare cases, personal influence seems to be important, but for the most part, people are advanced because of the competent performance of their jobs. The recent "Mary Cunningham case" shows how unfair or excessively intense competition can injure people in organizations.

Mary Cunningham was appointed to a major vice-presidency in the

Bendix Corporation shortly after her graduation from Harvard Business School. Because the appointment appeared to be irregular and because several long-time employees of the company had been passed over, the affair became a matter of considerable speculation and gossip. Eventually Ms. Cunningham was linked romantically with the president of the company, although there was no tangible evidence of such an alliance. The rumor itself was sufficient to disrupt company operations, and the president saw fit to deny it publicly.

The denial seemed only to fan the flames, and shortly afterward Ms. Cunningham was forced to resign, while Mr. Agee, the president was placed in a very insecure position because one of his major appointments had not worked out. There was no evidence whatsoever of Ms. Cunningham's incompetence, and at no time was it ever alleged that she could not do her job. The point was that she had won a competition, and the people who had lost felt very urgent about defeating her. This kind of competition can harm a company severely.

It became clear that the opposition to Mary Cunningham was because she was a woman. Her case illustrates the situation of women entering the ranks of corporate executives. Discrimination is not dead. However, Mary Cunningham was competent enough to be selected as a vice-president by Seagram's, a major corporation. Once again, she is free to advance her career. The moral of the story is it is important to remember that the higher the stakes, the rougher people play. You must test yourself to discover the level of competition you can handle and not permit yourself to compete for positions if you cannot deal with losing.

Cooperation

Even though competition is an important feature of organizational life, organizations do not reward people who continually disrupt operations. You are expected to cooperate with others to help accomplish company goals even while you are competing for advancement. It is also assumed that if you oppose what the organization does, you will leave it. Frequently, if you compete so hard that you interfere with company operations, you will be dismissed. Your cooperation should be obvious, your competition unobtrusive and fair.

Collusion and Conspiracy

A few organizations resemble medieval dukedoms. They are filled with cliques struggling for power and conspiring to topple various executives so that one of their members can move into a position of power. Communication in these organizations is characterized by conspiratorial talk, details of the private lives of executives, and plans for embarrassing them. A great deal of energy is devoted to private collusion, often at the expense of doing the required work well.

If you find yourself in such an organization, it is probably sensible to try to get out. Collusion and conspiracy work only for a short time. Even if you get into power because of a conspiracy, if the mood of the organization is conspiratorial you will last only a short time, until someone else topples you. Furthermore, if you expect favors from the person you supported in a conspiracy, you may be disappointed; once in power, she or he will find it important to mend fences with those who opposed her or him, and those who were supporters may be sacrificed to the goodwill of former opponents. It may be impossible for you to stay out of conspiracies if they are characteristic of the place you work, but such an atmosphere is infrequent, and you may be better off unemployed temporarily than if you tried to withstand it.

Personal Loyalties

It is easy to be loyal to your boss, particularly if she or he has honestly rewarded you. A fair share of loyalty to your supervisor is important to efficient operations, as companies do not work well if bosses do not cover for their employees and if employees do not protect their bosses. The goodwill shared by an effective supervisor and loyal employees can be beneficial to both. Still, you do not owe your supervisor loyalty beyond the normal operations of the job. It is unfair for supervisors to expect employees to play a role in their personal lives or to use job loyalties in the social realm.

Becoming overcommitted emotionally to a supervisor can be dangerous because bosses come and go in organizations, and if you are too committed to your boss, you will find it very difficult to work with the person who follows, and your personal loyalties can place your own job in jeopardy.

Mixed Attention

Everyone has personal problems, but it is disruptive to the organization to bring them to work. Everyone has the right to decide how committed to be to his or her work. You have no right, however, to let your commitment to matters outside the organization affect the work of others. Most organizations are perfectly willing to accommodate to personal emergencies, like illness or the illness of someone very close to you. Recent studies have indicated that a stable social and family life is very important to your continued quality performance on the job. However, if your primary commitment is to happiness in the family, you may have to cut back on this priority to advance in the company, because the obligations of the new job may well interfere with what your family has come to expect from you. The same holds true if you are very committed to some hobby, recreation, or political or community activity. It is absolutely essential to make a decision about how much you wish to commit yourself to your job and to confine your ambitions to jobs that you can reasonably perform. You cannot have the best of all of the worlds in which you live.

Gossip and Rumor

People have a tendency to talk in order to resolve uncertainty. Davis Riesman, in his book *The Lonely Crowd* (New York: Doubleday, 1950), refers to the "inside dopester," the person who has all the important information about everything that is going on in the organization. Inside dopesters are sometimes accurate, sometimes not, but those who have inside information have been known to trade information for favors from others. It is hard for executives to provide enough information to meet the needs of employees. Thus those who can convince others that they have accurate information become very powerful.

Sometimes it is improper for management to release information.

When people are concerned about how their fellow employees are being rewarded or punished, for example, the release of personal information could be both embarrassing to the individual and damaging to the organization. It is not customary in most organizations to release anything relating to the relationships between individual employees and management. But it is precisely this kind of information about which most people are concerned, and the individual who acts as if she or he has the information is regarded as an authority. For one thing, this information, true or false, satisfies people's need to know. For another, there is a latent fear of what she or he might say (or know) about anyone that keeps everyone a little on edge. What keeps both gossip and rumor flowing in an organization is the desire to predict the future.

Management often makes errors in its release of information. Very often, they gloss over company difficulties that could be handled directly. It is not that they lie, but they tend, often, to leave out details that are very important to employees. The problem is that there is usually someone who is in a position to know and who is willing to talk. All it takes to get a rumor going is one person confiding in another. Investigative reporters know that in every organization, there are people who harbor a grudge against someone. To settle the grudge, they may release information embarrassing to the person distasteful to them. Some rumors start because an employee resents being passed over for promotion. Some rumors start simply because someone overheard someone talking publicly about matters that should have remained private. The point is that someone will find out and someone will talk, and the organization's best antidote is massive doses of truth.

At time of crisis, rumors usually fill the air. When there is a danger of cutbacks or the company is having financial problems, when the economy is in trouble, or when sales are dropping, everyone wonders what will happen to his or her jobs. At times, it is most important for the company to keep quality information flowing. Sometimes rumors are so debilitating that they actually cause the organization to get worse. If employees feel that the next workday may be their last, they are not likely to dedicate themselves to the accomplishment of organizational objectives.

It is easy to admonish people to check their facts, but frequently facts cannot be checked. In fact, sometimes it is the people who know the facts who start the rumors. There really is no way to stop gossip and rumor in an organization, but there are some things you can do to protect yourself from their effects:

1. Before you believe a rumor, try to figure out what the person who told it to you stands to gain if you believe it.
2. When you hear a rumor, try to figure out what you stand to gain if you believe it. If you understand that sometimes you believe things because they make you feel better, then you can help yourself to avoid wishful thinking.
3. When you hear a rumor, ask if there is any way the person who told it to you could really get the information. Often you are relieved to discover that there is no way that the rumor spreader could actually know the facts.
4. Before you pass on a rumor, ask yourself how the person you are going to tell it to might benefit from hearing it and how you would benefit if you passed it on. You might discover that it is wasteful and unnecessary to tell anyone.
5. Before engaging in gossip, ask yourself how you would feel if you knew that people were talking about you.

These questions will help you discover that most gossip and rumor are not worth the time it takes to listen. Gossip and rumor change nothing for the good, but they can have an insidious effect on the operation of an organization. If you are worried about keeping your job, your best bet is to work hard and get your résumé updated.

STRESS AND BURNOUT

You live a good deal of your life in the place where you work. It is important that you get some satisfaction out of being there. Otherwise your life will be filled with stress, and you can suffer burnout. The following list of cautions was provided by a corporate stress counselor. Each category deals with a major source of anxiety and stress. If you remember some of the issues, you can help yourself to remain relatively calm. But keep in mind that complete avoidance of tension is undesirable. You should probably not regard your job as a potential source of inner peace. It should provide you with some dynamic satisfaction. On the other hand, if your job is destroying you, if you feel burned out, unable to handle tasks and to enjoy challenges that once excited you, then you will need to do something about the way you view the world. Effective communication is important in overcoming stress. It is not the only way to handle it, but if you combine it with restructuring your thinking, setting different objectives, and experimenting with new possible sources of satisfaction, you may be able to readjust yourself when you feel the symptoms of burnout creeping up.

• *Mobility in organizations means that you will frequently suffer emotional separations.* Therefore you need to be careful about what you expect from the friendships you make on the job. It is important to have people you can rely on working alongside you, but it is dangerous to depend too heavily on anyone. Transfers, promotions, departures, and terminations happen suddenly and unexpectedly. You will need to have enough associations so that the removal of one or two reliable companions will not be a shattering experience. Keep a calm and friendly demeanor to everyone you can, for any person around you can develop into a responsible associate.

• *Moving to a new job is a time of important social decisions.* When you move to a new organization you will experience considerable stress. Your old friends and supporters are not available to you. You will have to make new friends quickly. One of the more unusual things that happens when a person enters a new company is that people who, themselves, are relatively friendless will make the first advances. People who are secure in their relationships will hold back. Thus, it is possible to make serious mistakes in personal associations during the first few days on a new job. By confining yourself to business and reserving social engagements until later, you will have a chance to size up your work associates so that you can make productive decisions.

Remember that it is generally dangerous to select your closest friends from among the people with whom you work. The possibilities for competition and disappointment are very great. By considering your fellow workers as a source of allies rather than friends you can orient yourself to the inevitable competition you will face with them, and spare yourself the disappointment that comes when conflict of interest destroys a friendship.

• *It is a good idea to avoid complicated and unnecessary relationships within the organization.* Both spouses employed at the same place doing competing jobs, or attempting to maintain some kind of love affair in the midst of work, can escalate stress to the point where it is unmanageable. When spouses work together, they cannot be properly respectful of the aspects of the other that brought them

together in the first place. Forming intimate relationships with the people with whom you work can have serious repercussions.

• *Your career will place pressure on your family.* It is very boring for family members at home to listen to you discuss your job. A steady diet of "shop talk" makes those not involved feel as if they are second-class citizens. On the other hand, it is very difficult to avoid discussing what you have done all day. Sometimes a paradox is established, where the partner at home complains about the shop talk, but if there is no shop talk, the partner complains of being left out. Furthermore there are normal tensions in the family associated with mundane matters like paying the bills and raising the kids that require full participation from everyone. To have a major member of the family using up all the available emotion worrying about the job makes the others involved feel very insecure. The insecurity is transformed into anger, and soon tensions on the job create tensions at home. In fact, at least one reason for the breakup of so many families in recent years has been tension on the job carried into the home.

• *Sex can be more trouble than it is worth.* The *Playboy* image and the women's movement both suggest that free sex is a potential source of joy and fulfillment. Lord Chesterfield's admonition is more likely the case: "Intercourse, ridiculous! The pleasure is momentary, the position is ridiculous and the cost, abominable." There are always sexual temptations on the job, and sex is one way to compensate for defeats in other areas of life. On the other hand, sexual relationships are hard to manage at best. They take a good deal of time, and when they are formed with people with whom you work, they can make you very apprehensive and set off distracting jealousies. This may sound moralistic, but top executives really take a dim view of organizational disruption caused by people who cannot manage their love affairs. Furthermore there is no enemy more lethal than a rejected lover. You are better off forming such relationships outside the company.

Daniel Yankelovich in *The New Rules* (New York: Random House, 1981) points out that the present attitude toward sexual relations is the result of a general trend toward a quest for personal fulfillment. Yankelovich believes (and many authorities share the view) that our decades of economic affluence have brought most Americans to the point where they demand fulfillment through relationship rather than through the ownership of things. The result is a kind of restless search for satisfying relationships with an emphasis on sexual and emotional fulfillment. This trend probably motivated both the Playboy Philosophy and Women's Liberation. In fact, it is a kind of disappointing to reach for a goal that can never be attained because it can neither be described nor sought directly. By attempting to exert control on your own choices, you can at least remove your quest from your work place and take it where it cannot further complicate the difficult task of succeeding on the job.

Thus the admonition is clear. Regard the opposite sex with respect, avoid sexist attributions, socialize in public places, and confine your liaisons to people whose names you never mention on company property. Some authorities warn men to beware of women who use their sexual capabilities unfairly to advance in the company. Some authorities warn women about letting themselves be victimized by less competent men who use emotional relationships to keep women "in their place." The organization is not the place to carry on the battle of the sexes. Androgyny may be a few years down the road, but by thinking of your colleagues as fellow workers rather than potential lovers, you can spare yourself a good deal of unnecessary stress.

● *You must not expect too much.* During the 1960s and the early 1970s, many organizations tried to make themselves more efficient by encouraging employees to participate in various group dynamics and sensitivity-training projects. The T-group movement and the advances of humanistic psychology as advocated by Abraham Maslow and Carl Rogers suggested that employees who were open and trusting with one another were likely to be more productive. The evidence, however, indicates that none of the various kinds of humanistic movements seemed to have any major effect. In fact, there is some reason to believe that the whole idea was a dangerous reversal of the notion that because the successful employees of a smooth-running organization seem to get along well, an organization could be made to run smoothly if employees could be trained to get along well. We noted the fallacy in this kind of reasoning in the previous chapter.

While sensitivity training and encounter groups, along with related movements like EST, transactional analysis, various forms of meditation, and Lifestream, are now generally conducted outside the organization, the residual of all of them is the concept of *actualization*, a notion that still pervades organizational literature. The "actualized person," according to those who believe in this concept, is one who has realized his or her full potential, who can relate well to everyone, who derives real satisfaction on the job, who gets full gratification from sex, who has many close friends, who can express feelings constructively, and who is open and honest with everyone. The actualized person is essentially one who has pursued happiness and caught it.

Many people pay large sums of money to engage in various kinds of public and private therapies that offer actualization as their end result. However, back in 1936, Wendell Johnson (*People in Quandaries.* New York: Harper and Bros.) created the concept of IFD Disease: *I* stood for *Idealization*, *F* for *Frustration*, and *D* for *Demoralization*. According to Johnson, if you expected too much or if you could not make your expectations concrete, you were likely to be continually frustrated. Too much frustration, Johnson believed, led to demoralization and the inability to function on your own behalf. Psychiatrists report that a great many people become very depressed because they cannot achieve what they believe to be actualization.

The antidote to actualization is formal goal-setting, exemplified by "management by objectives." MBO is a process in which supervisors set goals for their work units, help their employees set goals for their work, and engage in a system of regular diagnosis and evaluation to make sure that goals are accomplished. The best-managed organizations in the country operate on an MBO formula. The advantage of MBO is that you can derive consistent rewards for work well done because you know what work must be done and you know what "well-done" looks like. Furthermore MBO focuses your attention on the concrete elements of your job, rather than on the elusive qualities of actualization. One of the best ways to manage stress is to work through your goals to make sure they are realistic. It is much more important to require yourself to do the do-able than to dream about accomplishing the desirable.

• *Be aware of the effect economics will have on your life.* Actualization was a dream offered in the days when we seriously believed that there was no end to the expansion of our economy. In a world of unlimited resources (and cheap gasoline) it was possible for everyone to live in a good climate, work short hours, have worthwhile activities to fill leisure time, and good friends available with whom to share. Good recreation, good art, good sex, were goals for everyone because we did not have to preoccupy ourselves with getting and spending.

When it became clear that this kind of world was no longer possible, it was necessary to revise the myth. The notion of "self actualization," so boldly offered in the 1960s turned around to a goal of professional success. The goal of owning a home characteristic of the 1950s turned around to a goal of finding a decent place to live.

The beginning of the 1980s is a time of revision. There are vast changes already in motion in politics, religion, economics and life style. By the end of the decade it will be more clear what the consequences of the cataclysmic changes in world economy and resources will be on our personal lives. The only thing we can do now is to be alert and realistic and above all, to understand that our chances are best when we seek the attainable rather than the desirable, and think carefully about the way we proceed. This will save us from the worst kind of burnout, the disappointment that comes from having no victories at all.

• *You will need to find satisfactions off the job.* There are a few people who are able to invest their entire life in their work. For most people, however, work is not normally a legitimate substitute for family, friends, and hobbies. Most organizational psychologists are suspicious of the person who seems to be involved only in work. Workaholics are usually very successful, but even they have considerable excitement and variety in their lives. In fact, most workaholics use their jobs as a source of fun as well as a source of success.

Most people need variety as well. It is easy to become bored when you invest most of your time in your work and use your home only as a place to rest up before going back again. Your home should distract and refresh you and provide you with some alternative goals and challenges and some different kinds of successes. The variety of dealing with matters at home should refresh you and help clear your mind so that you can do better on the job. In many ways, home acts as an incentive to do well on the job.

The "Peter principle," that people rise to their first level of incompetence, inevitably pushes people into stressful situations. Stress results when you cannot handle your problems. Once you reach the point where your problems begin to pile up, the stress from one set of problems makes the solution of another set of problems more difficult and as your failure ratio mounts, your ability to succeed is reduced. Thus effective problem-solving in the home can encourage you to do well on the job, and success on the job should help you to work out matters at home. If you have everything invested in the job, your chances of losing are increased (although the magnitude of your victories, rare as they might be, might also be increased).

• *You should maintain reasonable human relations on the job.* There is no point in feeling tense about matters that are of no consequence. Getting along with the people around you in small ways is important to your bigger successes. *Etiquette* may be an old-fashioned word. However, the courtesies people observe with one another are really never out of date. Opening doors for colleagues, greeting people pleasantly, and being able to engage in respectful conversation with them helps you to feel secure about the people around you. Being humane to others gives you the image of competence and makes you appear to be a person of goodwill. People like to be listened to, smiled at, and responded to as if they were decent and intelligent. You can cultivate some of the attitudes of courtesy by following these recommendations:

1. When someone is talking, try to understand what she or he is saying. Observe the courtesy of asking questions about it. A good question is a sign of respect.
2. People do not like to look like fools. If you disagree with their ideas, do so by presenting reasoned argument accompanied by evidence. Do not use words like *stupid* or *incompetent* about others, to their face or behind their back.
3. If you must offer criticism, do so gently. *Criticize only when you can recommend a solution.* Do not offer unsolicited criti-

cism. You do not have the right to interfere with other people in that fashion.

4. When groups of people are talking, be careful not to exclude individuals from the group. Some people are shy and could use the encouragement of having remarks addressed to them. From time to time, you could even ask for their opinion.

5. It is a good idea to remember people's names and to be able to associate their names with some aspect of their life. If you can remember who works where, who is responsible for what task, who has a son about to graduate, a daughter about to start a new job, or some major aspect of their life, then you can direct encouraging talk to them when you see them.

6. People's tastes should be respected. The wishes of anyone who indicates that off-color jokes are distasteful should be honored. He or she has the responsibility to avoid groups that are exchanging such jokes, and you have the obligation not to pressure him or her into listening. It is also a good idea not to tread on people's ethnicity, religion, or politics.

Courteous attention to the dignity of others will help win your their respect.

• *Alcoholism and drug abuse are sometimes serious problems for people in organizations.* In addition, some people have emotional problems. There are two issues here. First, you have to make sure that you avoid such problems. Second, it is stressful to try to help these people. It is also dangerous to get involved with people who have severe problems, because if you are not a trained therapist, you can make mistakes that make the problems worse. You may need to

extend tolerance and understanding to people who are emotionally ill, but most important, you have to be sure that they do not interfere with your own work. There is no point in feeling mounting stress because of problems imposed on you by other people who cannot help themselves. This may sound a bit inhumane, but it is not humane to encourage people in self-imposed adversities.

The decision to use alcohol or drugs as a way of relaxation is a personal one. When their use becomes a real problem, it is important that professional help be found at once. If you feel yourself slipping into habitual patterns of drinking, marijuana usage, or even dependence on prescription drugs, it is a good idea to seek help. In fact, it is important to learn how to utilize professional help. There are a great number of popular "therapies" advertised that promise to cure everything that ails you. A good physician, however, can be a legitimate starting place in your personal therapy. She or he can call in various specialists to help. Most large companies have physicians on the premises, and they also maintain programs designed to help those employees who need assistance with their emotional problems.

• *As you become more successful, you may make enemies.* Most people are bewildered when they discover that someone doesn't like them. What other people think, however, is very unpredictable. Envy and jealousy are hard for people to control, and if you do well, someone will resent it. There are people who try very hard to depress others who are feeling good. Others revel in the misery of their fellows. Most of the people you encounter on the job will be very much like yourself. They will want things to come out their way, they will work hard and compete fairly, and they will not try to injure you to express their own hostilities. You need to understand, however, that some people will develop irrational hostility to you, and as you become more and more successful, these hostilities may become more frequent and intense. You needn't feel any guilt. If you are convinced that you competed hard but fairly, you can regard their hostilities toward you as their own problem and you can protect yourself from their talk.

STRESS AND COMMUNICATION

In this chapter, we have tried to explain some of the personal issues you may encounter on the job. Each of them presents you with reasons to manage your talk in order to be more effective. The people around you can help you or interfere with your success, depending on the way you deal with them. An effective communicator can motivate people to be helpful.

Many people tend to resist that idea of managing their social and interpersonal talk. They regard it as "manipulative" and unethical. Consider it this way, however: it really is impossible to manage other people. All you can manage is yourself. But if you can manage yourself to be considerate of others, to appeal to their needs while you seek your own, and to learn how to address them so they can understand, then they will voluntarily commit themselves to cooperation with you. Your private talk should be as carefully considered as your public talk. Consider the notion of *negative spontaneity*. Instead of blurting out what you think when you think it, try to figure out what would hurt the other person and *avoid* doing that. This simple act of management will make you a considerate and responsible person, whose accomplishments others will be happy to associate themselves with.

SUMMARY

The most structured interpersonal situation on the job is the orientation of new employees. Formal orientation is handled through the handbook and the training period, but each person in contact with a new employee can help indoctrinate him or her in the way things are done in the organization.

Giving rewards and punishments present some serious problems for supervisors. Rewards and punishments should be given for good reason, and the competition for them should be fair. Delivery of good and bad news should be characterized by directness, good reasoning, and public statements that are designed to quell rumors and gossip.

Care should be taken with personal associations on the job. It is wise to avoid intense commitments to the people you work with. Social and political life in the organization can get blurred and have a serious emotional effect. Formal programs designed to manage human relations on the job have not been very successful, but management by objectives has helped employees to avoid frustration and to pinpoint the ways in which they can be successful.

Gossip and rumor are generally destructive forces. It is sensible to examine your own motivations before taking gossip and rumor seriously, and to avoid passing it on. Try to get accurate information, and where information is unavailable, protect yourself.

People with severe problems may turn to drugs and alcohol or show signs of mental illness. Courtesy to them is important, but you cannot act as their therapist because you may make the situation worse.

If you are attentive to the social details of your work place and treat people with courtesy and consideration, you can induce others to participate with you in the accomplishment of success. By respecting the dignity and rights of others, you can appear to be responsible and your advancement will be made much easier.

READINGS

A good source of information on the variables that influence interpersonal communication in organizations, including a discussion of roles, trust, communication networks, and barriers to communication, can be found in Harold P. Zelko and Frank E. X. Dance, *Business and Professional Speech Communication*. New York: Holt, Rinehart and Winston, 1978. See Chapter 9, especially. Abne M. Eisenberg, *Understanding Communication in Business and the Professions*. New York: Macmillan, 1978, Chapter 2, discusses perception in interpersonal communication and shows how such behaviors as smiling, eye contact, gesturing, touching, shaking hands, speaking style, vocal quality, and mode of dress affect interpersonal relations.

Some good information on the nature of stress, fear, and anxiety and how to cope with them can be found in Charles Spiegelberger, *Understanding Stress and Anxiety*. New York: Harper & Row, 1979. Ogden Tanner, *Stress*. New York: Time-Life, 1976, offers a simple explanation of how the pressures of daily life affect the body. A more technical work, Joseph L. Kearns, *Stress in Industry*. London: Priory Press, 1973, shows how stress operates on various levels of management. Useful advice on how to deal with personal stress can be found in Theodora Wells, *Keeping Your Cool Under Fire*. New York: McGraw-Hill, 1980. This book provides exercises for dealing with the daily pressures encountered on the job.

A good statement about shyness and how it operates can be found in Gerald M. Phillips, *For Shy People*. Englewood Cliffs, N.J.: Spectrum Books, 1981. This book offers advice on how to improve your interpersonal skills on the job, in the home and community, and in general socialization. Ronald B. Adler, *Confidence in Communication*. New York: Holt, Rinehart and Winston, 1977, is a simple program of assertiveness training that you can do on your own.

Chapter 7

Cooperative Decision-Making and Problem-Solving

THEORY OF GROUP PROBLEM-SOLVING

The American philosopher John Dewey, in his book *How We Think* (Lexington, Mass.: D. C. Heath, 1933), claimed that individual problem-solving consisted of five steps:

1. The individual recognizes that a problem exists. Something appears to be impeding progress.
2. The problem is specified. (An impairment is found.)
3. Various solutions are examined.
4. A solution is selected.
5. The solution is tried and evaluated for effectiveness.

In organizations, groups of people like committees, task forces, boards of directors, or planning groups come together to make decisions, generate policy, revise operations, or solve problems. Their task is to fulfill an assignment from some authority. They do it best by following an orderly procedure, generally based on Dewey's five steps in individual problem-solving. Sometimes groups meet on a regular basis because it is their job to deal with problems as they come up. Other groups are brought together to deal with special situations. Rarely do problem-solving groups have the power to put their solution into operation. Their job is to arrive at a solution and present it to a decision maker who has the authority to make it operational.

Operations planning is another kind of group enterprise, usually conducted in conjunction with some kind of computer-assisted technique designed to facilitate administration and to help administrators by predicting possible outcomes. Typical of these procedures is PERT/CPM (program evaluation and review technique/critical path method). PERT/CPM systems use the mathematics of probability to schedule and deploy resources and to detect flaws in plans.

Group problem-solving in most contemporary organizations is based on a synthesis of Dewey's system with PERT/CPM models called *standard agenda*. In most organizations, there are six basic issues that are commonly considered by problem-solving groups:

1. How can we best revise our goals?
2. How can we increase productivity, improve distribution, deploy personnel better, or reduce costs?
3. How can we deal with emergencies inside the organization?
4. How can we deal with changes in conditions outside the organization that affect the organization?
5. How can we plan effectively for the future of the organization?
6. How can we take advantage of unexpected opportunities to improve the organization?

The main advantage of using groups to solve problems is command of details. Most organizations are so large and complex that no one person can know enough to deal with the kinds of problems with which they are confronted. There are so many possible points of view that must be considered in order to make an informed decision that it is irresponsible to believe that one person alone could do it. Thus problems are referred to groups of people made up of profes-

sional and technical personnel, administrators, planners, fiscal specialists, and whoever else is required, so that as many points of view as possible can be taken into account in a solution. People who seek change in organizations find it necessary to work through groups. An individual with a brilliant scheme or the creative idea of the half century now finds that her or his thought becomes the agenda for a group of specialists.

A carefully selected group respects the interests of everyone involved without giving undue advantage to one position. The process of group problem-solving is, in that sense, essentially democratic, although it does not function in the way our government does. In government, pressure groups seek the attention of legislatures, and people with points of view seek the attention of voters. Eventually people are selected for their positions by majority vote. However, once they take office, they, too, are required to function as administrators working through problem-solving groups. Even legislators must have groups of people working on problems and making recommendations about the legislation that is needed. Organizational problem-solvers work through consensus rather than majority vote, for it is important to avoid splitting the organization into factions.

Organizational problem-solving has a further responsibility. Once a solution is built, it must be defended in front of whoever has the power to put it into operation. Much of the presentational speaking we discussed in Chapter 5 takes place after a committee or task force has come up with a solution. Thus there is an unbreakable connection between problem solving and argument. Aristotle said they were counterparts. Persuasion is required before action can be taken. Problem solving must take place so that persuaders can have something about which to persuade. By eliminating formal argument from the problem-solving process, participants can revise, correct, reshape, and structure solutions without involving personal feelings or making irrevocable decisions. At some point, however, a decision must be made between "Yes, we will do it" and "No, we will not." It is at that point that the persuader has his or her day.

ISSUES COMMONLY INVOLVED IN PROBLEM SOLVING

Some problems in organizations can be solved by a simple process of fact-finding or evaluation. Questions like "What is the state of sales in the Coshocton branch?" can be answered by means of organized data-gathering. A question like, "Are the salespeople meeting their quotas?" can be handled merely by a comparison of sales to quotas. It is what to *do* after a problem has been discovered that is the legitimate business of problem-solving groups. Impairments are the substance of problem-solving discussion. Sometimes groups must seek facts and sometimes they must evaluate, but their real task is to recommend solutions to problems.

A problem begins when people start to sense that something is wrong. Once an impairment has been discovered, the problem can be referred for solution. Remember that an impairment is something happening or not happening that interferes with organizational operation. There are three steps in the discovery of an impairment.

1. Discovery of the situation: something happening or not happening.
2. Connecting the situation with something injurious to the organization.
3. Identifying the problem to be solved.

For example,

Situation: The company's bank balance is falling.
Injury: There is not enough money to buy materials for production.
Problem: How can we get the materials we need?

Situation: The prices of our products were raised.
Injury: Sales are falling.
Problem: What can be done to improve the balance between sales and prices?

There are a number of other problems that could have been associated with the situation, each of which may have demanded a solution. The decline in the company's bank balance may have resulted in problems in meeting the payroll. The overall situation in the company may have been a consideration for the board of directors. The main idea is that a connection must be made between a situation that can be observed and an injury that can be identified.

The details of problems may vary from organization to organization, but the types of problems encountered are consistent in all organizations. The following list gives most of the major problem areas grouped by categories:

1. Goals
   a. Are present goals still worth accomplishing?
   b. Are new goals necessary?
   c. Are goals attainable?
2. Goods and services
   a. Is there a demand for what we provide?
   b. Are we getting the message about what we provide to the people who might be interested in it?
   c. Are our goods and services priced properly?
   d. Are our goods and services of sufficient quality?
   e. Are our goods and services obsolete?
   f. Are there goods and services we ought to be providing?
   g. Are our customers and clients sufficiently satisfied with our goods and services?
3. Administration
   a. Is management effective in making decisions?
   b. Is management effective in meeting emergencies?
   c. Is management effective in resolving conflicts?
   d. Is management effective in transmitting decisions?
   e. Is management effective in carrying out decisions?
   f. Is management responsible to stockholders?
   g. Is management responsible to the community at large?
   h. Is management effective in recognizing problems?
   i. Is management effective in planning for the future?
4. Finance
   a. Does the organization have enough money?
   b. Is money being properly allotted?
   c. Is money being properly invested?
   d. Is money being properly accounted for?
5. Personnel
   a. Do we have competent people in the organization's positions?
   b. Do we lose competent people at an excessively rapid rate?
   c. Do we obtain the people we need for the positions we have?

      d. Are employees doing their jobs?

      e. Are employees able to do their jobs?

      f. Are employees properly protected and motivated?

      g. Are relations with the union satisfactory?

6. Logistics

      a. Are goods and services being distributed effectively?

      b. Are materials being properly obtained and stored?

      c. Is information properly stored and easily retrievable?

      d. Is information being distributed effectively?

7. Physical plant and ambience

      a. Is the plant effectively laid out?

      b. Is there sufficient space for what must be done?

      c. Is the plant safe and comfortable?

8. Liaison

      a. Are proper relations maintained with the community?

      b. Are proper relations maintained with stockholders or the chartering or sponsoring body?

      c. Are proper relations maintained with competitors?

      d. Are proper relations maintained with employees?

      e. Are proper relations maintained with customers and clients?

      f. Are proper relations maintained with the government?

      g. Are proper relations maintained with the press?

      h. Is there a proper connection between organizational components?

9. Planning

      a. Are we able to accommodate to changes in the law?

      b. Are we able to accommodate to changes in the fiscal situation?

      c. Are we able to accommodate to social changes in the community?

      d. Are we able to accommodate to changes in supplies of raw materials?

      e. Are we able to accommodate to changes in energy supplies?

      f. Are we able to accommodate to future demands for goods and services?

Each of the questions must be worded so that the specific details are included. The following diagram provides an overview of the problem–solution process:

A Problem is identified, described, and referred to a problem-solving group			
What is the background of the problem?	What caused it?	What are its consequences?	What is its nature? Definitions, examples, statistics, citations that identify the problem.
How would we know the problem was solved?		What limitations must be imposed in solving it?	

The solution consists of				
Who?	must do what?	about what?	where and when?	under whose supervision?
paid for by?	to be evaluated in what fashion?	starting when?	content of presentation?	

Decision to be made by?

Operations plan

A problem can be identified anywhere in the organization. Once it is referred to a problem-solving group it is their responsibility to analyze the situation and to prepare a solution to the problem. Generally, they do not have the authority to declare that the solution will be put into operation, but they must present their case to the decision maker (or the decision-making body). Once the decision is made to go ahead, the matter is referred to an administrative body to plan, put into operation, and supervise. Members of the problem-solving group may be involved as individuals elsewhere in the process.

ADVANTAGES OF GROUP PROBLEM-SOLVING

There are a number of tasks that people work on best alone, for example, crossword puzzles, complicated layouts and designs, chess problems, artwork, and knitting. However, problems that involve the interests of many people must include many people in the solution. Large organizations are composed of people with diverse backgrounds and interests, each of whom regards the world from his or her own viewpoint. Engineers, accountants, design specialists, scientists, salespeople, secretaries, and supervisors will each have a different stake in the outcome of problem solving. Therefore, their ideas are very valuable in the process of solving the problem. Because they come from different backgrounds and have different interests, each can contribute information that others would not be aware of. In fact, insufficient variety in input is one of the major problems in group decision-making. When groups are made up of people who have similar information and who tend to think alike, a situation called *groupthink* comes about. The group shows little imagination, fears controversy, and usually reproduces past solutions. If people are included who are different in outlook, solutions can be broadened and made more effective. *Group thinking,* not *groupthink,* is the goal.

In addition to the personal interests of members, organizations have departmental interests that must be represented. A solution is not effective if it eliminates a difficulty in one part of the company only to create a serious situation elsewhere. For this reason, the interests of the various components must be represented in group problem-solving.

There is also a democratic advantage to having broad participation in problem solving. People tend to support programs they have had a hand in building. If the efforts of many people are combined in making plans, their cooperation in putting the plans into operation is virtually assured.

PROBLEMS IN THE GROUP PROCESS

There are some problems with group problem-solving. During its early days, many people regarded it as a cure for everything that ailed the organization. Social experiments involving group processes were tried everywhere, ranging from efforts to get blacks and whites to work well together to attempts to train executives to be creative in their decision making. It is, indeed, a useful method of solving problems, but it has its limitations, which must be taken into account before one develops expectations. Furthermore any method can vary in effectiveness depending on the intelligence and skill of the people who use it. Here are some of the most important hazards.

• *Groupthink is a constant peril.* When the problem solvers are too much alike, they tend to agree too much. When the problem solvers regard each other as social peers, they are afraid to disagree because they fear disagreement will cost them heavily in their social lives. When the problem solvers are relatively lazy, they will find it easy to come to agreement. Each of these three reasons contributes to the phenomenon of groupthink, which is the process of finding the simplest solution that the group can agree on and going no farther. Groupthink is superficial and uncritical, and sometimes it perpetuates destructive programs because the problem solvers are afraid to try anything new. Some social scientists believe that many of the major destructive decisions made during the Vietnam war were based on groupthink.

Groupthink also happens when the group is run by an authoritarian leader who has the power to reward and punish. When this happens, the members do not feel free to think independently. They try to find out what the leader wants, and they give in to him or her. Some authoritarians use groups to give the appearance of democracy to their decisions, but they want the people in the groups to learn to get along by going along. Whenever dissent is punished, the group process is subverted. In order to make a group work well, the members must be willing to sit and listen to opposing points of view, no matter how repugnant they find them.

• *Some people are unable to function in groups.* Some people are too shy to play a role in the group process. They may have a great deal to contribute, but they are afraid to contribute. Others may have something to say but have insufficient training to participate well. A third group of nonparticipants consists of individuals who are trained in individual kinds of occupations and who have no patience with the group process. No group can transcend the quality of its members. Consequently groups must be selected with an eye toward the competence of the members in participating in the group process.

• *Group activity takes a long time and is often boring.* Groups are sometimes tempted to jump to conclusions because it takes so long to give all points of view a hearing. Because everyone has the right to participate, it takes inordinately long to explore the various aspects of the ideas presented. However, to limit expression means to limit the primary strength of group problem-solving. Each phase of the group process must be played through to the end. It takes a long time to gather and evaluate information, to discover limitations, to set goals, and to test carefully each proposed solution against legitimate criteria for judgment. It takes a long time to prepare the final report in sufficient detail so that it properly represents the group solution. Group problem-solving is not an appropriate way to deal with problems if time is short and there is a pressing urgency for a solution. At such times, it may be necessary to rely on the wisdom and the resourcefulness of one person.

• *Group processes sometimes suppress creativity.* It is not clear that creativity is a virtue, but a great many people think it is. The group process tends to reduce the impact of creativity because proposals are so carefully examined. The bold idea and the imaginative solution are sometimes reduced to the mundane because of the care with which the group examines them. However, given the choice between a creative solution and careful planning, most executives prefer the latter.

• *Groups sometimes factionalize.* Group problem-solving is effective as long as the members retain their independence and respond as they choose to each issue that comes up. If a group splits into political factions, then decisions are influenced by considerations other than the best judgment possible. When individuals have loyalties to other individuals or to issues and causes that impede independent thinking, the group process is no longer useful.

• *Groups sometimes require people to work below their abilities.* When groups meet regularly over a long period of time, the members can become stereotyped. It is common in socialization to identify people with types of behavior or the performance of specific tasks. Such identifications are called *roles.* When individuals in groups become identified by their roles, their effectiveness is reduced. If one person is expected to gather the information whereas someone else evaluates it, the group loses major potential contributions from each. Groups work best when the members are willing to vary their roles to suit their opinions and their needs. Consider the number of things it is possible for people to do in groups. They can:

1. Raise questions about what is going on.
2. Ask for a review of agreements and disagreements.

3. Offer information.
4. Criticize or question the information that someone else has offered.
5. Offer opinions and defend them.
6. Question and attack the opinions of others.
7. Offer standards for evaluation.
8. Make evaluations.
9. Offer ideas for possible solutions.
10. Question ideas raised by others.
11. Propose ways to evaluate solutions.
12. Discover limitations on the group's activity.
13. Play devil's advocate for unpopular ideas.
14. Support ideas offered by others.
15. Provide services like keeping records, making phone calls, conducting interviews.
16. Provide leadership when necessary.

Maximum group effectiveness is achieved when the members are versatile enough to fill all of the above roles.

THE ORDERLY PROCEDURE OF
GROUP PROBLEM-SOLVING

Most groups come together because their jobs require it. Supervisors and technical personnel from various departments and divisions meet regularly to handle the problems that affect them in the course of their work. Sometimes executives have to appoint special groups. Commonly they select people with skills and knowledge appropriate to the problem to be discussed. Sometimes groups are made up of trusted advisers (like the president's cabinet). Sometimes groups can be formed of people who volunteer to work. In formal organizations, groups come into existence only at the direction of an executive. Groups that form and attempt to solve problems outside legitimate organizational procedures are generally regarded as subversive and not to be trusted. Problem-solving groups are not like social-action groups in the community. The latter are made of people with an axe to grind. They have no status, and they must appeal to the goodwill or the good sense of legislatures or executives in order to get a hearing for their ideas. Groups in industry have status. They are entirely task-oriented, and they know where their solution is going before they begin their work. In fact, knowing where their solution is going and who they have to please often shapes their work.

Social and political groups in the community are voluntary. Members come and go. It often requires considerable political skill to find rewards sufficent to keep any kind of permanent group in place. For that reason, voluntary groups are confronted with a great number of problems that problem-solving groups in industry do not encounter. Most important is that community groups must lobby for status. Since they have no official position they must devote a good deal of work to gaining attention and finding people to take them seriously. Groups on the job are taken seriously from the start, and they have attention because the work they do is important to the company. In fact, when industrial groups turn political they experience their most serious problems.

Problem-solving groups often deal with the same kinds of issues time after time. Sometimes it is easy to solve problems simply by discovering their nature and applying the solution typically used for that kind of problem. Groups are severly taxed when they are confronted with new problems that require the integration of information and ideas unfamiliar to anyone in the group. At times like these, effective leadership is imperative.

One of the chief obligations of the leader is to see that the group uses a logical and orderly pattern of problem solving. When groups fail, it is most likely because they were disorderly, either in defining and explaining the problem or in developing solutions. When one of the logical steps of problem solving is omitted, groups tend to get confused, and their solutions are defective because key elements are missing. The issues in group problem-solving follow in orderly sequence. Although it is possible to take the steps out of order, groups seem to operate best when they follow the steps of the deliberative pattern. The group's course of action is to:

1. Be sure what the nature of their task is.
2. Discover its problem and phrase it as a question, the answer to which is the group's output.
3. Acquire detailed and reliable information about the problem.
4. Set goals against which a solution can be evaluated.
5. Discover the restrictions that constrain its problem solving.
6. Construct a solution and test it against its potential for accomplishing the goals.

Once these steps are accomplished, the group must prepare a forensic statement designed to convince the decision-making authority that put them in motion that their solution is worth adopting. To do this, they must follow the steps detailed in Chapter 5.

Step 1

The group must be sure about their task: what is to be done and for whom, when it is to be done, and what form it is to be in when it is delivered. When the group meets for the first time, they must discuss the nature of their task and prepare questions to ask the authority who got them together so that they understand completely what they are to do. Most groups begin with some sort of *charge*. A charge is nothing more than a set of directions to follow. It is often in the form of a memo that calls the group's attention to some problem and requests that the group do something about it. The group must discover what is required: a formal policy statement, a new program, revision of procedures and policies, an emergency directive, or precisely what is wanted by the charging authority. The group must be prepared to ask questions until this matter is perfectly clear. Here is what the group must find out before they move on to the next step:

1. Where is the problem located? Is the problem presumed to be one of personnel, equipment, procedures, logistics, finance, what? How does the executive view the problem? What is his or her preliminary view of its nature?
2. What are the committee resources and privileges? When and where is it to do its work? Can it visit the site of the problem, interview people, hire research personnel? What information does it have access to? Is its work to be considered overtime or part of the regular job? What expenses may it incur and how is it to report them?
3. Does the executive want a policy statement, a revision of procedures, a set of regulations, personnel recommendations, or what? What does the executive propose to do with the report when she or he gets it?
4. Is the report to be delivered in writing? If so, in what form? Who is the intended reading audience? Who will be available to help produce the written report, for example, secretaries,

clerks, editors, or artists? Is it to be typed or printed? What method of duplication is required? Is any particular format required (as in the case of grant proposals)? What is the minimum and maximum size of the report?

5. Is an oral presentation to be made? Under what circumstances? Who is to make it? Where and when? Who will be the audience? What will they do with the report? Will there be questions and argument?

6. What is the deadline? Is there any leeway?

7. Will there be regular contact with the charging authority? What is the group to do if they have questions during the process? How will the executive back up the group if they get into trouble while working on the problem?

8. What are the privileges and perquisites available to the group? What personal expenses may they incur, like meals, refreshments, or coffee? Are they to meet on or off the premises?

Being sure of the rules before the group starts work prevents frustration later in the process. It also reduces the chances that the group will have to make false starts or pause in the middle of its deliberations to work out what are by then trivial details.

Step 2

The group must phrase a question, the answer to which will be the basis for their final report. Questions must be direct and specific and phrased in concrete language. This is not so easy to do. It is fairly simple to phrase general questions, like "Should we . . . ?" or, "What should we do about . . . ?" but questions like these are clichés, and they are not helpful in the process of problem solving.

The question must guide the group to the discovery of relevant information. It must direct them where to look and what kind of evidence to seek. The nature of the impairment must be specified, or some idea must be given about where to look for the impairment; for example, "The group will look into the matter of delayed shipments into Regions 6, 9, and 14," focuses the group on shipping to particular places, but it does not really say what the group is to do. "Look into" is a sloppy phrase.

The charge by the executive should guide the group to the precise nature of its activity, such as, "The group will prepare recommendations for the chief of operations relevant to eliminating delayed shipments into Regions 6, 9, and 14."

The group may evade responsibility if it phrases the question, "What can be done about delayed shipments into Regions 6, 9, and 14?" This is a legitimate question, but the passive voice in which it is phrased leaves in doubt the issues of who is to act. A group can wander far afield unless it knows who will eventually act. Recommendations made for people not interested in receiving them are not helpful as solutions to problems. For example, delayed shipments could probably be eliminated if the salespeople were directed not to take orders for those regions. Groups can also confuse themselves by personalizing their wording: "What can *we* do about delayed shipments into Regions 6, 9, and 14?" This question would mislead the group at the outset because the group itself can do nothing. Someone has the power to act, not the group, and so the group should specify who has the power in its wording of a question.

A final statement useful to the group might look like this: "What can the chief of operations do to eliminate delayed shipments into Regions 6, 9, and 14?" This question refers to the impairment and to the agent who can act. It restricts the group to particular kinds of solutions relevant only to the scope of authority of the chief of operations. The question is not two-valued. It is not phrased, "Should the chief of operations eliminate delayed shipments?" It allows various operations to be explored, including the possibility of the chief of operations' making recommendations to other people about the roles they can play in ending delayed shipments. It also allows for the possibility that the group will discover that delayed shipments are not really a problem and that the group can come up with a "null finding," that is, "Nothing needs to be done about delayed shipments." The group has been guided to a *possible* impairment, but they have not begged the question by deciding what the impairment is in advance of gathering the facts.

In order to phrase a question properly, the group must be sure that

1. The problem area is named specifically.
2. The authority who is to act is named specifically.
3. The problem is worded in open-ended fashion so that no possibilities are ruled out in advance.

Most questions fit a formula where A = the charging authority; B = the person or persons who will act; C = the group itself; and D = the general area of the impairment. The formula is that A wants to know what B recommends that C do about D. The group must avoid two-valued wording to prevent polarization of the group. They must avoid the passive voice in order to keep the question specific. They should be sure that they are recommending a solution and not preparing a battle plan for themselves.

Step 3

The group must now make the problem specific by gathering facts and evaluating them. By gathering information, they can develop a concrete idea of the nature of the impairment: where it is located, how severe it is, what its impact is on the organization, whether it has occurred before, how it has been handled in the past, whether other organizations have ever experienced it and what they have done with it, and so on. Once they have gathered all this information, they have the opportunity to reword their question so that it is considerably more specific. Their rewording will take into account whether they want to work on the symptoms of the problem, the causes of the problem, or both. It will also permit them to deal with emergencies, chronic difficulties, or both. The group defines its terms, using both lexicographical and operational definitions. It gathers examples, creates or discovers statistics, and examines the opinions of authorities, applying the criteria provided in Chapter 5 to separate relevant and useful information from irrelevant or defective information.

Once the initial set of facts is gathered and evaluated, the group can move on to a consideration of the relationship between the symptoms and the causes. Facts can generally be grouped into two categories: information about the nature of the problem and information about the cause of the problem. The group can choose to work on the symptoms of the problem only, or they can try to eliminate the problem by eliminating the causes, or they can attempt both. If the problem arises from something over which they have no control, like federal law or postal regulations, they may have to work on the symptoms only. If the problem results from defective regulations inside the organization, they may work on the causes as well.

If the problem appears to be one of faulty supervision or incompetent personnel, it is not wise to tamper with major components of the organization. The group will be responsible for making good guesses (hypotheses) about causes and solutions as they decide precisely what action to take. Following are some questions that groups can raise about their information to improve their chances of success in correctly specifying the problem.

1. Does the information we have uncovered lead us to some reasonable assessment of the cause of the problem? How sure are we?
2. Do the causes we have discovered lie within the scope of authority of the person for whom we are making recommendations? Can our authority act on the recommendations that may arise from our assessment of cause?
3. Do the causes we have discovered lie in some discernible component of the organization with whom our authority has contact (for example, personnel, accounting, sales)? Do they lie entirely outside the organization, and should they be construed as matters over which we have no control?

The answers to the preceding questions provide a basis for rephrasing the question. For example, if the group discovers that one of the problems underlying late shipments is the federal regulations governing the transshipping of merchandise, there is very little that can be done about it, but if the group discovers that one problem is the tendency of the shipping clerks to set aside shipments to those regions because it is too difficult to handle the paperwork when they have to use a partial truckload, then the organization does have

control. In the first case, the group would seek alternatives, such as "How can the chief of operations direct personnel to alternatives to shipping by truck?" In the latter case, the wording might be "How can the chief of operations improve the performance behavior of the shipping clerks in regard to shipments into the regions in question?"

The information the group has leads them to some hypothesis about a type of solution that might work, given the problem as defined. Each recommendation the group wants to make could be considered a separate question, and as a matter of fact, recommendations could be made about both alternatives to trucking and improvement of the performance of the shipping clerks. There are two major cautions to keep in mind, however:

1. The group will never have enough facts. It is possible for a group to evade its responsibility by claiming that it does not have enough information. The statement, "We cannot decide until all the facts are in" is a copout, along with the statement "We can't do anything until we get our research proposal funded." The group must be prepared to meet the deadline with the facts it has. Keeping conclusions tentative permits new information to be brought into consideration during the later phases of the discussion process.
2. The group can open the fact-finding process any time it wants to, and it has the privilege of changing the question whenever the facts seem to warrant a change. That is one of the main virtues of group problem-solving. It is not necessary to make a commitment to the nature of the situation, or even to the solution, until the moment it must be put into operation.

Groups have the option of keeping in touch with the executive who charged them for advice about when they must act, how they can get more information, and whether the executive approves of the changes in orientation that they think are justified by their information.

Step 4

The group must establish some standards for a solution. The standards include a specific statement of how they will know whether the problem has been solved. What, for example, would be the state of shipments into Regions 6, 9, and 14 that would indicate that there was no longer a problem? This kind of specific statement will help the group later on to test individual proposals. Each proposal could be assessed as to its potential to reach the goal specified.

Some groups like to phrase goals in fuzzy terms, for example, "We believe that there is no good reason for the delay in shipments into Regions 6, 9, and 14 and that the shipping clerks should, in the future, be more efficient." A statement like this is neither a solution nor a statement of goals. It is a moralistic expostulation with no value whatsoever in problem solving. What is needed is a statement like "When there are no more reports of delays of shipments into Regions 6, 9, and 14 than of delays to any other region in the company, then we would know that we have a solution, and when the reports of delays are no greater than the average of the other regions, we would know that we have a quality solution." Making abstract words more concrete helps the group generate tangible goals that can be achieved. The problem is to avoid idealistic statements that frustrate solution-finders because they simply cannot be achieved, no matter how much effort is made.

The following indicates a useful specification of goals for the shipping problem:

1. A solution should guarantee that all material shipped into the regions in question will reach the customer in the time that is average for other regions.
2. A solution should guarantee that the warehouses in the regions will cooperate in expediting shipments.
3. The solution should provide a manual of instructions for shipping clerks, to guide their behavior in routing shipments.

The three goal statements are based on the discovered facts. There is one small problem, however, and that is that the goal may be impossible. After the goal to be accomplished has been specified, it must be further examined so that it does not violate the limitations that necessarily apply to solutions.

Step 5

Step 5 involves the discovery of those limitations. Remember that when we discussed making proposals, we pointed out that a proposal was weak if it brought along problems greater than those it was to solve. In the case of the goals set for the shipping problem, there is a question of cost. Would it be of value to the company to speed up the shipments, but at such an expense that the loss would be even greater than that of the late shipments? If there are restrictions on the amount of money to be spent, the group should know them. There are other limitations that must be examined also. Limitations are presented by

1. *Funds.* If the solution costs more than it saves, than it should be rejected.
2. *Logistics.* If the solution requires more space, movement, or technical processing than the premises can provide, it cannot be considered a good solution.
3. *Personnel.* If there are no people qualified to implement the solution and/or if they cannot be trained and/or if it would cost too much to train them, the solution must be rejected.
4. *Technical skill.* If there is insufficient technical and professional skill available to implement the solution, it must be rejected.

In addition to impediments to solutions imposed by practical matters, there are problems outside the organization that have to be faced. For one thing, a solution cannot break the law. For another, there may be some human considerations that the group should keep in mind, issues of safety, respect for persons and privacy, and so on that would stand in the way of possible solutions. The union contract may forbid certain kinds of activities, as well. The examination of a proposed solution should include an assessment of whether or not it would meet the goals specified and an assessment of whether it violates internal or external limitations.

Step 6

Solutions can come in big lumps or small fragments. One person may have an inspiration and provide the entire solution, or the solution may be built piece by piece from proposals made by various members of the group. Steps 1–5 tend to prevent the politicizing of the group. By the time a group reaches the solution phase, they should be quite objective about what they are trying to do, and no one should have a commitment to a specific proposal. In fact, excessive commitment to one's own idea is an ego problem that the group can do without. The idea of the group process is to eliminate this kind of personal involvement. It is not likely that passionate argument can be generated around the issue of the steps a shipping clerk is to follow in trying to route shipments more rapidly into some obscure county.

Broader questions may result in more provocative kinds of solutions. If the group finds it necessary, for example, to examine the whole warehouse system on which shipping is based, some elements of the organization may have a vested interest that will be unsettled by the prospect of major changes. However, even in this case, the group should have enough tangible evidence to cope with emotionally based objections. The group should feel responsible only to the charging authority. If others are upset with their work, it is up to their superior to defend them and to take the responsibility for their solution, if he or she approves of it. If he or she does not, there is no real harm done (except for the time spent), and the group can be given a new or modified charge and sent back to the proverbial drawing board. This happens frequently in organizations. If the members of the group refrain from talking about the details of their problem solving, it is possible to transmit very provocative ideas and have them modified into workable solutions. If group problem-solving becomes excessively public, the opportunity to be tentative no longer exists. One of the major problems with so-called sunshine laws is that committee deliberations need to be private in order to permit the examination of a maximum number of points of view. Once a person is required to speak out in front of an audience, she or he becomes identified with what has been said, and it is very hard for her or him to back away from it.

The remaining step of the problem-solving process, presenting a proposal, is detailed in Chapter 5. If a written report is required, refer to the appropriate section in Chapter 9. For a detailed discussion of the steps in the standard agenda for group problem-solving, refer to *Group Discussion: A Practical Guide to Participants and Leaders* by Gerald M. Phillips, Douglas J. Pedersen, and Julia T. Wood. (Boston: Houghton, Mifflin, 1979). The steps of group problem-solving are logical and coherent. Review the steps by examining how the process worked in the solution of a real case:

TRAFFIC IN HOUSE BAYOU

Luke A. Head, the city manager of House Bayou, has received several complaints from merchants recently that traffic congestion between 4 and 6 P.M. has prevented people from coming downtown to do their shopping. They complain that the sudden and unexplained influx of traffic has deterred people from their usual trips downtown for dinner and shopping, particularly on Monday and Thursday nights, when the stores are open until 9. They claim that the problem is costing them heavily, and they demand action. The city manager refers the problem to the city traffic commission in a memo asking them to "consider" the problem.

The chairman of the traffic commission, Mort R. Karr, requests clarification. On behalf of the commission, he wants an interpretation of "consider." His memo reads, "Do you want a proposal for action, an ordinance, or what?" Mr. Head replies, "Whatever you think proper to reduce the traffic flow." Mr. Karr notes that Mr. Head is begging the question and jumping to a solution when he indicts traffic flow as the source of the problem. Mr. Karr suggests that there may be a still more fundamental cause, that is, whatever is causing the increasing traffic flow.

The next step for the commission is to word the problem. Tentatively, they ask: What can the commission propose to the city manager and the city council that would be useful in quelling the merchants' complaints? They decide that the merchants' complaints are the symptom they need to work on for the moment.

The commissioners interview the complaining merchants. They ask the merchants to show their comparative sales figures to document the allegation that they are losing money. They discover that there has been a drop in general sales of more than 3 percent, as well as a comparative drop of 11 percent in the evening hours. The loss in dinners for the restaurants is considerably higher, nearly 17 percent. The commission agrees that the merchants have a problem.

They next check with the police to see if there has indeed been a change in traffic patterns. They discover that not only has traffic increased during the 4–6 P.M. hour by more than 30 percent, but that the police have responded by instantly banning all downtown street-parking. As private commercial and public parking lots can handle only about 55 percent of all parking during the shopping period, banning street parking accounts for considerable losses in sales.

The commission decides to find out what has occasioned the

heavy traffic flow. They discover that the factory on the north edge of town has added a shift, starting at 5 P.M. This means that traffic has started pouring in from the south at about 4 P.M. and moving down from the north at about 5 P.M. Because of the one-way street plan, one north–south street is congested for one hour, and then the other north–south street is congested for the second hour as one shift moves in and the other moves out. The bulk of the workers at the factory live in the residential areas to the south of the town. There is a way to get to the factory without passing through the town, but it adds approximately seven miles to the trip.

The commission decides to investigate the total parking potential in the downtown area. They discover that there are five churches with parking lots for about 450 cars within two blocks of the downtown area, and that there was also space in office-building parking lots for another 100 cars. The high school stadium is located three blocks from downtown and has spaces for 250 cars. Incidentally, they also note that although the police have banned on-street parking during the rush period, no police have been assigned to facilitate traffic flow during the congested period.

The Commission decides that they can reword the problem as follows: "What recommendations can we make to anyone about how to facilitate traffic flow in the downtown area between 4 and 6 P.M. weekdays and also to provide reasonable parking facilities for shoppers?"

They decide that their solution, insofar as possible, should be privately financed, should involve minimal law enforcement, and should not interfere with the rights of householders.

They decide on the following:

1. Police officers are to be reassigned from desk duty to traffic control during the congested hours.
2. Negotiations are to be conducted with the churches, the school district, and the owners of the office buildings to make their parking lots available during rush hours.
3. They propose a system of private, guarded lots, with the merchants providing a fund for maintenance because of excessive wear and tear. Shoppers are to be permitted to park free, provided they show a ticket giving evidence that they have been shopping at one downtown store. Merchants are to fund a shuttle-bus service to the lots for persons with packages.
4. They request that the factory do what it can to encourage

their employees to use the town by-pass on their way to and from work.

The commission's plan is accepted and put into effect; at this time, it appears to be working successfully.

EFFECTIVE COMMUNICATION IN GROUP PROBLEM-SOLVING

Even though group problem-solving is a collective effort, individual members can make things go more smoothly if they observe some suggestions about how participation can be made most effective.

• *Members should be prepared for meetings.* If the group leader is following a systematic agenda, the members will know in advance the topics for discussion at a particular meeting. If the leader is not following a systematic agenda, the members should insist on it.

When members know what is to be covered and how much time will be devoted to each topic, they can prepare notes about what they want to say, look up information, and prepare themselves in a number of other ways. Even if it is not possible to get an advance agenda, the logic of the process should suggest what is to be covered at each session.

• *Members should cultivate a speaking style appropriate to discussion.* The talk in discussion is essentially conversational. Members may present ideas, but they are not giving formal speeches. Although disagreements will occur frequently, they should be presented gently and tentatively. Such a statement as "I have some data to add" is more effective than "Smith left out a lot when he gave his report." Members should avoid direct confrontation, personal insults, and excessive displays of emotion.

A good guide to the style most useful in discussion is provided by Irving J. Lee's book *How to Talk with People* (New York: Harper & Row, 1950). This book refers to the proper approach to discussion as the "shy, Socratic approach." Speakers must allow for the possibility that they may be wrong, and they must accept responses to their ideas with goodwill. All contributions should have an air of tentativeness. Members should not be intimidated into silence by excessive anger and direct personal attacks. Remarks can be somewhat

more spontaneous than in formal speaking because everything can be modified and corrected. The directive to follow is "Do not suppress what is on your mind. If it seems relevant, say it and participate in modifying it."

• *Groups work best when the members are physically comfortable.* Group problem-solving should not be an endurance test. The executive who charges the group should be sure that there is a comfortable work space available for them. Comfortable chairs and tables are essential. The group should work out the smoking problem. These days, disagreements between smokers and nonsmokers can seriously disrupt a group. Smokeless ashtrays are one way to handle the issue. Coffee and soft drinks should be available for those who require them.

Business lunches are normally not productive. Although it is possible to talk about some business matters at lunch, the ambience and noise at most eating places tends to discourage talk, and the alcohol common at such lunches tends to impede thought. Lunch served in the conference room is somewhat more effective. It is most productive, however, for groups to use the lunch hour as a time to break from their deliberations and spend some relaxing social time. Formal breaks should be provided frequently during discussions, about fifteen minutes every two hours.

• *Group members have a collective responsibility.* It is very difficult for group members to cast off their history and commitments and to dedicate themselves solely to the business of the group. Furthermore, it is important that biases be made public so that the group can take them into account in their solution. People are picked to participate because they represent various points of view. Thus it is important that those points of view be expressed.

However, group members must understand that their main responsibility is to the group. When they subordinate matters of common interest to their own personal desires, they attack the comfort and convenience of their colleagues and subvert collaboration. Every effort must be made to find areas of agreement leading to consensus, and where conflicting points of view cannot be reconciled, the group should carefully indicate the reasons that the opponents cannot come together. Understanding the nature of a conflict is sometimes as important as actual agreement.

• *Members should attempt to provide a variety of services to the group.* We pointed out earlier in this chapter that members should try to avoid becoming stereotyped by the nature of the comments they make. Members who allow themselves to participate by saying what is on their mind usually acquire skill in offering a number of different types of contributions to the group. The discussion leader has the obligation to invite members to contribute and particularly to urge members to make types of contributions that they do not normally make.

• *Careful records should be kept.* Although it may not be necessary to keep minutes or to transcribe the group's deliberations, someone should have a record of the agreements made along with the reasons for the agreements, as well as an indication of what issues have not been resolved and what the major points of contention are. It is also helpful to keep some kind of file of the facts that the group has uncovered. Careful records will prevent arguments later about what was said. Sometimes it is necessary to reconstruct history to remind the group's members of what actually went on.

Tape recording is not a good idea because the members will want to keep their ideas tentative. People are often intimidated when they believe that their errors will be forever recorded. Furthermore, because much of what the group says should be confidential, a tape recording in the wrong hands could be quite embarrassing.

• *Confidentiality should be maintained.* It is not good practice to discuss what people say in the group with those outside the group. Very often, people say something they wish they hadn't. They deserve the right to be able to back off from such remarks without having to account for them outside the group. In fact, the luxury of error inside the group is what makes the group process so productive. If people do not have to defend their foolishness, they are much more likely to cooperate in making it more sensible. In addition to all this, in serious matters the press ought not to be able to eavesdrop on the deliberation. The premature publication of comments may force the group to an unproductive solution.

• *Authority must be established within the group.* Groups are an ultimately democratic institution, but they require leadership. Someone must be in charge, seeing to it that the agenda is followed, that deadlines are met, and that people have a fair opportunity to talk and to resolve conflicts. Leaders are customarily appointed because of their position in the organization.

• *Conflict should not be allowed to disrupt deliberations.* Disagreements are useful only if they are resolved. Leader and members alike must concentrate on reconciling opposing points of view. Members should be encouraged to object and then submit their objections to the cooperative arbitration of their colleagues.

The most difficult conflict to resolve is direct confrontation between people. When members of the group attack each other it destroys the equilibrium of the group. People tend to take sides and the smooth flow of problem solving is disrupted. For this reason, group leaders must nip personal clashes before they begin. The best way to do this is to become a spokesman for both sides. When two members confront each other, the leader can intervene and rephrase each member's remarks, removing the personal references and innuendos. By maintaining this kind of control, the leader will suggest to the members that they should cease the personal attacks. If this does not work, the leader has the obligation to silencing both parties until they can proceed with decorum. There is a good reason for not letting the atmosphere of discussion get too loose. It is to guarantee the leader the control she or he will need to prevent harmful conflict.

• *Participation can be satisfying, but the group should not be regarded as a source of personal gratification.* When a group performs successfully, the members usually feel good about it. They tend to like and respect one another, and their morale is sufficiently high so that they will welcome another chance to work together. This kind of goodwill is an *outcome* not a precondition. Group output cannot be improved by making the members like each other. In fact, the many different techniques designed to make members like and respect each other have not produced the desired effect.

Members often make friends with one another and socialize outside the group. The development of personal associations is not a group goal, however. What goes on outside the group should not be permitted to affect group deliberations. In fact, the leaders should be particularly attentive to clique formation and should not permit power blocs to disrupt the cooperative efforts of the group.

SUMMARY

Group problem-solving uses the steps in thinking described by John Dewey, combined with systematic-logic methods like PERT/CPM. People in groups pool their ideas in order to come to consensus on some solution to a problem submitted to them by an executive or a supervisor. There are standard issues that might be dealt with in group problem-solving as well as effective procedures for handling the issues. The content of discussion may vary from group to group, but the pattern of group problem-solving remains consistent, no matter what the problem.

Groups start with a "charge" an organizational directive to solve some problem. They deal with questions related to product and services, distribution, relationships between components, finance, management, production, facilities, and logistics. Virtually all organizational problems relate to the maintenance and the satisfactory operation of the organization. Personal issues are important only if they have something to do with the general good.

Group problem-solving reduces the negative effects of authoritarian control; however, when excessive agreement takes place, the group can also become authoritarian and subvert the possibility of creative thinking. Groups should pool the interests of people with diverse backgrounds, training, and experience. Collectively, the group can discover matters not visible to an individual problem-solver.

Some of the problems that affect groups are the time it takes to obtain a solution, the tendency of the group to suppress brilliant individual effort, the possibility of factionalizing, and the pressure to push people into stereotyped roles.

Most groups follow six orderly steps in problem solving. A problem is identified, it is defined, facts are discovered and evaluated, goals are set, limitations are discovered, and a solution is constructed.

Once the solution is agreed on, it must be presented to the decision-making authority, orally or in writing or both.

Group members should develop a personal style of contribution that facilitates group cooperation. They should be gentle in disagreement and considerate in questioning. They must take care not to let their personal likes and dislikes interfere with their attitudes toward issues inside the group. Groups work best when they are led in an orderly and effective way, and when they have records to use to remind themselves of what they have done.

READINGS

There are a number of good books about group problem-solving. A simple sociological explanation can be found in Gerald M. Phillips and Eugene C. Erickson, *Interpersonal Dynamics in the Small Group*. New York: Random House, 1970.

An introduction to discussion preparation and detailed information on the standard agenda can be found in Gerald M. Phillips, Douglas J. Pedersen, and Julia T. Wood, *Group Discussion: A Practical Guide to Participation and Leadership*. Boston: Houghton, Mifflin, 1979.

An excellent statement about leadership and membership behaviors illustrated with transcripts can be found in Harvey J. Bertcher, *Group Participation: Techniques for Leaders and Members*. Beverly Hills, Calif.: Sage Publications, 1979.

A simple and cogent statement about participation style is made by Irving J. Lee, *How to Talk with People*. New York: Harper & Row, 1950. Although this book is thirty years old, it is still the best reference for the kinds of speech behaviors that get the best results in problem-solving groups.

Chapter **8**

Communication
in Management

THE LEADER–MANAGER

This is a chapter on leadership. Managers are leaders. Leaders have responsibility to direct the performance of people. Managers must be leaders and administrators. They must supervise work and they must manage records, reports, and the details of the work.

Leadership is the element vital to successful organizations. Traditionally, people have believed that leaders were born. Good family, good education, and a spark of something or other called *leadership ability* were what distinguished a leader from a follower. This narrow view of leadership came from the hierarchical nature of society. In recent years, however, advances in technology and complications in the organizational world have made leadership a meritocracy. People can become leaders if they qualify. They must be technically competent and must have the ability to direct the behavior of other people. They must be able to say the right things at the right time, be firm in the face of unrest, and conciliatory to frustration and despair. They must be tuned in to the needs of the organization and know how to integrate the work of many people to meet those needs. In addition, they must be skilled followers of the leaders next above them in the hierarchy.

Democratic leadership functions in an ambiguous society where prizes are available to everyone, but in limited number so that competition is necessary to win them. The leader manages the competition. It is a society that says that personal gratification is available but withholds it from all but those who are able to surmount the difficulties in their path. Leaders motivate others to work for gratification. It is a society that praises individualism but requires people to work together. The leader combines the individual efforts of people into a collective enterprise. Those who seek to lead must be adaptable and smart, and they must be skilled communicators.

Those of us who have been raised in the television era are used to problems being presented and solved in a limited period of time. Our programs start at 8, reach a peak at 8:30 and solve the problem by 8:59. Life in the organization is not like that. Problems are rarely solved. Situations are dealt with, and crises are met, but the main work of the organization is the step by step movement toward the accomplishment of goals. Leaders must be aware of both internal and external forces which produce situations that require action.

REQUIREMENTS OF A LEADER

Our society is characterized by a surplus of options and a demand for the quick resolution of problems. Companies compete for our attention (and money) and confront us with overwhelming possibilities for personal choice. We are presented with varieties of cars, clothing options, food choices, and recreations. Even the choice of a career or a mate requires us to face a bewildering array of alternatives.

At the First Global Congress of the World Future Society held in Toronto in the summer of 1980, Robert A. Wilson, President of the Northland Bank of Calgary, Canada, gave an address in which he discussed what managers of the future would have to face. These issues are the substance of managerial communication:

• *Managers must cope with increasing demands to participate.* Advances in technology plus the complex challenges to resources rule out one person-rule in corporations. Everyone, literally, wants to get into the act. Companies encourage participation through "management by objectives" programs and "peer evaluations."

Workers want a say in the programs that affect them, and they seek unions to represent them. Consumers demand that companies provide products of good quality that are safe. Stockholders want to influence the way things are done. Furthermore management decisions cannot be made on intuition. Evidence is necessary, and managers of the future must be able to sift through the evidence, listen to conflicting points of view, and reconcile many ideas into a unified policy. Once a decision has been made she or he must integrate people into the broadest possible consensus in order to achieve organization goals. She or he must do all this without generating potentially destructive conflict.

• *Managers must be oriented toward planning.* Managers must be able to project the effects of today's decisions on tomorrow's conditions. They must be adept at coping with both the expected and the unexpected, both inside and outside the organization. That means that they must be able to cope with changes in society, technology, and the attitudes of people. Managers must have a long-range view of the direction in which the organization is going, so that they can make adjustments to accommodate to future problems. To accomplish this, they must have enough imagination to anticipate problems, know how to use the information from experts, and be able to avoid wishful thinking. Realistic appraisal of options must characterize their work. They must be able to generate hypotheses and test them carefully, and most of all, they must be able to admit their errors and recoup their losses.

• *Managers must recognize that government will play an increasing role in the operation of organizations.* Government is required to save organizations from destructive competition, to protect the consumer from exploitation, to preserve resources for the common good, and to provide direction for the entire society. This does not mean that organizations deliberately act against the interests of the people. What it means is that organizations necessarily take a narrow view of society because their interest is in their own progress, even at the expense of others. The goals of individual organizations must be coordinated so that society benefits because only if society benefits will the organization thrive. It is the objective of government to integrate the efforts of the individual components of society. Thus managers must overcome their suspicion of government and learn to deal with it.

• *Managers must be able to handle information.* The computer has replaced the hunch. Managers can no longer rely on intuition for decisions. Furthermore every manager is responsible to someone else, and every decision must be defended with rational argument and supported with valid proof. Thus managers must know where to find

data as well as how to evaluate it. Furthermore information is often so complicated that managers must rely on advisers for interpretation. Management is only as good as the information by which it is guided; thus the selection of competent advisers and the ability to communicate with them are important components of successful management.

• *Managers must keep an eye on the market and avoid smugness.* Contemporary marketing is characterized by intense competition. Most manufactured products face competition from foreign companies as well as domestic ones. Some companies tend toward monopoly (energy producers, for example), but government shows every evidence of managing such monopolies as they did the so-called public utilities. Managers must take a long-range view of marketing, stay tuned to local needs, and be able to adjust production to accommodate to demand. Through imaginative collegial management, new markets must be opened, and through the use of persuasion, old markets must be expanded.

• *Managers must be able to work with a shortage of capital.* Most corporate expansion took place in a fuel-rich economy. When energy is inexpensive, there is usually enough money to go around. However, with the shrinking of energy supplies and the attendant inflation, capital is restricted. Managers must be able to plan to use the amount of money available to meet their needs and prepare for the future. They must be able to set priorities and allot limited resources so that company goals are accomplished.

• *Managers must react to economic fluctuations.* Swings between inflation, depression, and expansion of the economy are very rapid. Managers must be able to adapt their decision making to those rapid changes. They must know how to take advantage of rising and falling interest rates and be able to manage inventories to take advantage of tax laws. Fiscal changes provide a topic for planning and discussion. By coordinating rapid moves with long-range goals, managers can maintain and expand production and profits despite an adverse economy.

• *Managers must recognize that they live and work in a milieu that affects their operations.* Multinational corporations must maintain many styles to fit the local communities in which their components reside. Even companies that have no international connection must take community attitudes and commitments into account as they make their plans. More and more, citizens are responding to corporate decisions with objections and criticism. Managers must be able to make contact with their communities and integrate community attitudes into decision making designed to provide a comfortable relationship with the communities in which they are located.

Leaders of organizations must be both politicians and persuaders. They must be attentive to the messages they receive and send, inside and outside the organization. Leadership *is* communication. Leaders direct, inform, guide, counsel, persuade, argue, cajole, reason, inspire, plan, talk, listen, and order. Their competency in thinking problems through is revealed by their talk. It is for this reason that this chapter presents a model of organizational leadership as skilled communication.

THEORY Z: WHAT WE CAN LEARN FROM THE JAPANESE.

William Ouchi, in his new book, *Theory Z: How American Business Can Meet the Japanese Challenge* (Reading, Mass.: Addison-Wesley, 1981) points out that American industrial society is composed of self-interested individuals, competing with each other. This, he argues, is a society that has no freedom. Japanese industrial society, on the other hand, is an enterprise that emphasizes the relationship between members of the organization. Communication is a prominent feature of Japanese industry. In one sense, it is part of the culture in which people hold their jobs for life. In another sense, it is a feature of a society in which people define their own success through the success of the organization to which they belong.

In the simplest and most direct sense, Japanese employees are interested in doing what they can to help their country succeed. By the same token, their managers regard the individual workers as experts in their work and they are thus, interested in what the workers have to say. The "quality circle" is a simple method by which every worker who wishes to do so can make his input and have his influence on the decisions of management. Whether they are individually rewarded does not matter. The fact that they have helped their company advance is the basic reward.

Those who have observed the operation of Japanese management first hand testify to the fact that Japanese managers do not try as hard as American managers to be friendly, "one of the folks." Rather, they are genuinely respectful of the knowledge and experience of their employees, and they are not at all embarrassed to ask for help when it is needed. The net effect is to discourage entrepreneurial attempts to achieve personal success at the expense of others. Harmony is the goal, and cooperation the guiding force.

Oddly enough, a characteristic feature of the most successful forms of management in Japan stems from the American Group Dynamics movement. The idea of decisions being made at the bottom of the organization, then passed upward for approval is a major component of success. The American tendency today is to hand decisions down and expect compliance. American management, however, is often remote from the workers, built out of careful engineering and statistical analysis, yet unrealistic because it does not take into account the life that the workers lead in the shop. Because the decisions are not generated from those who are affected by them, it is often virtually impossible for American workers to comply with the requests or demands made of them. Quite the reverse is true of the Japanese. Decisions are made by the people who are bound by them, fulfilling the basic belief that people work best when they have had a hand in making the decisions by which they are bound.

General access is another component of Japanese management. It is part of management to be in contact with the workers. In the United States, supervisors are often separated from the workers, and it requires considerable effort for a worker with a message, however, important, to work through the red tape and bureaucratic channels to get to the person in charge. Even then, the worker who does so jeopardizes his or her future status, since any managerial personnel bypassed become resentful because they have been ignored.

There are two other aspects of American management that are self defeating. First, American managers are rewarded because of short-term gains. Japanese management, on the other hand, has the option of planning a long term campaign, and temporary setbacks do not disrupt the structure. The managers, in fact, are in constant touch with the workers to see how things are going and the workers get first-hand information so they are not surprised by changes. American management, on the other hand, reserves the right to reward and punish because of short-term success or failure, and workers are constantly "laid off" because of a miscalculation by a manager for which they must pay the price. The second component of American management that is self-defeating is that American managers do not like "bad news." Japanese management is aware that they will get constant negative messages, and they are prepared to cope with the negative by using every bit of employee wisdom they can find.

Ouchi seems to feel that part of Japanese success is due to the fact that they are a society in which conflict can be resolved before it burns up society. They are not a "frontier society," as he puts it. Certainly Japan as a society does not have the communication tradition of the United States. It is traditional to believe, in fact, that Japan is a sort of totalitarian, monolithic society in which the government controls. This is far from the truth. Half of Japan's workforce is employed by small companies that cannot guarantee employment. Furthermore, the large companies are engaged in competition for both domestic and overseas markets that make American competition look like tea parties. In the final analysis it appears that the characteristic difference is the way management regards the worker. Workers who feel they are worth talking to tend to talk, and usually they have something important to say. Once they discover that management uses what they learn from them, workers are ready to comply with formally organized efforts to use their ideas. Thus communication becomes a tool of management designed to bring about effective utilization of the most important resource a company has, the workers.

In the years ahead, the Japanese style of management will exert greater influence on trends in the United States, and we can expect more influence to be exerted by the workers. Managers will need to learn how to carry on effective communication with their employees, and the material we presented in the last chapter will take on considerably greater importance. The manager who is able to use systematic group problem solving effectively will be the manager who gets the greatest input from the workers, and will, thus, have the greatest pool of constructive ideas with which to work.

THE PROPER AUTHORITY OF LEADERSHIP

There are a variety of positions from which someone can lead. Most obvious are the positions assigned on the organization chart. Leadership can come from a job description that requires the individual to lead. We must take care, however, to distinguish leadership from administration. An administrator fulfills his or her job description by performing functions, checking schedules, and keeping records. The administrator works "by the book" to make sure that organizational regulations are complied with. A leader, however, directs and guides to make sure that the work done measures up to standards. Furthermore a leader is able to leave "the book" when necessary to handle problems imaginatively. What is called *management* is a combination of leadership and administration.

Leadership is a condition characterized by respect. A person can be called a leader only if he or she has followers. A person who directs the behavior of truculent and submissive people cannot be called a leader. A leader has the trust of the followers. They believe that she or he is qualified to make decisions and is fair and able to make decisions that benefit them. They are willing to take the advice, follow the orders, and implement the directives of the leader because of their respect for him or her and his or her record. Leadership can be attained by

1. *Demonstrated ability to process information.* People who know what needs to be known and where to find it are often regarded as leaders.
2. *Ability to respond to individual needs.* The person who seems to understand the pressures under which people work and takes them into account in directing activities tends to be regarded as a leader.
3. *Ability to conciliate.* The person who can end disputes, leaving the combatants relatively satisfied with the outcome, and who can bring about consensus in the face of conflicting opinions is seen as a leader.
4. *Ability to fight and win.* People often gain positions of leadership because they are able to advocate an idea and get it adopted in the face of opposition. The problem with this kind of leadership is that if the program advocated by the leader fails, the leader may find himself or herself out of power.

5. *Displays of charm, friendliness, and wit.* People with social skills that make them appear humane and considerate are often regarded as leaders. In most organizations, even if these people do not occupy leadership positions on the organizational chart, others usually come to them for advice and help or seek their company for encouragement and goodwill.

Once leaders achieve their position, they must carefully balance their own authority and their responsibility to their own leader. Leaders must be very careful about staying within their scope of authority. The PERT/CPM process used in many large organizations specifies the legitimate range of authority for supervisory positions throughout the organization. The limits of responsibility must be respected, for people resent it when others intrude on areas that are legitimately theirs and for which they are held responsible.

People can exert leadership without holding a formal position. In fact, one of the most serious problems faced by a manager is how to use the authority of the people in the organization who develop their own followers through strength of personality and ability to exude goodwill. In democratic societies, a leader without a formal position could become the head of an opposition party threatening to those in power. Such a situation is intolerable in a formal organization, which demands the attention of everyone in it to the accomplishment of established goals. For this reason, most organizations are carefully attentive to those employees who show talent in leadership. It is an objective of most personnel policies to discover such people and integrate them into the management structure. If they cannot be formally worked into management, the process of group problem-solving can use their talents and their leadership constructively in the accomplishment of corporate goals.

COMMUNICATION BY MANAGERS

The leader–manager maintains control through communication. Followers respond to the oral and written directions of the leader. Leaders are able to transmit information so that people can understand it, and they are able to observe and listen in order to receive communication from those they supervise. The process of leadership is not mystical. It can be observed and evaluated. Consider the following list of possible communication goals for a leader. Assess your own capabilities to discover what your potential is. And remember that you can learn techniques to help you attain every one of the possible goals.

1. A leader can guide behavior by giving advice without appearing to order or direct.
2. A leader can correct erroneous behavior without upsetting the person corrected.
3. A leader can use a performance evaluation to motivate improved performance, even when the performance evaluation is in the "best" category.
4. A leader can give a reward without making the recipient smug.
5. A leader can give instructions clearly and anticipate mistakes before they happen.
6. A leader can referee a conflict without angering either party.
7. A leader can stimulate people to meet emergency situations.
8. A leader can persuade followers to do more than they believed they could.
9. A leader can engage in friendly persuasion without trying to destroy the opposition.
10. A leader is tolerant of differences and respectful of the opinions of others.
11. A leader is able to maintain equity in the distribution of rewards and punishments.
12. A leader does not gossip or spread rumors.
13. A leader provides accurate and complete information.
14. A leader can give reasons for her or his decisions.
15. A leader is able to spot potential in followers.
16. A leader knows how to ask questions and whom to ask.
17. A leader is able to encourage others to be leaders.

Leadership can be learned. With reasonable technical knowledge and competency, people who desire to be leaders can be trained in the techniques of skillful management of communication to achieve the goals in the above list.

When a person is in a position of leadership but is unable to lead, we have a "Peter principle" effect. The Peter principle operates when a person has been given a job because of technical skill or seniority but does not have the communication skills required to do the job. Such individuals may be able to handle the paperwork, but they do not win the respect of their employees and they never qualify for advancement. They may get ulcers, suffer from stress, and burn out. Here are some of the ways people can get into positions of authority for which they may not be qualified.

1. *The cousin with the old school tie.* Nepotism and tradition sometimes influence decisions about who should be promoted. In some organizations people are selected for leadership positions because of the school from which they graduated or because they are related to some powerful person in the organization. Leadership exerted by such people is often characterized by evasion of responsibility and abdication of authority either to strong people whom they supervise or by deference to their own supervisor.

2. *It's my turn.* Some organizations base promotions into leadership positions on seniority. There is nothing intrinsically wrong with taking experience into account in making advancement decisions, but sometimes such decisions are made on seniority alone, without reference to competence. Such people are often very defensive about their positions and feel threatened by the competent people they supervise.

3. *I passed the exam.* The principle on which the civil service operates is that it is possible to measure leadership through a

paper-and-pencil examination. Clearly, however, what examinations measure is knowledge about what a leader must do, not the ability to do it. Thus basing promotions solely on examinations often puts people into positions of leadership who are unable to act, even though they may know what actions are required.

4. *I need the pay.* Sometimes people seek positions of leadership because it is their impression that leaders get more pay. They can offer convincing arguments on their own behalf; however, their motivation is not the challenge of leaderhsip but the dollars alone.

5. *Throw the rascals out.* Some people think the way to attain leadership is to lead a successful rebellion. Although this rarely happens in formal organizations, a great many people think it is possible. As a result, many leaders find themselves confrontcd with a hostile opposition. The problem with winning a post by destroying its previous occupant is that you do not have the loyalty of the followers of the previous occupant, who can rise up and throw you out.

6. *You can if you think you can.* Some people aspire to leadership because of a sincere interest in accomplishing some goal. They are so zealous in their quest to accomplish the goal that they lose sight of the human relations so important in leadership. They exploit and punish their followers and eventually fail in their quest.

7. *Do it by the book.* Compliance with regulations can sometimes push people into leadership positions. Competent administrators are required in some positions, but contact with people cannot be accomplished by the book. Excessive attention to regulations can frustrate employees and subvert the activities of the organization.

8. *Perks and privileges.* Some people are lured into positions of leadership because they think it desirable to be seen by others as a leader. They want the carpet in the office, the expense account, the best secretary, and the power to get other people to do what they want. Unfortunately power confers responsibility, and if leadership is exercised only to your own advantage, followers will not cooperate.

9. *We are one big happy family.* Some people achieve an influential position because of their ability to act like parents. They

serve as fathers or mothers to their employees, who respond by acting like children. Employees of such leaders must be constantly supervised, and particular attention must be paid to emotional needs. The whole business gets so distracting that organizational objectives are sacrificed.

Composite leaders combine a little of all the preceding. In addition to having technical and communication skill, they are able to work well with others. They have usually earned their position through service and competent work. They have a sense of right and wrong and are upset by incompetency. They are idealistic and also able to nurture their followers to do the work required to accomplish the ideal. They like the money, the perks, and the power that come along with leadership, and they use these confidently and well.

PERSONNEL PROBLEMS

The most serious problems faced by leaders come from the people they lead. Not everyone who works is totally dedicated to the organization. A great number of them cannot see beyond their own interests. By thinking of themselves all the time, they reduce their chances of advancing their own cause, but they do not know this. Leaders must deal with a wide range of opposition and resistance. By understanding the causes of inadequate performance, leaders can work out strategies of motivation and compensation designed to overcome personnel problems.

The Adversary

Some workers regard their work life as a game of cops and robbers with the "boss." The leader is seen as a cop whose main job it is to catch the workers doing something wrong. These kinds of workers put up constant resistance, for they see every organizational requirement as a way of getting more work for less pay. Their paranoia is particularly strong at evaluation time. The leader has the problem of convincing these people that leadership is not policing and that the effort spent on concealing things from the boss would be better spent actually doing the work.

The Specialist

Some workers are exceptionally skilled at what they do. They regard the leader as an amateur, not qualified to evaluate them and actually a bit jealous of their skill. They patronize the leader and try to bowl him or her over with technical talk. Such employees know that if the leader would only leave them alone to do their work, things would be all right, but they suspect the leader of trying to sabotage them. These employees must be convinced that the leader respects their technical competence and regards them as valuable members of the organization.

The Unionist

In companies with collective-bargaining contracts, some employees regard their membership in the union as more important than their job. They spend their time advocating causes and stirring up dissent. Most stewards are sensible and cooperative, but some of their followers resent the company and regard cooperative union leadership as subversive.

The Child

Leaders with a fatherly demeanor often make children out of their employees. Some employees are children to begin with, however. They seek approval for everything they do. They constantly need permission to think for themselves, and they try to be dependent on their leader for advice about their personal lives. However well these people do their work, they are a nuisance to supervise. The leader must convince them to grow up and assume responsibility.

Beetle Bailey

There are a few workers who are good-hearted "goof-offs." They are cheerful, pleasant, and fun to be around, but they do almost nothing. They spend time at the water fountain, take long coffee breaks, volunteer to solicit for the charity drives, and have a kind word for everyone. They are difficult to supervise because they are so hurt when they are reprimanded.

The Burnout

One of the most serious problems for the leader is the once-competent worker now burned out. Virtually all conscientious workers reach a point where their job is impossible to do. Skilled leaders can find alternatives for these people. Recent studies show that if people are moved into different jobs when they start to burn out, they can be motivated to become productive once more. The leader must make the decision about how and when to intervene.

The Senior Citizen

Some workers become premature pensioners. They have been on the job for a long time, and as they approach retirement, they do less and less work. Although most older employees are immensely productive, these few place considerable stress on their colleagues, for someone must make up the work that they don't do. The leader must somehow motivate them back into a reasonably productive workday.

Eddie Haskell

We remember Eddie Haskell on the old *Leave It To Beaver* television show as the chronic apple polisher. Leaders have a problem to begin with because they never know whether friendly overtures are sincerely motivated or strategies to gain favor. The apple polisher is constantly seeking special favors but usually not as a reward for good work. A leader must take considerable care in making exceptions for anyone, for once a special privilege is given, it is usually requested again and again.

I Want Out

Some workers simply do not like their jobs. They would prefer to be doing something else, somewhere else, although they may not know what. They limp through the day making a minimal effort. They cling to their jobs because they have nowhere else to go and they need the paycheck. Sometimes a leader can be of most service to these people by helping them to transfer to another kind of job or even helping them to find a job elsewhere. Sometimes all the discontented worker needs is some reinforcement of his or her own competence.

The Genuine Worker

In the final analysis, the leader has no choice but to regard each employee as what the job description says she or he is. The minimal expectation of every employee is that he or she will do at least the minimum required on the job for which he or she was hired. The first responsibility of the leader is to get the workers to do what they are supposed to do. The effective use of rewards and punishments can often motivate high-quality work. Most people respond to incentives to get ahead, and if the workers think their leader is fair and they have an even chance to display their skill, they will work hard and support the organizational effort.

Leaders are also required to conform to their own job description. They must see to it that everyone under them produces what is necessary to accomplish the tasks of the department or division. By understanding their own jobs, leaders become able to explain the contribution that each worker makes to the accomplishment of mutual goals. Leaders also provide a model for their own workers in the way they respond to directives from their own superiors.

LEADERSHIP OF PROBLEM-SOLVING GROUPS

Frequently those who occupy managerial positions must lead problem-solving groups. This requires particular skill, for often the success of the group depends on the technique used by the leader. There are a number of tasks that the group leader must do in order to ensure effective performance. They must

1. Overcome groupthink and urge members to be appropriately critical.
2. Overcome the resistance that some members will offer to the group process by persuading them to play an active role.

3. Be prepared at all times to orient members to where the group is on the agenda.
4. Offer periodic reviews of what the group has accomplished and what remains to be done.
5. Manage traffic so that talkative members do not subvert the rights of quieter members.
6. Be able to use democratic methods when things are going well and authoritarian methods when things are going poorly or when there is urgency in finishing the job.
7. Be prepared to ask questions that motivate continued discussion.
8. Argue on behalf of unpopular ideas to guarantee that important points of view will get a fair hearing.
9. Manage logistics, make sure the discussion room is comfortable, and make sure that refreshments are provided and that people go home at a reasonable hour.
10. Make sure that records are kept.
11. Support positive contributions and discourage disruptions.
12. Maintain liaison with other components of the organization.
13. Represent the group in public.
14. Manage the pace, slowing things down when the group seems to be jumping to conclusions and speeding things up when the group seems to be caught in a boring loop.
15. Make sure the final report is prepared properly.

The formal function of the discussion leader can be best accomplished by following the steps of the standard agenda and preparing questions and statements designed to guide the members through those steps. The leader should be particularly alert at points of transition from one phase of discussion to another. At those times, a careful summary of past accomplishments is required. This can be followed by a statement of the problems to be solved in the next phase of activity.

THE INTANGIBLE CHARACTERISTICS OF LEADERSHIP

Leadership can be described by acts. Acts of leadership include conveying information, giving advice, modifying attitudes, giving instructions, persuading, issuing orders, and conciliating. The intangibles are "judgment calls," like the ability to move when moving is required. Part of what makes a good leader is the ability to understand what other people are saying, both directly and indirectly. A good leader should be able to spot signs of trouble in employees and make a good assessment of what is necessary to overcome the difficulty. For this reason, leaders must be good observers and good listeners. One of the most important aspects of leadership is getting a maximum understanding of what other people are trying to say.

Leaders are constantly confronted with having to make judgments about competence. These are not so difficult when they involve merely routine jobs, but most jobs in industry today are not routine. Each of them contains a finite body of work that must be done, but there are also intangibles like the ability to handle the unexpected, ability in human relations, and the ability to respond to pressure. It is very hard for a leader to know what it is reasonable to expect.

Once the leader has made a judgment on competence, he or she must consider what it would take to get the person properly trained. This requires motivation. The person selected for a job must want to do it; otherwise training will not be effective. Generally a person will resist assignment to a new task unless some reward is promised. The intangible "we will consider it at promotion time" is sometimes not convincing.

Another persuasive job for the leader is to convince her or his superiors that things are going well. Executives normally do not get firsthand information about how things are going in the divisions under them. They rely on reports from the supervisors of those divisions. Persuading the boss that things are going well is a major act of leadership.

Leading also has an emotional component. Leaders often need to justify their actions publicly and privately. Every decision potentially annoys someone, who must be calmed. Every action demanded of employees must be motivated. When someone is dismissed, others may fear that they will be next. They must be reassured. Leaders must have a steady supply of logical supports that they can use to justify their decisions.

Most important of all is the ability of a leader to *distinguish the desirable from the do-able.* The leader cannot afford to waste time taking employees on blind-alley trips to impossible objectives. The leader must be careful not to undershoot, but he or she must also be careful not to try for too much. Realistic goals can be achieved.

Goals achieved motivate people to seek the next goal. The essence of the management-by-objectives system is to generate solid leadership by setting attainable goals. Leadership is the art of the possible. Management, the combination of leadership and administration, is a challenge to everyone who works. Most people aspire to it, but few are willing to discipline themselves to learn to do it. We have used the word *leader* here synonymously with manager, for we feel that leadership exercised through communication skills is what makes the difference between shuffling paper and truly leading other human beings.

PARLIAMENTARY PROCEDURE

Leaders are often required to preside over formal public meetings. Although most organizations do not follow parliamentary procedure to the letter, they do demand that some of the basic regulations be followed. Parliamentary procedure is actually a general language of meetings. Everyone knows the essentials, and so large groups of people share the rules as they meet to decide on major bits of business. If you need to know the details of parliamentary procedure, see Henry Robert, *Rules of Order Revised* (Chicago: Scott, Foresman, 1980).

Parliamentary procedure is a commonsense method of allowing a large number of people to participate in doing business. Its purpose is to protect the rights of minorities and individuals while permitting an assembly to do its work.

1. Parliamentary procedure enables a large group of people to transact business with speed and efficiency.
2. Parliamentary procedure protects the rights of individuals.
3. Parliamentary procedure keeps a group together by providing a formal method by which conflict can be legally resolved.

Parliamentary procedure has five basic principles:

1. Only one subject can be considered by an assembly at any one time.
2. Every proposition presented to an assembly is entitled to free and full debate.

3. Every member has rights and obligations equal to those of every other member.
4. The will of the majority must prevail, as long as it does not deny the minority its right to try again.
5. The particular interests of individuals must be subordinated to the rights of the assembly.

There is a standard order by which business is brought before a parliamentary body.

1. *The meeting is called to order.* This means that the formal agenda and the rules of parliamentary procedure must now be followed. Once the meeting is formally called to order, the chair has the right to rule on all parliamentary matters, subject to whatever advice she or he wishes to seek. Some organizations retain a consultant called a *parliamentarian* to provide advice to the chair. The parliamentarian has no status except as adviser to the chair.
2. *The minutes are read.* The minutes are a record of the last meeting. They can be corrected by vote of the assembly. Once they are approved (as corrected) by a majority vote, they become part of the permanent record of the assembly.
3. *Reports are presented by relevant officers and committee heads.* The first reports come from vice-presidents and the treasurer, followed by heads of standing committees and finally by heads of special committees. The assembly must accept the reports by majority vote. Acceptance does not mean that the assembly approves the reports, merely that they can now become part of the record.
4. *Old business is conducted.* During old business whatever was on the floor when the last meeting adjourned is disposed of. If the organization uses an agenda, whatever was on the last agenda that was not completed is considered in order. Any motions postponed from the last meeting may be considered.
5. *New business is considered.* New proposals and motions specified in committee reports or reports from officers may be considered or entered on an agenda for consideration at the next meeting.
6. *Adjournment takes place.* Simple adjournment is sufficient when the organization meets regularly. If the organization is

meeting for one time only, adjournment means that the organization will never meet again. Organizations established for one series of meetings usually declare an agenda of meetings and specify an adjournment time. Sometimes organizations prefer to recess. When it convenes again, it returns immediately to what it was considering at the time of the recess. Even though a week or more may pass between recessing and reconvening, the two meetings are regarded as one meeting.

7. Some meetings provide for business "for the good of the order" between new business and adjournment. Customarily nonmembers may not be present during these sessions, which are characterized by members' making statements about problems in the organization.

All business at a parliamentary meeting is carried on through *motions*. A motion is merely a proposal that an assembly take some sort of action. A motion is decided by a vote. There are four main kinds of motions:

1. *Main motion.* A main motion has as its object bringing up a proposal for action for the consideration of the assembly. Only one main motion may be considered at any one time. Every other motion must relate either to the main motion under consideration or to the privilege of the organization. A main motion must be disposed of (passed, defeated, postponed, tabled, and so on) before another proposal can be made.

3. *Subsidiary motion.* Subsidiary motions relate directly to the content of the main motion. They may be presented while the motion is on the floor. They include such motions as amendments, postponement, and tabling. They either modify the content of the main motion or dispose of it in a special way. They may be proposed in a hierarchy; that is, several can be on the floor at the same time. In the chart of parliamentary motions, Table 2, we present the order of precedence of subsidiary motions.

3. *Privileged motion.* Matters of privilege take precedence over all other business. In addition to such matters as adjournment, they include questions of proper order and the privileges of persons in the assembly. They, too, follow an order of precedence.

4. *Incidental motion.* Incidental motions follow no order of prec-

edence. They have nothing to do with the content of the main motion, but they may affect the manner in which the main motion is handled. They are mostly procedural in nature.

Motions have a standard order of procedure. Consider the following dialogue as an example of how motions are handled:

Member: Mr. Chairman.
Chairman: The chair recognizes Mr. Schmidlapp.
Member: Mr. Chairman, I move that the assembly authorize the expenditure of $1,500 to fund the annual awards dinner.
Chairman: It has been moved that the assembly authorize the expenditure of $1,500 to fund the annual awards dinner. Is there a second?
Member: Mr. Chairman.
Chairman: The chair recognizes Ms. Finster.
Member: I second the motion.
Chairman: It has been moved and seconded that we authorize the expenditure of $1,500 to fund the annual awards dinner. Is there debate?

The members of the assembly can then argue the issue, or they can

1. Amend the motion by adding, deleting, or substituting words. (Change $1,500 to $2,000, for example). An amendment may also be amended, so that at any given time, there may be a motion, an amendment, and an amendment to an amendment on the floor.
2. Refer the motion to a committee for consideration. The assembly can do this even though two amendments are under consideration.
3. Postpone consideration of the motion, even after a proposal has been made to refer it to a committee.
4. Table the motion. Once it has been tabled, another main motion is required to get the motion back under consideration.

The whole process seems very complicated, but it is actually quite simple. There are several ways to dispose of a motion. One is to defeat it. Another is to pass it. But there are intermediate possibilities requiring various forms of consideration. In order to take advantage

Table 2. Chart of Precedence of Motions and the Rules That Govern Them

Motion	May Inter-rupt the Speaker	Requires a Second
Privileged Motions		
1. Fix a time at which to adjourn	No	Yes
2. Unqualified adjournment	No	Yes
3. Recess	No	Yes
4. Question of privilege	Yes	No
5. Order of the day	Yes	No
Subsidiary Motions		
6. Lay on or take from the table	No	Yes
7. Call for the previous question	No	Yes
8. Limit or extend the limit for debate	No	Yes
9. Postpone to a specific time	No	Yes
10. Refer to committee	No	Yes
11. Amend	No	Yes
12. Postpone indefinitely	No	Yes
Main Motions		
13. General Main motions	No	Yes
Specific main motions		
a. Reconsider	Yes	Yes
b. Enter on minutes to reconsider	Yes	Yes
c. Rescind	No	Yes
d. Expunge from minutes	No	Yes
e. Adopt a resolution	No	Yes
f. Qualified adjournment	No	Yes
g. Create an agenda	No	Yes
h. Amend by-laws	No	Yes
Incidental Motions		
Suspend the rules	No	Yes
Withdraw a motion	No	No
Object to consideration	Yes	No
Point of order	Yes	No
Parliamentary inquiry	Yes	No
Appeal decision of the chair	Yes	Yes
Division of the house	Yes	No
Division of a question	No	Yes

Note: Organizations may have special policies in their by-laws that take precedence over this table.

Debate	Vote Required	Motions That Apply
Limited	Majority	Amend, reconsider (debate on amendments)
No	Majority	None
Limited	Majority	Amend (debate on amendments)
No	Chair	Appeal chair's ruling
No	Chair	None
No	Majority	None
No	Two thirds	Reconsider the chair's ruling
Limited	Two thirds	Amend, reconsider (debate on amendments)
Limited	Majority	Amend, reconsider, previous question
Limited	Majority	Amend, reconsider, previous question
Yes	Majority	Amend, reconsider, previous question
Yes	Majority	Limit debate, previous question, reconsider
Yes	Majority	All
Yes	Majority	All
Yes	Consent	May be vote if question is called (majority)
Yes	Two thirds	All
Yes	Two thirds	All
Yes	Majority	All
Yes	Majority	Debate on subsidiaries only
Yes	Majority	For regular agenda only, all motions apply
	Two thirds	For special agenda only, all motions apply
Yes	Two thirds	Follow procedure in by-laws
No	Consent	Two-thirds vote if demanded, no subsidiaries
No	Consent	Majority vote if demanded
No	Two thirds	Reconsider
No	Chair	Appeal the decision of the chair
No	Chair	Decision of authority referred to by chair
Limited	Majority	All except amendments
No	Chair	Majority vote if demanded
No	Majority	Amend

of these other possibilities, allowance is made for postponement, which allows members to think about the motion for a while; referral to a committee, which permits open discussion not subject to parliamentary procedure; or tabling, which, in effect, turns the motion down but keeps the door open to reconsidering it.

Virtually all of the subsidiary motions, as well as the main motion, permit debate. Debate should commence with the person who proposed the motion. It is customary then to recognize, alternately, persons for and against the motion. If any member is mentioned by name during the debate, she or he has the privilege of requesting the right to respond. When the debate is over, the chair takes a vote by voice. If the voice vote is not clear, the members may call for a division of the house, which requires a vote by another means. Once the vote is completed, the chair announces the result and moves on to the next item of business.

Debate can be limited in a number of ways. A subsidiary motion may impose time limits on debate; time limits may be imposed on each member as well as on the total time allowed for debate. An incidental motion permits dividing a main motion into parts and considering the parts one at a time. The assembly even has the privilege of demanding that the agenda be followed, for if it seems to stray from procedure, a member can call for the order of the day and force the assembly to comply with procedure. Finally, debate can be ended by "the previous question," a motion that proposes that the assembly vote on whether debate should be ended. If the assembly approves "the previous question," a vote is taken on all of the subsidiary motions in descending order and then on the main motion itself.

Amendments are the most important subsidiary motions. The purpose of a motion to amend is to clarify or modify a proposal so that it is generally more acceptable. An amendment must be germane to the main motion; that is, it must be on the same topic. It can be hostile, but it must relate to the same subject matter. Amendments may

1. Add words to the motion.
2. Delete words from the motion.
3. Substitute words in the main motion.

In complicated main motions, amendments may refer to whole sections or clauses. Only two amendments are permitted on the floor at the same time. An amendment to an amendment may refer only to language proposed in the amendment, never to the main motion.

The logic of precedence is really very simple. If you study Table 2 for a while, you will discover what your options are at a parliamentary meeting. Parliamentary procedure is fairly easy to learn by participation, as long as the chair is sophisticated in its use and can instruct the members of the assembly in proper procedure.

By-laws are the rules by which an organization operates. They are the fundamental agreement about the purpose of the organization and the business it is to do. Membership in an organization with by-laws presumes a willingness to observe the by-laws. By-laws are the equivalent of a constitution or a corporate charter. By-laws should designate

1. The name of the organization.
2. Its purpose (to sell merchandise, to provide service, to meet specific needs of the members, and so on).
3. Rules and regulations about membership: who may join, how they join, who certifies them as eligible, what are the special classes of membership (if any), what is the term of membership, what are the obligations of the members including dues and initiation fees, how the dues are altered, how the membership qualifications are altered, how to maintain good standing, how members are expelled, and how members may resign.
4. Officers: who they are, what they do, how they are elected, and what their term of office is. This section may read like a set of job descriptions. President, vice-presidents, secretary, and treasurer are commonly included. Paid positions, like executive secretary, may also be described. Refer to the *Rules of Order* for standard descriptions of the duties of office.
5. Executive board and board of directors: how selected, what are their duties and obligations, how vacancies are filled, and so on.
6. Fiscal matters, including procedures for audits and the rights of the members to know the organization's fiscal condition.
7. Committees and their duties: what the standing committees are, how special committees are generated and charged, how reports are given, and what is the authority of committees.
8. Statement of parliamentary authority: what reference work is to be used to resolve disputes over parliamentary procedure.

9. Parliamentary procedure: meeting agendas, special revisions of procedure, and the establishment of rules for particular meetings and standing rules.
10. Procedure for calling regular and special meetings, the preparation of the agenda, and the procedure for passing legislation.

There are standard procedures for nominations and elections. In general, the nominating and electing procedure is provided for in the by-laws. In most organizations, nominating committees propose slates of officers, and nominations are permitted from the floor. A second is not required for a nomination.

The following chart shows how members can take action for special purposes.

Motion	Purpose	Effect
Table	Permits more urgent business to be considered.	Delays action on the motion.
Previous question	Secures an immediate vote on pending business.	Ends debate.
Limit debate	Restricts the time for debate.	Speeds up or delays action.
Postpone to specific time	Allows time for informal discussion.	Delays action.
Refer to committee	Permits extended consideration.	Delays action.
Amend	Improves the motion.	Changes original motion.
Postpone indefinitely	Prevents a vote.	Suppresses the motion.
Point of order	Calls attention to a violation of the rules.	Keeps the group observing parliamentary procedure.
Appeal decision of the chair	Permits the assembly to question the chair's authority.	Enables assembly to rule instead of chair.

Motion	Purpose	Effect
Suspend the rules	Permits action not permissable under the rules.	Secures action not provided for in by-laws or parliamentary procedure.
Object to consideration	Prevents wasting time on objectionable business.	Suppresses the motion.
Divide a question	Enables the assembly to consider the parts of a motion.	Sets up an agenda of a series of motions to consider.
Division of the house	Determines the accuracy of a vote.	Secures a vote by a method other than the one used.
Nominate	Presents the names of a candidate.	Starts the electoral process
Request for information.	Obtains information about the content of a motion.	Clarifies confusion.
Parliamentary inquiry	Obtains procedural information.	Advises memberships on what follows next
Fix time to adjourn	Permits the meeting to continue legally.	Establishes formal meeting procedure.
Adjourn *sine die*	Sets no time for the next meeting.	Puts organization out of business.
Recess	Permits an intermission in the meeting.	Business picks up where it left off
Question of privilege	Corrects an undesirable condition.	Permits member to request adjustment for comfort and convenience.
Order of the day	Secures adherence to procedure.	Ensures law will be followed
Take from table	Continues the consideration of a postponed motion.	Allows assembly to consider business at its pleasure

Motion	Purpose	Effect
Reconsider (may be made only by member of winning side)	Reinstates a defeated motion.	Secures further debate and another vote.
Reconsider and have entered on minutes (winning side only)	Permits reconsideration at the next meeting.	Permits time to consider before reinstating a defeated motion for debate and vote.
Rescind	Repeals action taken.	Reverses decision of the assembly

There are some terms that participants in a parliamentary meeting should know the definitions of:

1. *Committee of the whole.* A special case established by suspension of the rules, that permits the assembly to consider a motion as a committee, without being bound by parliamentary rules.
2. *Floor.* The privilege to speak without interruption. When a member has the floor, he or she cannot be interrupted except by following specified rules.
3. *Privilege.* Refers to the comfort of the members: lighting, the repetition of comments that were not understood, the regulation of heat, the stopping of confusing noise, and so on.

Although parliamentary procedure is an old and traditional form of doing business, a great many organizations still employ it. Because it is the way of doing business for most corporations and boards of trustees, it has status at law. People who aspire to executive positions or leadership roles should be familiar enough with parliamentary procedure so that they can run a meeting if they have to.

THE PUBLIC RESPONSIBILITY OF LEADERSHIP

Public relations is one of the most difficult tasks of leaders. When a person represents an organization to the public, everything he or she does is in the name of the organization. The public tends to be suspicious of large organizations and of the people that represent them. In a sense, the public relations mission is very much like that of a diplomat representing a country in foreign lands.

Dealing with the press and the public presents some serious ethical issues to a leader. When the company is able to release all of the relevant information, then there is no problem. The company's representative merely presents it, using the best evidence, answering questions, and in general, doing a good job of persuasive speaking. Even then, the public may not be convinced. Investigative reporters and consumer advocates offer powerful opposition to many public statements.

Some organizations feel that they cannot release complete information because it would harm the company's operations. Whether they are right or wrong is immaterial. If you are representing one of these companies in public, you will need to search your own conscience and make a decision about the extent to which you wish to be associated with the dissemination of partial truths or distortions. Most companies live in a kind of neutral state, however. They have very little contact with the public until something unusual happens. Then they don't quite know what to do. When there are suspicions of pollution, rumors of a layoff, the possibility of a takeover by a foreign conglomerate, or a serious accident in the factory, someone must come before the public and the press and represent the company. Good news hardly ever requires such public representation. In this chapter, we are discussing the leader–manager, who in this case, must establish public relations policy on the spot in response to an unexpected event.

Writing press releases requires great skill. The Three Mile Island nuclear accident in March 1979 gave a good example of virtually all of the errors that can be made in releasing information. For one thing, the company responsible really did not know what had happened. They kept reassuring the public, some people suspect, because they wanted to reassure themselves. The governor's office was concerned with preventing panic, but even more concerned with protecting citizens. As a result, errors were made on all sides. When the representative of the Nuclear Regulatory Commission arrived on the scene, he felt that he had little alternative to telling the unvarnished truth. The problem was that by that time, everyone was so confused that no one could recognize truth. Pressure was mounting for answers, and no one even had good questions.

Public pressure keeps organizations honest. It was public pressure that helped break the Watergate story and public pressure that generated the recall system used by car manufacturers to handle defective products. The problem with public pressure, however, is that it is imposed only when something unusual happens. The old journalistic saying is that "If dog bites man, that is not news, but if man bites dog, it is newsworthy." For organizations that keep regular contact with press and public, most releases are in the "dog-bites-man" category. Hardly anyone is interested, and not much of the information reaches the public. It dies in the wastebaskets of newsrooms around the country.

It is important to keep regular contact with press and public, however. In the first place, regular contact ensures responsible contact in time of emergency. Trust built up over a period of time can guarantee honest treatment when the going gets rough. Through a system of meeting the public and holding open houses and factory tours, and through a flow of news about promotions, union negotiations, production breakthroughs and innovations, and changes in the company's fiscal policy, the name of the organization becomes respected, and the public relations officer gains credibility.

It is never sensible to try to conceal information, however negative it might be. It is equally bad to distort information or to tell outright lies. Someone is bound to find one. It is hard enough to get people to believe the truth. All it takes is one error in a public release, and doubt is cast on every other word that comes out of the company. The general rule is to present information systematically when there is no trouble in order to pile up a data base. For example, a rumor

circulated in a small town that the factory, the town's largest employer, was about to go bankrupt. The factory employed about 25
percent of the workers in the community, and its closing would be
a disaster. The town was in a state of panic. The public relations
officer, however, had built a relationship with the local newspaper
editor. He had released quarterly fiscal reports to the press for over
twenty years. When the rumors reached their peak, the public relations officer issued another fiscal report and asked the editor to
compare it with previous reports to see if there was any sign of
financial trouble. Not only was the editor able to present hard facts
about the financial structure of the company, but she was also able
to editorialize on behalf of the company by explaining the honest
news relationship that existed. No one could find out how the rumor
started, but it died down quickly and business went on as usual.

Sometimes, in extreme emergencies, it is hard to know what to
say. The rule of thumb is to say what you know and to promise more
later. Explain what you plan to do to get more information, and try
to give a realistic estimate of how long it will take. (Some newspapers
will even use such an estimate as news—"Company to Release Facts
on Tuesday" makes an attractive headline.) Rather than releasing
half-baked information or euphemisms, you are better off saying
what you know and don't know.

The press cannot be expected to advertise your organization or
product. Self-serving statements are generally cast aside, and media
people become suspicious of companies that produce a steady stream
of artificial stories designed to attract attention to their products or
services. Media people are accustomed to this kind of "puff" from
celebrities and politicians, and when business people try it, they
acquire the reputation of being manipulators, and their important
releases are not taken seriously. The best way is to weld a responsible
and honest relationship so that when it is important that people believe you, they will. You can ask for a few lines for good old Gert
Green on her retirement and send a picture along with the announce-
ment of the opening of the new branch. Gert will get her lines; if the
new branch is going to employ locals, it will probably get space also;
and if the editor knows you to be honest, she or he might even run
your picture and help your institutional image. Press people, in
general, are very smart, cynical, and suspicious. They are trained to
spot phonies, and they very much appreciate open and honest treatment. They will generally respect reasonable requests to keep things

"off the record," and they will be patient with you at crisis times if they believe you are doing your best.

It is somewhat more difficult to deal with television than with the printed press. For one thing, a TV story takes time to plan: it requires pictures, pictures require cameras, and cameras require logistics. Local stations are always interested in something dramatic, but often you will have to cooperate by providing them with the time and the facilities to do their filming. If there is a fire on your property, you will not be able to keep them out, and you will have no control over what they do. Even when they interview you, no matter how much sensible information you give, a good deal of it will end up on the editor's floor. They can give you only thirty seconds to a minute, hardly time to explain anything worth explaining. When you are responding to a TV interviewer, redundancy is crucial. You must remember that you are allowed a thirty-second message; keep repeating it in many different ways, so that no matter what gets cut, the essence of your message will reach the air. You may have to rely on the local press to correct the record if the TV station distorts your message.

Some companies produce attractive visuals to accompany press releases and community information. If the organization has money to spare, there is nothing wrong with this, but in general, most general information released is wasted. Anyone really interested in the company and its condition will want more detailed information than is found in the publicity brochures, and she or he will not be concerned with the pictures. Large numbers of people are probably not apt to read the illustrated report of what goes on at the Wombley Widget Corporation. Often, expensive visuals become children's cutouts. Sending visuals with newspaper stories is often wasteful because papers generally prefer to have their own people take the pictures. Public relations films are useful, however, in presenting the company name to service clubs, schools, and civic and charitable organizations.

When you represent an organization that uses public funds, you must be particularly careful. Many states have laws requiring open meetings of boards of directors of public organizations, when decisions are to be made. No reporter would demand to wander about and watch you do your daily business, but public business is part of the public record, and it is useful if everyone involved knows it. Any attempt at deception or secrecy can seriously hurt the organization, for it would be interpreted as an attempt to hide some duplicity. The best advice to public participants is to cultivate a little skill in public speaking, so that what they say will sound sensible to those who happen to be listening.

The best public relationships can be destroyed if you lose your temper or demand that press people do your bidding. At times of crisis, it is easy to lose control. At those times, you will need to use the respect you have built up in the past to gain some time to get your statements together. Even when the press is hovering over you and demanding that you say something, you will need to think through your main idea, fit it into a structure, and select some very responsible information to prove your point. An honest statement well delivered will win you respect, even if people disagree with you.

The public responsibility also extends to appearing as a formal speaker before civic clubs, charitable dinners, and the like; serving as a master of ceremonies; appearing at career days at the local school; and sometimes even judging the local beauty contest. At times like these, what you learned in Chapters 3, 4, and 5 will be very useful to you.

SUMMARY

Leadership is defined by more than position on an organization chart. A leader need not have a position. The occupant of a position who cannot lead is an administrator. The manager is a combination of administrator and leader. Managers can be trained. The act of managing is defined by the ability to respond to particular situations. The manager of the future will handle participation by employees and the community, plan for the long and the short run, work harmoniously within government regulations, manage information competently, respond constructively to capital shortages and changes in the economy, and adapt to local conditions.

Managers derive their ability to lead from their command of information, their ability to respond to individuals, and their ability to stand for ideas and defend them well.

The ability to communicate effectively is the hallmark of good managers. Leaders must be able to motivate competent behavior by those they supervise, be able to reward and punish fairly, and be able to make decisions about who is competent to do what. The inability to handle the tasks of leadership associated with a position fulfills the Peter principle.

Managers achieve positions in many ways, some of them unfair.

Managers should hold their positions because of their competence and their ability to lead. Leaders have a sense of regulation and order combined with optimism and enthusiasm. They need not have consummate technical skill, but they must have an overview broad enough so that they can understand what everyone does and why.

Managers have a number of problems dealing with their employees. Not everyone is dedicated to accomplishing organizational goals, and managers must be alert to the possibilities of improving the performance of the employees who is not functioning well. Intangibles in the leadership process are the ability to identify competence, the personality to motivate desire, and the ability to make quick decisions in emergencies. Leaders must be able to get along with other leaders, including their own supervisors.

Leaders also have a highly sensitive public responsibility that should be characterized by honesty and openness. Public messages must be handled with a maximum of tact and respect for everyone involved.

READINGS

Realistic advice on the leader's responsibility to the agenda and the members of the organization can be found in Thomas M. Scheidel and Laura Crowell, *Discussing and Deciding: A Desk Book for Group Leaders and Members.* New York: Macmillan, 1979. Gerald M. Phillips, Douglas J. Pederson, and Julia T. Wood, *Group Discussion: A Practical Guide to Participation and Leadership.* Boston: Houghton Mifflin, 1979, offers specific advice to leaders about techniques in the various stages of discussion. Simple advice on how to improve leadership skills is found in Arnold Schneider, William C. Donaghy, and Pamela Jane Newman, *Organizational Communication.* New York: McGraw-Hill, 1975, pp. 147–178.

A good primer on how to manage a meeting and use parliamentary procedure is Henry L. Ewbank, *Meeting Management.* Dubuque, Iowa: William C. Brown, 1968. A more complete work, which includes advice on how to plan various kinds of meetings, arrange logistics, prepare agendas, and publicize programs, is William T. Carnes, *Effective Meetings for Busy People.* New York: McGraw-Hill, 1980. Sales meetings and workshops are discussed in detail. A good, brief discussion of the chairperson's obligations at a public meeting and of following up and evaluating the success of meetings can be found in Anthony Jay, "How to Run a Meeting," *Harvard Business Review,* Vol. 54, March 1976, pp. 43–57.

Some practical techniques that leaders can use to evoke creative problem-solving can be found in James L. Adams, *Conceptual Blockbusting.* New York: Norton, 1979.

A quick and simple explanation of techniques of meeting the press and the public is Chester Burger, "How to Meet the Press," *Harvard Business Review,* Vol. 53, July 1975, pp. 62–70.

A brief review of Japanese-style management can be found in Randy Hirokawa, "Improving Intra-Organizational Communication: A Lesson From Japanese Management," *Communication Quarterly*. Vol. 30, No. 1. Winter, 1982.

Chapter 9

Basic Writing
in the
Organization

In this chapter, we offer some specific advice on how to produce the written documents required in organizations. Specifically, we deal with

1. Memos.
2. Business letters.
3. Instructions, policies, and procedures.
4. Evaluations and reports.
5. Abstracts and précis.
6. Articles for publication or formal oral presentation.

MEMOS

Memos are bits of written conversation. They are short notes used to handle simple business that is not urgent enough for a phone call or complicated enough for a letter. They are generally used for one of the following reasons:

1. To announce some activity or action.
2. To confirm some agreement made orally.
3. To suggest a simple action.

4. To make a date or an appointment.
5. To remind someone of something.
6. To confirm the receipt of some document.
7. To issue simple instructions.
8. To convey a secondhand message.

Memos have some important advantages over other kinds of information procedures. They are more effective than phone calls because they save time. Phone calls often require small talk and sometimes trap you into distracting discussions for which you are not prepared. The same is true of personal contact. It takes time to arrange to see a colleague, and it requires that you move from your office to hers or his. Once you are there, you must deal not only with your business but with the business the other person wants to bring up. However, you can send memos at your convenience, and the recipient can read them at his or her convenience. Exceedingly busy executives needn't read them at all, because the business they deal with usually can be delegated to a subordinate.

The most important advantage of memos is that they provide a written record of business transacted. You can keep a file of memos, check off responses to them, and keep track of simple business by reviewing them. If some detail needs to be checked, you need not rely on your memory.

Memos are not appropriate for carrying on extended argument or negotiation, nor can they be used to present complicated proposals or explanations.

Every memo must contain the following information:

1. The name of the writer.
2. The name of the person who receives the memo.
3. A simple statement of the subject of the memo.
4. The date of the memo.
5. A legible message.
6. A distribution list if copies are sent to other people.
7. Sometimes a method for acknowledging receipt or replying.

Following are some sample memos.
To announce an activity or action

From: Ed Mann
To: Rita Boock   Date: July 29, 1982
Re: New Policy Activation
Effective tomorrow, the policies outlined in Report C233.6 will be in force.
Please start keeping records under those policies at the start of the business
day. Initial and return to acknowledge receipt.

E.M.

The recipient of this memo can have a photocopy made of the
initialed copy so that both individuals have a record that the information was sent and received.

A memo confirming an agreement:

From: Arthur Mometer
To: Ernie Erway
Re: Confirmation of phone conversation, July 26, 1982, 11 A.M.
Date: June 26, 1982
Confirming our agreement to share facilities and expenses during our visit to
Coshocton sales meeting, July 15. I will reserve hotel room and exhibition
space; you arrange transportation for us and the display materials. Estimated
departure time 9 A.M., July 5.

A.M.

cc: Ben Kroll

Mr. Kroll gets a copy of the memo because he handles expense accounts. If Erway sends a similar memo, each man can check to make
sure they have the same information, thus reducing the chances of
error.

A memo offering a suggestion:

From: Max Zupper
To: Sally Fortt
Date: May 19, 1982
Re: Changes in menu format
When you print up next month's menu cards, I think you should use an Ameri-
can eagle motif or some patriotic thing to go along with our store promo of
Fourth of July Specials. Get me some samples and call me when they are ready.

M.Z.

Sally got her materials together and sent the following:

From: Sally Fortt
To: Max Zupper
Re: Proposals for menu format
Date: May 24, 1982
I have three alternative layouts for June menu formats. I need a half hour for the presentation. I'll be in at 10 A.M., May 31, unless I hear otherwise.

S.F.

Max doesn't need to do a thing if the date and time are all right. If they are not, he can either phone or send another memo. Because the date was all right, he sent the following memo:

From Max Zupper
To: Sally Fortt
Date: May 29, 1982
Re: Meeting on menu layouts
Just a reminder that we are getting together at 10 A.M. to discuss your layouts. I can give you an hour if you need it.

M.Z.

Memos are sometimes used for serious business when you want to be absolutely sure that a record is kept so that the precise message can be checked. Here is an example of an instruction:

From: Sue Perman
To: Cal Lumny
Date: February 16, 9:15 A.M.
Re: Release of information to representatives of other departments
Effective immediately (see date and time above), do not release financial information to anyone requesting it. If financial information is requested, you are to refer the requester to Noah Vale, who is in sole charge of information. This is particularly important for salary information. Please sign receipt form accompanying this memo.

S.P.

cc: N. Vale

This memo is designed to stop rumors about salaries that have been stirring up trouble in the company. Responsibility for information leaks must be fixed, and so a specific procedure has been declared. The memo was delivered by Mr. Piffai's secretary and a receipt signed.

The secondhand-message memo is a good way to check gossip and rumors without getting involved in extended discussions. For example,

From: Rita Boock
To: Lena Genster
Date: January 14, 1982
Re: Grapevine
I just heard from an "unnamed source" that you had given notice. I'd like to talk to you about this, and if it is not true, I would like to stop the rumor. Call me if you care to.

R.B.

This kind of memo puts the ball squarely in the other person's court. If Ms. Genster is indeed about to leave, there is no need for her to reply. If she is concerned about false information, then she can call and discuss it with her supervisor, Ms. Boock. No acknowledgment is necessary.

Good memos carry a message in one paragraph or less. There is no need for supports. Memos do not work well if they are more than one paragraph long. The following checklist will help you evaluate your own memos for accuracy and completeness:

1. Who is to receive the memo? Why a memo instead of a phone call or a visit?
2. What is this person to know or do? (Memos should not be sent about attitudes or beliefs.)
3. When, where, why, with whom, how, for what purpose is this person to know it or do it? (None of this needs to appear in the memo, but you should know it to be sure that you get a complete message written. Once you have answered the questions, you can decide how much you need to tell your reader.)
4. How will receipt be acknowledged?
5. How will you know that the recipient knows what you want him or her to know or does what you want him or her to do?

In addition, you should

1. Make sure that your final memo contains
   a. Your name.
   b. Your respondent's name.
   c. The date (and time, if relevant).
   d. A statement of contents or topic (re:).
   e. The message.
   f. Information about who received copies.
2. Make sure you initial your memo before you send it. Before you initial it, check it for grammar, punctuation, and spelling.
3. Make sure you have a copy of your memo and make a note on it of how you sent the original (office mail, messenger, drop in message box, and so on).
4. If you requested a reply, note it on your calendar so you can investigate if the reply does not come.
5. If your memo made an appointment, be sure to pencil it on your calendar. Do not make it permanent until you get confirmation.

Memo writing is not the most challenging kind of writing you will ever have to do, but skill in writing memos can save you time and reduce your tensions on the job.

BUSINESS LETTERS

Business letters are used to exchange information with people, mostly outside the organization. Every business letter represents the organization because it is on organization letterhead. The writer of a business letter has a responsibility to act in line with organization purposes and in ways creditable to the organization when she or he employs that letterhead.

Business letters can handle most specific business. Tentative plans can be made in person or on the phone and confirmed by letter. If business is urgent, it is usually handled by some sort of personal contact, and a letter is used to confirm agreements so that a permanent record is available.

To write an effective letter, you must

1. Identify the person or the position that is to receive your letter.
2. Decide on the information to be received as a result of your letter.
3. Select a pattern from those listed in Chapter 4 to provide organization for your letter.
4. Select a very few proofs or supports for your message.
5. State your message in three to five paragraphs. It is important to try to keep your letters to one page. Recipients of letters are usually in a hurry, and an extended letter can be very annoying. If there are a great many details in your message, include them in a document called a *report* and indicate in your letter that your recipient will find the details in the enclosure. That will spare him or her the necessity of sifting through a lot of information, and, at the same time, it will provide the detailed information.
6. Edit your letter for logic and supports and for grammar, punctuation, and spelling.
7. Have your letter typed in perfect form and proofread it. You can delegate the proofreading to a subordinate *if* you are sure that your message is correct. Proofreading each letter gives you one more opportunity to make sure that you have said exactly what you want to say.

In a business letter, you can

1. Request specific information from someone outside the company. "Please send me your latest catalogs and price lists . . . ."
2. Provide information requested from someone outside the

company: "You will find our latest catalogs and price lists enclosed. Please notice the price changes on items using . . ."

3. Acknowledge a routine situation (congratulations on opening a new branch, an excellent stockholders' report, and so on): "Congratulations on your appointment as advertising manager. You can count on us to continue to provide your company with the highest quality of paper and art materials . . ."

4. Comply with a legitimate request for action: "I have referred your complaint to the production manager, and I intend to check back with him in a week. I have asked him to check the shaft carefully and to investigate the cause of the binding."

5. Request legitimate action from someone else: "I would like you to examine the July sales figures again to be sure that they are accurate. Smedley suggested that some of the reports had been lost in the mail and that the sales in Wyoming and Utah were not included."

6. Discuss a disagreement arising in the course of business: "I regret that our warranty does not cover the situation you refer to. If you will check page two of the warranty document, it specifically states that immersion in water will invalidate the warranty."

7. Issue notification of the disposition of an order or request (back orders, routing followed, replacement numbers, and so so): "As you instructed, I have renumbered all of the widget bins to reflect the new catalog numbers. I have retained the old numbers in parentheses . . ."

8. Acknowledge an adjustment or a settlement of a grievance: "I am enclosing a check for $34.95 to cover the cost of purchase of a replacement for the defective appliance . . ."

9. Thank someone for service rendered: "Thank you for your prompt attention to my complaint. I appreciate the quick service and will keep it in mind when I examine my new purchase orders . . ."

10. Attempt to sell goods and services or explain the new goods services available: "You may be interested in a new item in our line. The Z91 exercycle (catalog sheets enclosed) is equipped with motorized pedals and odometer for a four-speed motor . . ."

11. Respond to or introduce an argument: "I do not think your proposal will work because . . ." (Try to handle it in a page and include a document with the details.)

There are standard patterns for opening business letters. The purpose is to declare the main message as quickly and clearly as possible. For example,

> "Your brochure entitled 'New Products for 1981' lists four models of the 617 Portobar. We are interested in obtaining specifications on these models."
>
> "In your letter of June 17, you requested information on our 617 Portobar. We are enclosing the following information . . ."
>
> "Your letter of May 5 requesting information on the status of your account has been referred to me, and I have the following details for you . . ."
>
> "On your invoice #24578 covering our November shipment, you list 500 of item #238 as shipped. We did not receive them . . ."
>
> "Regarding your inquiry about item #238 on invoice #24578 covering the November shipment, we have the following information . . ."
>
> "I have received the report from the warranty department on the toaster you returned on April 16. I have the following information for you . . ."
>
> "Your letter of April 9 was referred to our credit manager, who will . . ."
>
> "You sound as if you are having trouble out there in Coshocton. Remember, I was manager out there and I think I can help. Please check . . ."
>
> "Your letter of November 6 offering reasons for adopting the new return policy frightened me. I do not think we should apply that policy because . . ."

Notice how direct each of these openers is. Everything else in the letter supports what is in the first sentence of the letter. The reader knows immediately what the letter is about. The writer has no problem deciding what goes in and what stays out. Anything that supports the main message is in. Anything else is out. Anything that goes beyond one page is out.

Business letters are costly! A letter that takes fifteen minutes each from the writer and the secretary can cost anywhere from $15 to $50. If you figure in the cost of equipment and overhead, you must agree that business letters should not be sent unless there is a very important reason for them. If they are sent at all, they should be effective. If you have a position that requires you to write a large number of letters, try to establish forms for some of them, and ask your secretary to compose the greetings. That is, you may have a standard letter for referring complaints, one for reporting back orders, one explaining how you disposed of a question, and so on. You need only brief your secretary about how to put in the specific information. If your company has a word-processing system, all that is necessary is to combine the specific information with the format. This will materially reduce the time you need to spend on the simple letters and will enable you to give your attention to letters requiring unusual consideration and time. Advance planning on your part can reduce the cost of letter writing and produce better letters.

Check your letters against the following criteria:

1. A good business letter should identify the main message in the first two sentences.
2. A good letter contains one message in one page. (You can go to two pages in emergencies. If more space is required, submit a report along with a letter explaining why the report is important and how to use it.)
3. Edit out anything that would reflect unfavorably on your organization.
4. If your letter contains bad news, don't try to be cute about it. Bad news and good news should be given succinctly in the first two sentences.
5. Never send the first draft of a business letter. Make sure your message is the way you want it to be. Make sure your final draft is edited for typos.
6. Check a secretary's manual for information about salutations, headings, and signatures. Comply with standard practices. "Original" business letters are distracting.

There are some special considerations in writing letters seeking employment. Normally such letters are uninteresting. They are filled with clichés and they repeat information that appears on the résumé. Potential employers are besieged with letters, and they appreciate letters that get to the point. In fact, a good letter may make the difference in getting you an interview.

Write your letter after you have prepared your résumé. The purpose of the letter is to make a specific application of **your résumé** to the job you seek. In essence, you use a *forensic* pattern, in which you offer yourself as a solution to a problem the company is having, that is, a vacancy in the ranks.

Your résumé provides the data to support your argument. A good résumé has a specific statement about your educational and employment record. It is simple—one page, if possible (or one page, front and back, if you have a great deal of experience or many honors to report; if that is not enough space, you can indicate that more information is available and explain what it is about). Your résumé should be accompanied by a letter in which you formally state your interest in the job.

Dear Sir:

I am applying for the advertised position of laboratory technologist. My résumé is enclosed. Note that I have had considerable experience in laboratories under a great many different conditions. I am adaptable and could be useful to you in many ways.

I have participated in three experimental studies, which I could not detail in the résumé. My name was included as third author on all of them. If you are interested, I can send you the studies with a statement of the role I played in each.

Thank you for your attention to my application. I hope to hear from you.

Josephine Hrivanic

Notice that the letter is unassuming and informative. It is also brief. That means there will be a good deal of white space on the page on which it is written. Busy people like to see white space. It means that the letter is simple and will be easy to read. Cramped letters are confusing and intimidating to anyone who has a great deal of mail to process.

Examine the following résumé:

RÉSUMÉ

Josephine Hrivanic
1144 West 16th Street
Wombat, WN 9999999
Phone: (666) 555-7777

I am seeking a position as a research assistant or laboratory technician in a university or hospital facility. I am prepared to take an entry-level position if advancement is possible.

Education

Peden Tech	Major: Biochemistry
100 School Street	Minor: Statistics
Peden, WA 9999009	Activities: President, Woman's Vocational
Registrar: R. D. Fax	Society
B.S. conferred 6/1959	Honors: Dean's list, 1957, 1958, 1959.
cum laude	

Griffle High School	Major subjects: Science, mathematics
Muddy Road, R.R. 3	Activities: Varsity track, senior-class treasurer
Sludge, AR 1110009	
Principal: Jim-Bob Hoople	
Graduation: 6/1956 with	
honors	

Work Experience

Travesty Medical Laboratories	I performed blood series analyses, steroid
866 Colonel Sanders Lane	tests, and liver functions. I supervised three
Travesty, AR 20998876	technicians. I worked on two research studies
Supervisor: Saralou Hopper	with professors at Travesty University. I left
Employed: 7/1962–8/1970	to devote full time to my family.

House Bayou Hospital	I worked on a research program funded by
1929 Griffle Road	NIH. I performed all blood analysis tests as
House Bayou, LA 888888899	directed by project directors. I left because
Supervisor: Art Tifak	the project was completed and funding was
Employed: 6/1959–6/1962	terminated.

Skills: I can perform virtually all laboratory analysis tests. I have supervisory experience and can evaluate technician performance using quality-control techniques. I can type 60 w.p.m. and have minimal bookkeeping background.

Personal Reference:	Evan Slater, M.D. 929 Winston Rd. Slab Cabin, AR 8888877	Work Reference:	Alois Stanovsky, M.D. Travesty Community Hospital 980 Kidneystone Drive Travesty, AR 20998875
Work Reference:	Constance Mondor, M.D. Travesty University Department of Pathology Travesty, AR 20998873	School Reference:	Edna McNab, Ph.D. Department of Physiology Peden Tech Peden, WA 9999009

Additional references available on request.

The résumé could have been extended to a second page if there had been more education or employment to report. Notice that the résumé begins with a statement of the type of job desired. Special résumés can be prepared for various types of jobs. Notice also that specific skills are listed. This is nothing more than a summary of the best information that could be presented on the candidate's own behalf, an argument on behalf of employment. The way the résumé is laid out, the material is easy to read. There is no extraneous material. Four references are provided, and more are promised. In addition, a contact person is named to verify employment dates and graduation, if that is necessary. This example illustrates the following principles of résumé writing:

1. It must contain your name, phone number, and address. It should not contain personal information or information revealing your age, race, religion, or national origin. It need make no health statement. In the sample, Ms. Hrivanic indicates that she left her job to raise a family, but she gives no details about her present marital or family status. It is important to give a reason for leaving employment, but it is illegal for employers to inquire into family details. The applicant may supply the information at his or her option to explain gaps.

2. There should be a brief statement of your employment objectives. They should be compatible with the type of job for which you are applying.

3. Each school you attended should be listed, along with relevant information about your school record. The name of a contact person to verify your attendance should be included. (If the school officials during your time of attendance are no longer there, provide the names of current employees or list the position title of the person to whom inquiries should be sent.)

4. Information about your work experience should be provided: the name and address of your employer, the name of your supervisor (or someone who can verify your employment), the type of work done, and your reason for departing. It is not necessary to include your rate of pay unless your prospective employer requests it.

5. A résumé can include community activity, volunteer work, and so on, but only if they really support the application. Also in-

cluded could be honors and ahievements, as well as publications. In this case, Ms. Hrivanic chose to note her publications in the accompanying letter. Listing an excessive number of these kinds of things is pretentious. On the other hand, if the résumé does go to two pages, it might be important to include them in order to complete the page.

6. Special skills should be noted.
7. The names and addresses of at least one personal, work, and educational reference should be provided. (Be sure to check with the people you name so that they are alerted to the fact that they may receive inquiries.)

Remember that your accompanying letter can include information specific to the job for which you are applying.

INSTRUCTIONS, POLICIES, AND REGULATIONS

Instructions

Instructions must be carefully organized according to a chronological pattern. Before you write them, you must test them to be sure they work. There is nothing more confusing than an erroneous set of instructions. If you give instructions orally you can stop for questions and you can inspect the work. Written instructions provide no such options. Once they are written, they stand. Use the following guidelines to help you write instructions.

Step 1. Identify what the object, form, or situation should look like when completed. Describe the finished product, and if possible, include pictures and diagrams.

Step 2. Identify everything that must be done to achieve the goal. Do not leave out steps no matter how trivial they may seem. If someone had to do them in the oral trial, they will also have to be done when your written instructions are followed.

Step 3. Check the order of your instructions. Make sure nothing is missing. Do the task once more yourself, to be sure.

Step 4. Include a list of all the materials that will be needed to do the job.

Step 5. Include a statement about the kinds of problems that may be encountered on the job and what can be done to solve them.

Step 6. Give an estimate (maximum and minimum) of how long it will take to do the job.

If you have a long set of instructions, check them carefully to find places where you can summarize, for example, "Your object should look like this now."

Following is a set of instructions written by an industrial engineer. Try to follow them. Do not look at the diagram until you have attempted the instructions.

1. Obtain a plain white sheet of 8½" × 11" paper and place it front of you with the shorter side closest to you.
2. Check the surface on which you have placed the paper to make sure it is a hard surface on which you can write. If the surface is not hard, change to a hard surface.
3. Take a writing implement (#3 pencil, felt-tip pen) and hold it ready for drawing.
4. Locate a point 5" from the bottom of the paper and 1¾" from the left margin, and make a dot.
5. Draw a 2" square with the located point (Instruction 4) as the upper left corner. (You may use a ruler.)
6. Locate the midpoint of the upper line of the square you have just drawn (there should be 1" on either side of the point), and make a dot.
7. Draw a 2" line perpendicular to the upper line of the square, with the dot specified in Instruction 6 as the midpoint. One inch should be above the top line of the square and perpendicular to it, and one inch should go down into the square and be perpendicular to it.
8. Use the line you just drew (Instruction 7) as the left-hand short side of a 2" × 4" rectangle. Draw the rectangle, heading right on your paper.
9. Locate the upper-right corner of that rectangle (Instruction 8). Locate a point 1" to the left, and construct a vertical rectangle with a 1" base by drawing a line 2" up from the point and 2" down from the point so that there is a 1" × 2" rectangle going up from the common line and a 2" line cutting across the larger (2" × 4") rectangle (Instruction 8).

10. Locate the lower-right corner of the large (2″ × 4″) rectangle, and draw a diagonal connecting that corner with the upper-left corner of the 1″ × 2″ rectangle that extends above the large rectangle.
11. Locate the upper-right corner of the 2″ × 4″ rectangle (the midpoint of the line in common of the two rectangles in Instruction 9). Connect the point with the lower-left corner of the lower 1″ × 2″ rectangle by a diagonal.
12. Locate the midpoint of the left 2″ line of the upper 1″ × 2″ rectangle. From that line draw a 1″ line perpendicular to the line extending to the left.
13. From the left end of the line you drew in Instruction 12, drop a 1″ perpendicular line to connect with the top line of the 2″ × 4″ rectangle. You should now have a one inch square.
14. In the upper-left corner of the square you drew in Instruction 13, locate a circle (you may use a template or a compass) with a ½″ diameter, so that its perimeter contacts the upper and left sides of the square and the circle is contained entirely within the square.
15. Now, return to the left side of the large 2″ × 4″ rectangle. Locate the midpoint of that line.
16. From that midpoint, draw a line extending 1″ to the right and 1″ to the left. (The line should extend inside the rectangle for 1″ and outside the rectangle for 1″.)
17. Use that line as the top line to form a 2″ square (so that a 1″ square is enclosed inside the larger rectangle.

You have now completed your instructions. Please examine the diagram to check the accuracy of your work.

It is important to avoid relying on the reader's judgment. Make sure you edit out quality decisions and use numbers instead of estimates. Be sure to provide specifications for your materials (a piece of pine or poplar, 3′ × 4″ × 1″). When equipment is required, identify it and provide options (use a ½″ spiral or gouge drill bit). When you absolutely must use judgment statements, be sure to identify the problems that might arise and indicate that the finished product may not look exactly like the picture.

Be sure that you check through your technical terms and define them. In the instructions for drawing the diagram, for example, we could have defined *perpendicular, rectangle, template, compass,* or *diagonal.* Furthermore we could have provided a list of the materials

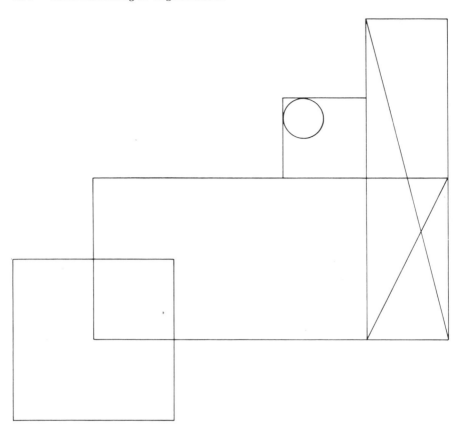

needed, which include "pencil, ruler, compass, template, and paper." We assumed you knew the meanings and that you had the materials available. That might not have been a tenable assumption. We also used the notation (″) to refer to *inch*. Actually, we were fairly safe, because we tested the instructions with students and discovered that they knew the meanings of the words. However, if you are not absolutely sure of the level of sophistication of your potential readers, be sure to define all technical terms in lay language.

Pictures and diagrams are important. Model airplane kits contain patterns on which the parts and pieces are assembled. You might not know what you are doing at any given time, but usually, if you follow the instructions, you get an airplane. Clothing patterns are prepared in much the same way, although they assume certain basic knowledge and skills in their instructions. Anyone who has tried to make clothing from a pattern, however, knows the importance of having a picture of the end product against which to test the work.

Job descriptions are actually special cases of instruction giving. It appears easy to write job descriptions, for example,

> The supervisor will direct the operations of all the employees in his or her division and will implement the policies of the company as they affect his or her personnel.

The problem with that description is that the supervisor does not know what is permitted. She or he needs operational definitions of *direct, operations, employees in his or her division, division, implement, policies of the company, affect,* and *his or her personnel.* That includes just about all of the words in the description. The following might help:

1. *Direct* means issue orders, observe work, correct errors, evaluate, classify, and recommend for pay increases, promotions, transfer, and dismissal.
2. *Operations* means all activities connected with processing shipments, filling out shipping forms, picking orders, packing orders, labeling orders, routing orders, and putting packed orders on trucks.
3. *Employees in his or her division* can be explained by attachment of the job description of each of the employees.
4. And so on.

One of the more important side effects of unionization in industry was pressure to write clear job descriptions, usually based on analyses of time and motion made by industrial engineers. It might not be possible to write precise instructions for executive, technical, professional, supervisory, and creative personnel, but you can approximate precision by being attentive to details.

To write a job description, you must first locate basic information about the job. You need to find out what the supervising executive expects the person to produce. You can do this by questioning the person who now holds the job about what he or she does on an hourly, daily, weekly, monthly, and occasional basis. Examine the time log form. Completely detailed time logs filled out for every hour of an eight-hour day, plus the additional questions about the regularity of duties will give a concrete idea of what ought to go into the job description.

Another source of data that can enter into a job description is the management-by-objectives agreement, if the organization uses an

Time Log for Employee

Employee will submit 8 of these forms, one for each hour

Fill out in hourly segments for eight-hour day*.

Name _____ Position Title _____ Date _____ Time _____

Activity	Number of Minutes	Purpose*	Priority	Interrupted by	For What Purpose?
Personal contact					
Letter written					
Letter read					
Memo written					
Memo read					
Document written					
Document read					
Phone call made					
Phone call received					
Filing and housekeeping					
Machine used					
Planning					
Meeting					
Slack time					

*Note other party in "Purpose" column for letters, phone calls, memos, personal contacts, meetings.

Employee will submit one of these forms along with the 8 hourly forms

List Tasks for Which You Are Responsible _____
Hourly _____
Daily _____
Weekly _____
Monthly _____
Periodically (state period) _____
Annually _____
Occasionally (how often and when) _____
Emergency (describe) _____
Fill in or Cover (for whom) _____
Voluntary _____
Other (explain) _____

On what matters is your decision final? _____
Whom do you supervise? (attach list and job descriptions) _____
How do you supervise? _____
Who supervises you? _____
List meetings and conventions attended _____
Detail work done at home _____
List travel required _____
Describe meal arrangements _____

MBO system. The objectives for a particular job provide detailed information about the nature of the job. If, for example, one of the objectives is "to increase the speed with which we produce the monthly report," then it is clear that a monthly report is one of the duties.

Phrase all duties in behavioral language. Try to eliminate fuzzy statements or references to personal judgment. For example,

> Bad: . . . is responsible for evaluating the employees he supervises.
> Good: . . . shall produce at intervals designated by his supervisor evaluation report forms (B27800, see example) for those holding the following jobs (attach list).
> Bad: . . . is responsible for the supervision of employees.
> Good: . . . shall assign tasks to employees holding the following jobs (attach list), oversee task performance, and evaluate task performance for same.

The concrete statement of the duty is longer than the abstract statement, and there is still ambiguity, but if it includes the forms to be filled out and the specific acts of supervision, the job description will be more clear to the person who holds the job. Job descriptions must be realistic, but not so precise that all discretionary judgment is removed from the employee. Most job descriptions do not give information about what constitutes quality performance and how substandard performance is identified. This is exceedingly difficult to do, but attention to MBO agreements will provide guidelines for evaluation. If it is stipulated that production in a given unit will reach a particular level by a given time, the employee understands what the goal of her or his supervision is. MBO agreements commonly specify the rewards for accomplishing the goals as well.

Policies and Regulations

Policies and regulations are difficult to write. For an example of detailed regulations and policies, read the rules of professional baseball. Examine particularly the instructions to umpires, for they provide information about how discretionary judgments are made. The rules of baseball were developed over a great many years, and they are revised every year to account for unforeseen circumstances. Thus the first rule of writing policies and regulations is to include some specification of how they can be modified and under what circumstances they should be modified.

Policies and regulations are customarily organized according to the set pattern. Occasionally charts and tables are provided, particularly when they include statements about who reports to whom.

1. Policies are the general guidelines by which the goals of an organization are to be accomplished.
2. Regulations are specific statements of how work is to be performed, including what is and is not permissible.
3. Policies confer discretionary power, and regulations limit it.

In most organizations, policies and regulations are contained in handbooks, often referred to as *regs.*

The following guidelines will be helpful if you must write policies and regulations:

1. They should be organized by systematic headings, with sections that are numbered and indexed:
   1.00 Personnel Policies
      1.01 Hiring Procedures
      1.02 Probationary Periods
      1.03 Orientation and Training Procedures
   Users of the policies should be able to refer immediately to the relevant sections. (No one, certainly, would want to read through them for fun.)
2. They should consist of authoritative statements, phrased unambiguously, from persons authorized to act. The writer of policies and regulations should not have to invent them. When you are asked to write such documents do not permit your personal attitudes to distort them in any way.
3. The title should contain a statement of the purpose of the policies and regulations, for example, "Policies for Hiring Hourly Rated Employees"; "Regulations for Installing Safety Devices on Machinery in Plant Number Four"; "Procedures for Preparing and Maintaining Permanent Personnel Records."
4. If there is a legal basis for the policies or regulations, it should be stated, for example, "The following regulations ensure conformance with the optimum standards of Code 2600 of the Commonwealth of Pennsylvania Regulations for Homes

Providing Day Care Services." If there are no legal bases, the source of authority should be stated, for example, "These policies regulate the line of authority of vice-presidents of the company pursuant to action taken by the Board of Directors on March 2, 1977." Copies of the statutes or the minutes of the meeting should be appended to the document in case someone needs to refer to them.

5. The consequences of violations of policies or regulations should be noted. There should also be a detailed statement on how violations are processed and whether there is a grievance procedure or an appeal privilege.

6. The effective dates of the policies should be stated.

7. Ways and means of modifying the policies should be provided.

8. A glossary should be provided containing all technical or ambiguous words. Operational definitions should be provided wherever possible.

9. There should be an index covering all imaginable situations so that occasional users can be directed immediately to relevant sections of the policies. Policy and regulation manuals are often quite thick, and quick access is necessary.

10. There should be a review of the policies in simple language at the beginning of each section, but it should be noted that these reviews are for clarification only and are not binding.

Most companies develop policies for personnel, space and logistics, production, finance, reporting and record keeping, information processing, controls over sales and merchandising, customer relations, community relations, and other considerations exclusive to the company. In general, policies are written in the active voice, so that the reader will know who is to act about what. For example, "Employees are not permitted to smoke on the premises" instead of "Smoking is not permitted on the premises."

EVALUATIONS AND REPORTS

Evaluations are narratives in which a state of affairs, a person, or a situation is compared to some standards. Customarily recommendations for action accompany evaluations. With personnel evaluations, for example, evaluators may recommend pay increases, transfers, reprimands, promotions, and so on. An evaluator has a choice of saying, "Continue what is going on," "There is a problem that needs to be solved," or "Things are going so well, so some reward is in order." The recommendation that a problem be solved usually results in the matter being referred to some problem-solving group to prepare a proposal.

Many evaluations are *pro forma;* that is, they take place but nothing much happens as a result of them. Often evaluations are based on complex forms which are sometimes filled out by supervisors, sometimes by professional evaluators or consultants, and sometimes by peers. In fact, peer evaluation and self-evaluation are becoming increasingly popular.

If one is writing up evaluation reports, the standards of comparison must be presented. In the case of evaluation of a production line, finite quotas can be set. Comparisons are then simple to make. All that is required is a table comparing numbers. In some cases, it is necesssary to justify the quota. The decision about whether there is a problem is left to experts.

In the case of a department like advertising or public relations, it is hard to conceptualize a quota. However, if a management-by-objectives system is used, each department head can work out goals for accomplishment during a given time period, and his or her work can be evaluated by the extent to which he or she has approximated those goals. Very often, evaluations are based on a simple formula of cost-effectiveness, for example: if a department does more work on the same money, its performance is rated as "good"; if the increase in work requires a commensurate increase in money, performance is "adequate"; but if either work goes down or expenditures go up, then performance is considered "substandard," and a problem is identified. Generally there are some goal statements somewhere in the policies and regulations that can be used as the basis for evaluation. For evaluation of individual employees, the job descriptions can be considered standards with which performance can be compared: if the employee does what he is supposed to do, work is "satisfactory"; if he does more than is required, work is "good"; and if he misses doing some of the work, then his work might be considered a problem to be solved. In using goal statements from policies or job descriptions, the writer's job is to make them operational. For example,

1. A social service agency has as its goal, "to provide counseling services to mothers on welfare in matters of child care, home budgeting, and mental health and to make recommendations to appropriate agencies for required services." The evaluater can use such a statement by counting the number of cases that have come in and the referrals that have been made. It would be difficult to assess the quality of the counseling given, but at least a check can be made on whether something is happening.
2. The goals for the community relations department of a large pesticide manufacturing company specify that the department is "to represent the company to the public and inform them how our product makes their life better." In actuality, the department tries to answer newspaper stories, rumors, and federal investigations with accurate information about the effects of the product and how wastes are disposed of safely. The work of the department could be evaluated by comparing charges and answers and by finding the positive statements made in the public press about the company.

Saving money, improving production, and intangibles like "improving morale" are often used as bases for evaluations.

Keep the following in mind when you write personnel evaluations:

1. You are obligated to make clear what the standards are for evaluation of the individual.

2. If you use the job description, operationalize each of the duties. Try to avoid mentioning abstract concepts like "quality" or "morale." Be sure to use standardized organizational criteria like attendance, tardiness, breakdown of machinery costs, and accuracy in submitting forms.

3. You can operationalize intangibles by applying the following questions:
   a. Is the time an individual spends on a task justified by the quality of the end product?
   b. Does the employee meet deadlines? If not, what extenuating circumstances are claimed?
   c. How does the employee's work compare with that of others doing similar work, now and in the past? Is there any good reason that he or she should not be able to perform as well as the average?
   d. What is the nature of the relationship between this employee, his or her peers, subordinates, and superiors?
   e. Have any exceptional events occurred involving the individual in question? What role did he or she play in them? (Be prepared here to illustrate the connection between the individual's actions and the outcome, good or bad.)

4. If the standards you are using are external, make that clear. Some jobs are governed by standards imposed by government regulations or professional societies. In such cases, these represent valid sources of evaluative material. (For example, the employee earned a special award from her professional association, or the employee was cited for failing to meet minimum state standards for performance.)

5. It is customary to permit the employee to reply. Under the Buckley Amendment, evaluative material cannot be concealed from the employee. It makes sense to permit the employee to read a draft of the evaluation and to allow him or her a rejoinder, particularly to uncomplimentary material.

Program evaluations are largely a search for impairments. You should take care, however, not to hold a program too rigidly to its specifications. Allowances must be made for changes in conditions and unexpected events that might alter program goals and operations. Your written report can follow the forensic pattern explained in Chapter 5. Be sure to identify the impairment by specifying the goals of the program and making some statement about how one would know whether the goals had been accomplished. You may find it necessary to indicate that the goals are no longer relevant, so that even if they are met, the program should no longer operate.

You can be quite extensive in listing the facts. An oral report must be confined to a brief period of time. In writing your evaluation, you can be complete in the presentation of your evidence. Once you have identified impairments, you may offer recommendations, although it is wiser to consult with the person receiving the report to see if they are required. Very often, the executive receiving the evaluation report may decide to refer it back to the program personnel or to establish a team to come up with recommendations. If commendations are in order, however, it is good practice to recommend them.

The result of a program evaluation is a project proposal. A project proposal, as we pointed out in Chapter 7, is the presentation of a particular solution to the problem specified in an evaluation (or other document dealing with impairments or anticipated difficulties). The project proposal is addressed to a decision maker or a funding agency. In either case, prepared forms are customarily provided. As a proposal writer, you should be particularly attentive to staying within the constraints imposed by the forms. It is also useful, if possible, to examine successful proposals that have been prepared on those forms.

We have told you that the person who proposes a program has the burden of proof to show that the change will result in conditions superior to those that prevail, so as to justify expenditures. The writer of a proposal has the additional task of filling the reader in on history. It is important that the reader know the proposal was conceived. Generally, decision makers are not present at the meetings at which the proposal was developed and planned; consequently they will need to know what was considered and the grounds on which components were rejected and accepted. For these reasons, the following are virtually always components of project proposals:

• *The background of the problem.* A brief history is offered of the conditions related to the problem. The history should include a narrative of the events that led up to the discovery of the condition identified as a problem. There should be a statement of how it was identified as a problem. The standards of evaluation used to judge the conditions should be presented and defended.

• *The nature of the problem.* The problem should be stated as succinctly and clearly as possible. There should be a statement of what is or is not happening and how it connects with the difficulty experienced by the organizations. Some conjecture should be offered about the possible consequences of doing nothing. All proofs should be arrayed following a set pattern. For example,

Problem	Effect
1. Delayed shipments	1. Costs the company $...... Loss of goodwill
2. Damaged shipments	2. Costs the company $...... Loss of goodwill
3. Erroneous shipments	3. Costs the company $...... Loss of goodwill

Evidence should be offered to document the effects. Careful descriptions in the form of narrative examples should be used to illustrate what is meant by *delayed, damaged,* and *erroneous.*

• *The details of the solution.* In this section, there should be a clear statement about who is to do what about what, when and where, and for what purpose, in addition to a clear projection of how doing it will eliminate the problem. Included should be a statement of how the changes can be evaluated. One possible way of doing this is to specify goals, "by this time next year, the situation should be as follows . . ." Some statement of urgency should also be provided, that is, how important it is that the organization get started on a solution.

Most program proposals are required to have an *operations plan.* These are difficult to do and often require the services of experts. An operations plan includes the following:

1. Statement of objectives (i.e., guideposts on the way to implementation).
2. Personnel required.
3. Space requirements.
4. Materials, machinery, and supplies needed.
5. Supervision required.
6. Reports and records to be kept.
7. Chain of command.
8. Accounting procedures (and possible sources of funds).
9. Method of evaluation.

A budget must also be included. The budget is prepared from a calculation of the costs of each of the listed components and the addition of a proportion of the overhead (fixed costs) of the organization. Special services of accountants and budget personnel will be needed, as there are some rigid legal restrictions that must be observed in budgeting. Budgets should also include special costs, including the cost of preparing and disseminating the proposal.

Technical reports are most often prepared to detail the outcome of experiments, trial runs, new machine designs, and other complicated activities carried on by specialists. They are written in two forms, one addressed to other specialists in the language of the specialization and others in lay language addressed to administrators not well schooled in the technical details of the project. Technical reports often look like doctoral dissertations. They employ highly specialized vocabularies. When technical reports are required in project proposals or in operations plans, relevant experts should be retained to prepare them.

Most of the data in technical reports consist of statistics, formulas, directions for technical operations, and charts, tables, and graphs. The level of sophistication of the eventual readers can be taken into account by the inclusion of summaries and abstracts directed at nontechnical readers. Guidelines for the preparation of technical reports can be obtained from the editors of the various technical and professional journals or from relevant government agencies. Here are some of the topics that might be covered in technical reports:

1. The effect that a new product or procedure will have on the company.
2. A description of how a new product will work.
3. Projections of the acceptance of a new product.
4. Estimates of the success of prototype models or designs.
5. Estimates of the nature of alteration in production required to produce a new product.
6. Description of the "present state of affairs" on the production line and/or the production of a particular item or an individual process.
7. Future projections of various sorts: actuarial estimates; technical projections of future influences; and scenarios of technical operations.
8. Descriptions of various experiments that are required or have been conducted.

9. Comparisons of processes, products, and operations with standards or the way they are done elsewhere.

ABSTRACTS AND PRÉCIS

We discussed oral briefing in Chapter 4. The abstract or précis is the written equivalent of the oral briefing. It is the *Reader's Digest* of the organizational world.

An abstract is a one- or two-sentence summary of the contents of an article, or a page or two summarizing a book. Abstracts can be illustrated by the two or three pages that dissertation writers are required to include with their document to summarize the contents for those who want to see if they want to read the whole thing.

Précis are somewhat longer, often a paragraph or two on each chapter in a longer work. Précis writing can be considered note taking that is later to be condensed into an abstract. The following is a typical abstract:

> Survey Report on Transportation in Forest Slough, Planning Commission. April 18, 1981. 230 pages. Of 500 citizens surveyed in relevant area, 40 percent were opposed to modification in existing transportation programs. Remainder propose various changes ranging in cost from zero to approximate tripling of transportation costs. No hardship areas identified, but special needs of aging population require maintenance of special services.

The précis of the same document ran to three pages. The headings used were the following:

1. Source of the request for the survey. (A paragraph on why the survey was made.)
2. Methods and procedures used in the survey. (A one-page review of the nature of the sample and the questionnaire design.)
3. Nature of the opposition. (A demographic review of who opposed and on what grounds, approximately one-half page.)
4. Summary of various proposals for improvement with cost estimates (about one page).
5. Recommendations of the commission (two paragraphs).

Technical documents are not designed to be read. They are constructed to be referred to by someone who needs specific information. Précis and abstracts help potential users identify what information is available in the longer piece of writing. The following questions should be answered in précis and abstracts:

1. What is the main message of the publication? What was the purpose of doing the work involved in its preparation?
2. In what form is the report made? What kinds of technical details are presented?
3. If the report is an argument, what are the main reasons offered for believing what is presented? Use a forensic pattern to organize the information.
4. What recommendations are made, and what is supposed to happen if they are accepted?

It is sometimes useful to let the writer of the main document check your précis or abstract to make sure that you have not violated the spirit of the original document.

ARTICLES FOR PUBLICATION OR FORMAL ORAL PRESENTATION

Technical, professional, and supervisory personnel have frequent opportunities to present their ideas to audiences of their peers. Professional associations maintain journals and hold meetings at which ideas can be exchanged and people can share their experiences and their findings. Many organizations provide special recognition for employees who are able to publish or to participate in professional meetings. Writing for these kinds of outlets is not the same as the more creative writing of the nonfiction published in popular magazines. We will not deal with the latter here. Our remarks are confined to the professional publication and dissemination of ideas.

In general, the same advice we gave about speaking applies to professional writing. You must make sure that your idea and your audience match. You have the option to select the journal or the association to which you submit your ideas. Be sure that you are familiar enough with the periodical or the organization so that you are sure that what you submit is harmonious with the kinds of things they commonly present.

Every periodical has a "flavor." Some print the results of experiments, others feature case histories, a few deal with historical or philosophical material. Recently a number of publications have devoted themselves exclusively to the presentation of material on the future. Publications and organizations can be defined by their audience. By discovering the kinds of people that belong to an association or the nature of the readership of a periodical, you can decide whether your material is appropriate.

Your major consideration should be whether what you have to say is important enough to warrant injuring a tree to get the pulp to make the paper on which it is printed. Highly scientific journals publish about 70 percent of the material sent to them. However, because most of the work comes from research funded by either industry or government, publication is a built-in feature of the project. Other professional publications print about 17 percent of what is submitted, so getting published is a highly competitive enterprise. Before you get involved, you must be sure that there is some satisfaction in it for you. Seeing one's name in print is gratifying to some. Others have jobs that offer them bonuses for publication.

Presentations at professional meetings are somewhat easier to qualify for. Usually professional organizations are divided up into sections or geographical regions for the purposes of convenience in examining program ideas. Find out the submission rules of the association to which you want to submit your material, and prepare a presentation according to their rules. Some require an outline. Others ask for a completed paper. Many of the technical reports and program proposals you prepare in the course of your job would qualify as papers at professional meetings. Remember that you will be doing an oral presentation, usually in a limited time period. The paper you prepare will be duplicated and distributed to anyone interested. You must prepare yourself to offer the main ideas of your paper within the time limits so that you do not infringe on anyone else's time.

Whether you write your information or present it orally, you are obligated to present material that is potentially interesting to someone else. The considerations of audience we explained to you in Chapters 3, 4, and 5 are particularly important for writing. Organizations and publications will reject idiosyncratic material designed to satisfy your ego. They look for clear identification of a purpose important to some segment of their readership. One journal editor remarked that when an article was published in his journal, it was usually so technical that no more than fifteen or twenty people actually read it. At professional meetings, only a few people will attend most of the oral sessions. However, the technical material important to specialists can have vast consequences. The journals and meetings are maintained so that specialists can be appealed to.

Here are some of the things you can write or speak about; you can:

1. Confirm something already known from another angle. You can perform a new experiment, make a new observation, or find a new idea to confirm something.
2. Criticize an idea. You can present standards for criticism and attempt to isolate strengths and weaknesses in someone else's idea, process, procedure, or experiment.
3. Add to history by filling in newly discovered details.
4. Cast reasonable doubt on some popular idea or assumption.
5. Report on your efforts (experiments) to connect two events in a causal, functional, or concordant way.
6. Introduce a new concept or theory to help clarify something that is not fully understood.
7. Replicate a previous experiment.
8. Offer a hypothesis and test it.
9. Explain a process.
10. Offer new ways to classify something.
11. Compare two ideas to show similarities and differences.
12. Propose and defend a solution to a problem.
13. Predict the future.
14. Advance and explain a theory.

All of these possible topics can be prepared by means of the patterns presented in Chapter 5. Follow these steps in your preparation:

1. Make sure you use one idea to a presentation. Be sure you can state your idea in one sentence. Use the previous list to help you explain. For example,
    a. I will show that Haskell's theory does not account for three important effects.
    b. I will explain the experiment conducted to examine the effect of spurkin on the production of breffinglass.
    c. I will show you how a replication of Fortescue's experiment casts doubt on its accuracy.
2. If you can state your idea in one sentence, you ought to be able to write a preliminary abstract (one paragraph) followed by a précis that will represent your outline. Once you have written the presentation, use the abstract to evaluate it. You can either revise your writing to fit your abstract or make slight revisions in the abstract to fit the article. If you find that much revision is necessary, you should reconsider the whole thing because you might not be clear enough in your own mind to publish.
3. Identify the kind of reader that might be interested in your idea and find the journal or organization through which that kind of person might be reached.
4. Examine material that has already been printed or presented to be sure that what you want to say is compatible. Find the format in which you are supposed to submit your article or paper.
5. Examine Chapters 3, 4, and 5 of this book, and prepare your article or paper according to the instructions presented there.
6. Ask some intelligent but uninformed person to read your first draft and to ask you questions. Make your revision so that important questions are answered.
7. Edit your work to remove fallacies and other possible sources of confusion. It is sometimes useful to have a professional editor examine the draft just before the final one.
8. Submit the article. Remember that it should be submitted following the instructions given by the journal editor or the program head. Make sure that it is produced in perfect form.

Your piece will probably not be accepted on the first try. What will happen is that you will get editorial advice. Sometimes this is a rejection; sometimes major changes are requested; and sometimes minimal changes are required before publication. Be prepared to redo your piece two or three times. Be particularly attentive to footnoting and documentation. Be sure to give proper credit for anything you may have extracted from the work of others. If you want to quote long sections from someone else's work, you may have to purchase permission. The editors can tell you how to do this. Remember that professionals are very egobound. They want their work to be read and used, but they want credit for it. It is better to credit too much than too little.

Also keep in mind the integrity of scholarly publication. Although there have been some scandals, for the most part editors of professional journals and program coordinators of responsible professional associations want quality material that is honestly produced, and that is useful to their readers or members. For that reason, most of them wouldn't publish their mother's work unless it met their standards. Most use a "blind referee" system, in which papers and articles, with all identification removed, are read and reviewed by specialists. The writer does not know who read her or his work, the reader does not know whose work she or he is critiquing. The editor or program coordinator then makes a decision about what to recommend.

If you seek to try your hand at this kind of publication, it is useful to talk to people who are familiar with the process before you make your try. Experienced authors can advise you about what kinds of frustrations you will encounter and how to handle criticism when it is received.

A WORD ABOUT WORD PROCESSING

A recent development in organizational communication is the word processor. A word processor is a "state of the art" computer designed to manage communication on simple and complex levels. A word-processing unit consists of a keyboard, a video screen, a device for maintaining programs and in most cases, a printer. Often these are connected to a central computer bank or message center, so that all data in a company is stored and available to anyone who needs it.

Some word processors work on a computer principle. They can be used to handle most computer problems as well as problems in written communication. Basically, however, the word processor is a fairly cumbersome device that takes up most of a fair sized desk. Words are stored, generally on "floppy disks," plastic platters that look very much like 45 r.p.m. records. Disks usually contain up to forty pages of information or more.

Specialized word processors like that designed by IBM are built to handle written messages exclusively. They provide the following services.

1. They can store text and display it on command on a video screen so that it can be edited. Words, phrases, whole pages can be inserted in the proper place, the machine adjusts itself to accommodate the new information.

2. By coordinating disks, information from two or more sources can be combined. For example, a list of names can be combined with paragraphs from a standard letter or report and a mass message devised, personalized for each individual to whom it is sent.

3. Most contain a dictionary of approximately 50,000 words and provide facility for the operator to include another 2,000 words for the purpose of checking spelling in a manuscript. When the word processor is doing its spelling task, each page is recalled and words that the machine does not recognize are highlighted so they can be corrected by the operator.

4. Special procedures are available for setting up tables, charts and graphs, detailed lists, and other long and routine operations.

5. The machine can be instructed to delete or add a line to a number of different documents.

6. Print-out can be stylized, centered, arranged with proportionate spacing, or the right hand margin can be justified.

7. Inputs can be made without stopping. Since the machine operates electronically, there is no need to be concerned about carriage returns or line changes.

8. The machine can arrange and number pages of text and print out final copy at an exceedingly rapid rate. Machines provide the option of using typewriter style type or print-face type. Some also provide the option of changing the size of the type.

There are a number of other features including accounting and billing capability, inventory capability, maintaining permanent records, inter-office communication of complicated material without requiring individuals to leave their station, long range communication, maintenance of central storage and retrieval facilities, calendar management, and the option of being patched in on an extensive remote computer network system.

The operation of word processors is not difficult, although many executives complain that their subordinates, department heads and supervisors do not understand the many applications for the equipment and so do not use them to capacity. Other executives report that secretaries skilled in operation of word processors often find themselves in supervisory positions. Those who know the technique and range of operation can provide important services to the organization.

We have only begun to comprehend the implications of the word processor. In the years to come more and more applications will be added, to the point where skilled operators and utilization specialists will find important career opportunities in the organization. More important, the word processor will revolutionize written communication by materially expanding the ability of individuals to combine information. More important, it will reduce routine tasks like typing and filing and provide employees customarily assigned to those tasks with the opportunity of growing into important communication positions.

There are a number of companies that provide word processors, IBM, NBI, Lanier, Wang, General Data Processing, Burroughs, Xerox, Radio Shack, to name a few. If you are interested in learning about the operation of word processors, most of these companies maintain regional field sales offices and conduct regular demonstrations of their equipment both on and off the premises. It is the opinion of the writer of this book that familiarity and skill with word processors will be a major obligation for the executive of the future.

READINGS

There are a number of specialized publications on business writing. Following are some of the most useful.

Lassor A. Blumenthal, *Successful Business Writing*. New York: Grosset & Dunlap, 1976. This book provides samples of a variety of types of writings, sales letters, complaints, inquiries, proposals, resumes and manuscript speeches.

Nelda R. Lawrence, *Communications in Business and Industry*. Englewood Cliffs, N.J.: Prentice-Hall, 1974. This book gives instructions for writing reports, letters, and memos, as well as minutes of meetings. It also contains workbook exercises on sentence writing and word choice.

Robert C. Cornwell and Darwin W. Manship, *Applied Business Communication*. Dubuque, Iowa: William C. Brown, 1978. In addition to standard advice on the techniques of writing for business, this book includes a section on how to avoid sexism in written communication.

Allen Weiss, *Write What You Mean: A Handbook of Business Communication*. New York: Amacom, 1977. This book includes a section on the audience for business writing and special advice on openings, closings, and transitions in letter writing. It also contains a special section on persuasive writing.

Thomas Pearsall and Donald Cunningham, *How to Write for the World of Work*. New York: Holt, Rinehart & Winston, 1978. This book offers considerable advice on style. It also includes formats for various kinds of business letters.

N. H. Mager and S. K. Mager, *The Complete Letter Writer*. New York: Pocket Books, 1976. This inexpensive little paperback is a compendium of formats for the writing of all sorts of business letters.

Edwin Newman, *Strictly Speaking*. New York: Warner Books, 1975. This book is unusually helpful in ridding your writing of clichés and meaningless phrases. A companion book is William Strunk and E. B. White, *The Elements of Style*. New York: Macmillan, 1979, which explains how to avoid the most common errors in writing style.

No office should be without a good secretary's manual and style guide. A particularly good one is Anna L. Eckersley-Johnson (Ed.), *Webster's Secretarial Handbook*. Springfield, Mass.: G. & C. Merriam, 1976.

Appendix A

Oral Reading

In the chapters on public speaking, we advised you that many times you will have to write a manuscript and read it aloud. In the final chapter, we suggested that you might want to read a paper at a professional meeting. This section deals with important considerations in reading.

You have often heard reports and speeches read in a monotonous, lifeless, boring manner. You may well have concluded that oral reading is inherently dull, yet you constantly listen to oral reading on the radio without being aware that the performers are reading from a manuscript. Good oral reading requires intelligence, concentration, and practice. It does not really require special techniques, but it does demand understanding of the material you are reading. Of course, if you wrote the speech or the paper, you *are* familiar with it. In those rare circumstances where you must present ghost-written material, you must be sure that you understand it thoroughly. If you need to read the words of some authority, you must be as familiar with the contents as you are with material you have written yourself.

Reading aloud is like public speaking because you use the same resources of voice and body to get and hold the attention of the audience. Oral reading is an extension of conversation. To be interesting, it demands variety in the voice and the facial expression and some body movement. The stilted effect that oral reading sometimes has results from excessive attention to reading words and not enough attention to your responsibility as a communicator. Remember that the audience need only be polite. If you want them to listen and understand, you must appeal to them by being interesting. Your material alone will not hold their attention unless they are very highly motivated specialists on the topic on which you speak. Keep in mind the following advice:

1. Make sure that your reading supports the main message of your presentation. It is tragic when a poorly written piece is read well, for all of the flaws in the writing are revealed. Practicing reading aloud will help you catch some of the problems in your presentation.
2. Look up the pronunciation of all unusual words. If you have the least doubt about how a word is pronounced, check it. The dictionary provides phonetic directions for pronunciation.
3. Study your sentence structure and make sure it is in oral form. When you write for a reader, you can use complicated sentences with dependent clauses. Speaking, however, is more episodic. It depends on short phrases clearly connected and easy to understand. Sometimes material that is written to be read has a kind of outline quality to it. Be sure that you connect your sentences with transitional words like *nevertheless, moreover, because,* and *for example,* so that the audience does not get a choppy effect.
4. Even though you wrote the piece, it is useful to make sure that your own ideas are clear to you. Nothing will reveal your confusion more than reading all of your errors aloud to an audience. Try reading your presentation into a tape recorder and and playing it back so that you can criticize it.
5. Make sure that you know what parts of the presentation you want to emphasize. On the manuscript you will use to read from, underline the sentences you think are important, and decide whether you will present them more loudly, inflect your voice, or use some other technique to make them important to the audience. In writing, you can use italics, capitals, and even different type faces to indicate important material. In reading, you must do it all with your voice. You can also draw slash lines (//) to indicate where you must pause. (/ = count one, // = count two, /// = count three.) In writing, you

use periods, commas, and paragraphs to indicate pauses. In speaking, you must impose the delays.

Do not try to sight read! Practice your material, if possible, with a critic, and at least tape it so that you can check it over. You will have to practice it a few times to make sure that it fits the time limits. Sometimes you will discover that it is important to edit out material to make your presentation fit; sometimes you may have the luxury of adding something. Practicing aloud will also identify the words and phrases that give you difficulty. You can change them rather than run the risk of mispronouncing or getting caught in a ridiculous spoonerism.

Practice with your manuscript on a lectern, if possible, so that you can move away from it. In preparing the final draft of the manuscript, use an "Orator" typing unit, with extra-large letters. Skip several spaces between lines. You will do a better job if you feel secure that you will be able to find your place if you step away or look up. You must be familiar enough with your material, so that you can get your head up and look at the audience from time to time. That does not mean you should try to memorize it.

Check your voice to see if you need amplification. It is useful to practice in the room in which you will make your presentation (or a similar room) to check the acoustics, find dead spots, and get information to give to an audio engineer who can set up a speaker system for you if you need it. You must be careful of your voice. Excessive strain can set off physiological changes that result in laryngitis, nodules, and more serious vocal disorders. There is no particular merit in trying to strain your voice if you have sound equipment available to you. Consider the following advice about the use of your voice:

1. Listeners find low pitch easier to listen to. Speakers tend to raise their pitch as they get involved and excited. If you find your optimum pitch and practice it, you will be able to return to it once you have emphasized material by raising the pitch. Regulating your breathing by marking breathing points on your manuscript will give you a moment to return to a more comfortable low pitch.
2. Vocal quality varies from person to person. If you feel that your quality is not satisfactory, there are specialists associated

with universities who can provide you with simple exercises to improve quality. Make sure that your nasal passages are open before you speak, and try to keep resonance out of the nasal passages. Some speakers make their sounds far back in the throat in a guttural fashion, and their talk sounds like a series of grunts. If you have to do a great deal of public speaking or manuscript reading, it would be useful to have a complete vocal analysis made by a professional.

3. Loudness can be easily regulated with an amplification system. Shouting is not a useful way of increasing loudness. Actors have exercises for projection that enable good ones to whisper and be heard in the back of a crowded theater. Many popular performers use audio amplification to expand their range of loudness.

4. Rate of delivery is the easiest aspect to control. You can do this with the slash system of marking we have already suggested.

5. Diction is important. Most people prefer to hear General American English because they are familiar with the sound of most of the words. Regional dialects and the excessive use of idiomatic expressions or technical jargon tend to confuse listeners. Try to get your pronunciation to conform to the directions in a standard dictionary. If you consistently mispronounce some sounds, you may need assistance to retrain the way you make the sound.

6. Delivery becomes an issue when it calls attention to itself or interferes with understanding or makes the speaker nervous. Attention to the details of delivery, however, can sometimes distract you from the content of your presentation. Those who have to make constant public appearances need to get specific training in vocal delivery so that it is not a constant source of worry.

7. Gestures should not be self-conscious. If you are standing at a lectern, most of your body will be concealed anyway. All you need to worry about is keeping your feet on the floor and not wobbling. If you are reading a manuscript, you will not want to move very far away from it. Keep in mind that if you let your arms and hands hang at your side, your natural need for emphasis will take over, and they will perform in ways that will help you.

8. It is important to keep an eye on the audience. You do not do this to detect what is going on. We have already told you that it is hard to interpret the meaning of audience action. Looking at the audience from time to time is a sign of respect. It means that you know that they are out there and you want them to understand, that you care about them. Make sure that you are familiar enough with your manuscript so that you can leave it for a moment from time to time to look at your audience.

9. You will not be able to exert too much control over your facial expression. However you look, you have looked that way all your life. Most people are expressive enough once they begin to concentrate on the content of what they are saying. Most audiences are willing to put up with anything you do with your face as long as it is not completely immobile.

Public presentation is performance. Performance skills can be learned. As a performer, you must be separated from the audience, not part of it. You must be in charge. You must have a message for the audience, constructed so that they can understand it, in words with which they are familiar. You must appeal to them so that they know that what you have to say is important, and you must put enough into the presentation of it so that they believe that you are important. That is why speech delivery is so important. When you write, your material can be artistically designed and set up in a neat, clear type so that it is easy to read. Punctuation guides the reader about when to pause and when to move ahead. The reader has the luxury of stopping and thinking, looking up unfamiliar words, and arguing back whenever she or he pleases. When you speak, all of the punctuation must be done by your voice, all of the explanations must be provided by you, and you must anticipate the questions your listener might ask.

If you want to be a performer, you must be trained, you must practice, you must experiment, and most of all you must rehearse. Most speakers in organizations do not have the time to take performance training, but they must take the time to rehearse. No matter what the form of your presentation, rehearsal will help you iron out the flaws and prepare you to meet most contingencies.

The Porto Bar Co:
An Experience in
Organizational Communication

In the following pages, you will become acquainted with the Porto Bar Co. Porto Bar is modeled after a real company. The information presented is real; the statements, memos, reports, documents that you will view are real. The work you will be asked to do is also real. When you are asked to judge the work of Porto Bar employees, you will be doing the same tasks as company trainees enrolled in a program of communication training. Later on, you will be asked to do tasks previously performed by Porto Bar employees. You will have essentially the same information they had. You may set your own time limits, but when you are asked to do pressure tasks, we will indicate the time limits within which Porto Bar employees had to work, if you care to test your own ability to work under similar stress conditions.

The advantage of the Porto Bar experience is that it will help you simulate real conditions in a corporation, without having your job at stake. It will enable you to take what you have learned to do in these pages and try to use it as you might be asked to use it if you were employed in a real corporation. We have already explained that you cannot learn to speak and write simply by reading. You need active experience under critical conditions. Your instructor can provide useful criticism and so can your colleagues. In the organizational world, there are no instructors; there are only man-

agers and supervisors. If you agree to take turns being the manager, each of you can also have a hand at administering criticism.

The people who are employed by organizations communicate daily in order to handle problems. We have explained that technical and professional competence is only part of what is required to be successful on the job. The Porto Bar experience is an adult "dungeon and dragons" game. You can add to it as you wish. You start with reality, and as you learn more about reality, you can extract experiences from other organizations and include them. Some groups have integrated Porto Bar with computer prediction and have tested their decisions against computer logic.

Porto Bar employees behave the way most employees do. They care about their company and they try to get along with one another, but sometimes their personal needs get in the way of their doing their jobs, sometimes they fight, sometimes they take days off at the wrong time, and sometimes they make totally stupid decisions. You will have an opportunity to monitor some of their decisions, and you will have an opportunity to evaluate some of your own as you deal with the problems inherent in any organization:

1. Obtaining relevant and valid information to use in decision making.
2. Hiring and orienting new employees.

3. Responding to changing conditions by making appropriate changes in the company.
4. Observing and evaluating employees and programs.
5. Solving problems, generating policy, and detailing program plans.
6. Making presentations and writing reports.
7. Managing the behavior of others.

The experience is best when done with groups of people acting as if they were Porto Bar employees and doing the tasks as directed. However, individuals can work their way through the experience as well. The experience was designed for training new junior executive employees in a large corporation. It was later adapted for use in classrooms in organizational communication. It is used here with the identity of the original company disguised.

THE COMPANY

Porto Bar is incorporated in a Middle Atlantic state. It is capitalized at $59 million and has annual sales of approximately $37 million. (The figures used here are based on December 1980. In subsequent usages, multiply all figures by the total inflation factor from December 1980 to the time of use. If specific prices are given, they can be changed to match prices for similar commodities at the time the experience is used.)

Porto Bar produces a product for apartment houses and condominiums called Porto Bars. They are segmented bars that can be built in according to particular apartment designs. Some models are built so that the resident can rearrange them to suit particular needs. They can be used as actual bars, as eating areas, as display counters, as room dividers, and for many other interior design purposes. The only other main competitor is Drinkomatic Corp.

In January 1981, the Porto Bar fiscal picture looked like this:

Salaries and wages	$ 9,940,000
230 production employees	
20 road salesmen	
45 executives and supervisors	
Benefits and personnel expense	$ 7,399,000
Production costs, including materials,	
equipment, and utilities	$12,944,000
Leases, rents, taxes, (including social	
security share, unemployment, and so on)	$ 4,364,000

INTRODUCTORY PROBLEM

The sales manager of the Porto Bar Co. is Van Garde. He super-vises a sales force of twenty and maintains contact with field ware-houses and building-supply jobbers and their representatives. About 38 percent of all sales come from direct response to advertising. Although the units are sold to contractors, advertising seeks to motivate requests for Porto Bar units from potential residents, and many ncw buildings install them as an attraction for affluent singles. Salespeople are required to serve as design engineers and to help contractors plan the use and installation of the units. Slightly more than half the sales of Porto Bar units are through major hotels and condominiums. These sales are handled by a vice-president and his staff, although Mr. Garde and the sales force are responsible for liaison and goodwill as well as technical information on these sales. The salespeople are paid only partially on commission. They also receive a salary for their service as design and installation specialists and as troubleshooters when problems arise.

Advertising is important because neither contractors nor potential residents normally think about installing portable bars in their living units. Warehouses and jobbers do not normally maintain field sales-people. They depend on people's coming to them and asking for what they want. Porto Bar advertises regularly in magazines ad-dressed to the trade, such as specialty magazines designed for build-ers, contractors, and jobbers, and it also advertises periodically in magazines addressed to potential customers like *Apartment Life* and *House Beautiful.* The competitor, Drinkomatic, depends en-tirely on pressure from potential renters or leasers, and it advertises in *Playboy, Gourmet,* and the *New Yorker.* Its advertising budget is clearly higher than that of Porto Bar, and there is reason to believe that its sales are considerably higher.

Recently Mr. Garde has had the uneasy feeling that sales have been dropping. Although he does not have detailed information, he has estimated a 3 percent drop in sales—not terribly significant, but still, in a time or rising inflation, there ought to be an increase in cash rather than a decline. He has discovered that the advertising budget has been constant at about $750,000 for the past four years. What has bothered him the most is informal reports from warehouses and jobbers that inquiries seem to be dropping off. Although there are enough orders stacked up to finish the year, there are, he thinks, ominous signs for next year.

For one thing, there have been a number of complaints from salespeople that their potential customers have expressed misconceptions about how Porto Bars are used. There is particular concern about whether or not they can be equipped with running water. (Most Porto Bar units have a running water and a refrigeration option. Small refrigerators are purchased from a separate contracter and mounted at cost. Sinks can be included and water run through hoses from the available water supply. Permanent units can, of course, be hooked up to plumbing at the option of the householder.)

Second, some of the salespeople have complained that the ads are attractive and dignified but that they do not explain the Porto Bar satisfactorily to potential customers. They point to Drinkomatic's advertising, which they claim has more impact. Even though Drinkomatic has not been working through jobbers, some salespeople believe that jobbers are becoming interested in taking on the Drinkomatic line.

Third, the vice-president who handles condominium sales has been making increasing use of salespeople in their trouble-shooting function. This presents two problems. First, when they are trouble-shooting, they are not selling. Second, the fact that they are trouble-shooting may indicate that something is wrong. Mr. Garde has called a group from his sales department together and asked them to function as a task force to consider the problem. (You can find instruction on how to proceed by referring to Chapter 7.)

During the first phase of this experience, regard yourself as a "consultant" on group problem-solving and organizational communication, called in to evaluate the discussions and deliberations of the task force. You may work individually or with a group. You will be presented with a series of statements made by participants in the task force meetings, which you must evaluate according to the criteria provided. Correct answers are provided following each set of statements. Try to take the steps one at a time, without looking ahead. The correct answers will also provide a rationale for the decisions. The answers were "keyed" by a group of business consultants who specialize in decision making.

Pay attention to new information as it is added. You will need all of the information you get. As you work through the entire experience, you will accumulate a great deal of information about the Porto Bar Co. and its operations. It is up to you and your group to sort it out and to use it as you need it. Your instructions for each section will be provided in the form of a memo from Van Garde to

"Consultants." You will also have an opportunity to look at Mr. Garde's memos to the task force. The purpose of this exercise is to train you for the tasks that lie ahead.

Memo C-1

From: V. Garde

To: Consultants

Here are some statements I have taken from the first thirty minutes of the task-force meeting. Help me classify them according to the following criterion code:

    B = The *one* statement that represents the best starting point.

    J = Jumps the gun. It is premature to raise this issue now.

    U = This is a useful early idea but not necessarily the best one with which to start.

    C = Cop-out. Passes the buck either by trying to blame someone or trying to pass the responsibility to someone else.

You can use the coding system to help you evaluate your own discussions

_____ 1. "What in the hell does Van really want us to do?"

_____ 2. "I think we ought to get on the salespeople and find out why they are fouling up."

_____ 3. "Van always pays more attention to salespeople than he does to us. Why should we do their work for them?"

_____ 4. "Someone ought to get that advertising manager out of here. He isn't worth a darn."

_____ 5. "This looks like a job for top management. There's not much we can do about it."

_____ 6. "I think we ought to meet regularly. Do you think Van will pick up the tab for lunches?"

_____ 7. "Why did Van think that we were capable of handling this kind of problem?"

_____ 8. "I think we'd better get out and get some information before we start doing anything."

_____ 9. "The first thing we need to do is get organized. Who's willing to take notes?"

_____ 10. "Van ought to do this himself. It requires an executive decision, not a committee meeting."

_____ 11. "Somebody ought to find out what's really going on in advertising."

_____ 12. "Do you think the company is about to go under? I start worrying when sales drop."

_____ 13. "Maybe we ought to start advertising like Drinko in some of the class magazines."

_____ 14. "What is the problem?"

_____ 15. "Don't you think there ought to be some salespeople in this group?"

Debrief: Memo C-1
Here is how I would have classified the statements. Do we agree?

1. B. *No group should start working until it knows what is expected of it. Someone must ask Van to be more specific, that is, to give the group a charge to carry out.*

2. J. *Maybe the salespeople are doing something wrong, but there is no evidence at all at the present time.*

3. C. *This does not seem to be the time for a paranoid gripe session. Furthermore, it rarely helps to attack the boss when you are required to produce some work.*

4. J. *There are no data about the advertising manager at all. It is premature to make this kind of statement.*

5. C. *You work for Van; Van has asked you to do a job. Trying to pass it on is a cop-out.*

6. U. *The person who made the statement may be trying to hustle some free lunches. On the other hand, it is important for a group to set a time and place for its meetings.*

7. U. *It is important that a group know its qualifications. Figuring out what Van thought the group could lead to a useful explanation of their task.*

8. U. *Of course, they need more information very soon. The first information they need is about what they are to do. Then they need information about what the problem is. See the discussion in Chapter 2 on how to phrase questions.*

9. U. *It is useful to get organized, and it is useful to have someone to take notes. There is some reason to classify this B, because someone will need to take notes as the group tries to phrase a memo to Van asking for a charge. We hope that the group does not automatically demand that a woman present take the notes.*

10. C. *If Van thought he could do it himself, he probably would not have asked the task force to deal with it. On the other hand, there is the possibility that Van wants to use the task force to ratify a decision he has already made.*

11. J. *This is premature. It is a question that the group will need to deal with later on perhaps, but the group cannot really specify substantive questions until it is sure what its task is to be.*

12. C. *This is entirely irrelevant. It distracts the group and could well get them discussing whatever rumors they have heard lately.*

13. J. *This is premature. It jumps to a solution before the group has the vaguest notion of what the problem is. Unfortunately a great many groups do jump to solutions, and a suggestion like this could seriously distract a group.*

14. U. *This is an important question. It should be asked the minute Van responds to the group's request for a charge.*

15. U. *This is a useful procedural question. Perhaps the group ought to include it in their memo to Van.*

Whenever problem-solving groups get together, they must get organized, set meeting times, and agree on an orderly procedure for doing work. They can't do this until they know what their work is. No manager should ask a group to do a task without specifying what the task will look like when it is completed. If you are asked to serve in a problem-solving group, insist on knowing what your objective is, what is expected, by when, for whom, and for what purpose.

Memo C-2
To: Consultants
From: Van
Here are three memos the group drafted to me, including the one they actually sent. Which do you think they sent and why?

Memo 1:   We'd like to know exactly what you want us to do. Why don't you give us some instructions?

Memo 2:   Please tell us our task and our deadline. Do you want a proposal, and if so, for whom? How do you want us to operate?

Memo 3:   Please answer the following questions: Do you want a proposal or just some suggestions? Where do you want us to meet? What expenses will you cover? What is our deadline? Who is in charge?

V.G.

Debrief: Memo C-2
    The group sent Memo 2. Memo 1 was too abrupt. Memo 3 was too detailed. The group should keep the privilege of selecting its own leader. Because the group asked the general "operations" question in Memo 2, Van will explain what is important to him.

Van has several alternatives. He can ask the group merely to gather information about the problem and describe the relationship between sales and advertising, from which he can generate his own solution. He has the authority to ask the group to focus on any aspect of the problem he chooses. In this case, he has some sensitivity to the problem and understands that he might have been part of it, that is, that the trouble is interpersonal, and thus he might be biased. For that reason, he sends the following memo:

To: Task Force
From: Van
Re: Your Charge

I want you to come up with a proposal for something I can do to help advertising and sales work better together. I don't know exactly what the problem is. Maybe there isn't one, but I feel that sales and advertising don't get along well together, and I think I have to take the lead, personally.

Take about two weeks. Give me a written proposal for something I can do, and don't take the problem upstairs. (Do not involve anyone on a higher level.) You can meet after hours because you will have to keep up with your regular work. I'll cover dinners sent in from Fannie's. Charge them to the company account. Use the west corridor conference room. You'll get a bonus for this work based on your salary, so be sure to keep track of your hours.

V.G.

Memo C-3
To: Consultants
From: Van

Can the task force use this charge to start its work. I want them to look for some impairment so that they can start to phrase a question on which they can base their discussions. The following statements refer to potential impairments: things that happening that shouldn't happen or things not happening that should happen that affect the company in some way. Check each statement and classify it according to the following code:

W = A statement not helpful in discovering an impairment.
X = A statement about something happening that shouldn't be happening.
Y = A statement about something not happening that should be happening.
Z = A potential impairment that does not now affect the company.

So that the Task Force can use your guidance in deciding on its question.

_____ 1. Salespeople are losing business.
_____ 2. Van is really uptight about this.
_____ 3. Sales and advertising aren't making it together.

_____ 4. It really is uncomfortable in the conference room with Bill smoking.

_____ 5. Business is lousy all over.

_____ 6. I hear they are making some big changes over at Drinkomatic.

_____ 7. I think the way Van runs the department stifles creativity. Personally I can't think positively when we have to deal with this kind of thing.

_____ 8. Porto Bar ads don't seem to have enough detail about the product.

_____ 9. I don't think Van and the head of advertising have very much contact with each other.

_____ 10. I've been generally upset with the way things are going around here.

_____ 11. I don't think we and the employees in advertising really know each other as people.

_____ 12. The warehouses and jobbers don't appear to have much contact with the company.

_____ 13. I hear salespeople are complaining. They have a tendency to cry a lot, but maybe there is something in what they are saying.

_____ 14. Do you think that trends in morality will affect the sales of home bars generally?

_____ 15. Somebody told me that high interest rates are going to have a real effect on slowing down new apartment and condo building.

Debrief: Memo C-3

1. X. *Lost sales means that the company is in trouble.*

2. Z. *At the moment, Van's stress must be regarded as a personal matter. You are advising him about his department, not about his personal life.*

3. W. *This is not a clear statement. Who is not doing what with whom? Personnel and conditions must be clearly identified.*

4. Z. *This is a personal inconvenience that must be worked out between the people involved. It affects the problem-solving process.*

5. W. *This is irrelevant at the moment. It may turn out later that what is happening is the result of general business conditions, but right now it cannot be claimed as an impairment in the company.*

6. Z. *This is interesting, but at the moment not relevant to Porto Bar.*

7. W. *This is a personal complaint.*

8. X. *If ads are ineffective or inaccurate, it could be a real problem.*

9. Y. *This could be a serious situation, if the two departments need to integrate their activity.*

10. W. *Aren't we all? But there is nothing specific yet.*

11. W. *The statement is not clear and therefore not useful.*

12. Y. *Because they account for a great many of the sales, this contact might be very important.*
13. X. *This is a good lead on something that might be happening.*
14. W. *This question should be addressed to a sociologist or minister.*
15. X. *Might lead to a useful inquiry about the effect of outside forces on the organization.*

The task force is about to begin the process of defining their question. Up to now, they have been ventilating their feelings and using words without pinning down the meanings. Take time out from your task, and try to sharpen your skill at operational definitions. Chapter 5 will help you. Following are some unspecific words extracted from conversations in the task force. They are offered to you in the context in which we found them. Try to write an operational definition for each one, and then provide an example illustrating the definition. Work on the italicized words in the following sentences:

The *mood* around this place is very *heavy* these days.
I think our major problem is *apathy*.
Employees are generally *alienated*. Maybe the salesmen aren't *involved* either.
Our big problem is how to get people to be more *productive*.

Here's an example:

What we need is more *commitment* from employees.

Commitment can be identified when an employee arrives at work and starts working before it is time to, stays late because she or he is concentrating on a task, and offers suggestions to improve the way things are done. For example, consider Bill Smith and the way he worked on the Barker case. He must have put in fifteen extra hours one week, and he wasn't asked to. He really got into the case and made it possible for the sales manager to get a very nice contract, and Smith didn't even expect a bonus. That's *commitment*.

You might find another way of putting this. The reason we asked you to do this task is because to respond properly to the next memo, you will have to operationalize some of the categories. Remember, an operational definition specifies behaviors that can be seen or heard.

Memo: C–4
To: Consultants
From: Van
Here are some proposed wordings of the problem with which the task force is going to deal. Pick the *best* one and classify it B. Those that are useful questions should be classified as *F* for fair. The ones you reject should be classified as poor: P_1 = too general, P_2 = polarizing, P_3 = begs the question, and P_4 = violates the charge. The best wording will specify who is to act and on what issues.

V.G.

_____ 1. How can Van get the advertising department to change the ads?

_____ 2. What are the problems the sales force is really having?

_____ 3. Should we change advertising copy to detail the adaptability of Porto Bars?

_____ 4. What can be done about the lack of articulation between sales and advertising?

_____ 5. How can Van get the head of advertising to check with him about the ads?

_____ 6. What can top management do to get sales and advertising to work together?

_____ 7. Should Van call the faulty advertising to the attention of the top brass?

_____ 8. What is the problem between Van and the advertising department, and how can it be solved?

_____ 9. What can Van do to convince advertising to coordinate their efforts more closely with those of the sales department?

_____ 10. What can be done to improve the advertising of Porto Bars?

_____ 11. Should Porto Bar ads be done by an outside agency?

_____ 12. What can be done to improve coordination between sales and advertising?

_____ 13. What should be the optimal relationship between sales and advertising in a fully functioning articulation design in a large corporation?

_____ 14. Should Van blow the whistle on advertising?

_____ 15. Should Van call the salespeople in for retraining in the use of advertising?

Debrief: Memo C–4
Here is some advice on operational defintions for the classification categories.

P_1 = *Any statement that refers to problems outside the Porto Bar organization or that does not contain any reference to items in the charge.*

P_2 = *Any statement that can be answered "yes" or "no."*

P_3 = *Any statement that assumes anything about the nature of the problem or its causes.*

P_4 = *Any statement that directs the group to do things either not included in the charge or expressly forbidden by the charge.*

  B = *The statement that specifies some action that Van can take to increase contact between sales and advertising.*

  F = *Any statement that refers to the problem of the relationship between sales and advertising and is open-ended, although it may not specify who is to act.*

1. P_3. *This begs the question because it has not been demonstrated yet that the ads are at fault.*

2. F. *The group will have to deal with this problem sooner or later, but it refers to a small and specific part of the problem.*

3. P_1. *"We" is not defined, and there is no real relationship to the charge.*

4. P_3. *We do not know yet that the problem is one of articulation. Van expressly states in his charge that he does not know what the problem is.*

5. F, *possibly* P_3. *Checking over the ads may be one way of improving contact, but there appears to be some begging of the question because we do not yet know that there is any problem with the ads, or that the head of advertising does not check with Van.*

6. P_4. *Referring the problem to the top is expressly forbidden by the charge.*

7. P_2, P_4. *For the same reason as 6, and because it requires a yes/no answer.*

8. F. *This is, of course, the question, but as it is phrased, it does not direct the group toward the charge, that is, a proposal for Van.*

9. B. *This was selected as the best wording because it simply repeats the statement on the charge in question form.*

10. P_4. *This clearly lies outside the capability of the group. They were not charged to make recommendations to the advertising department.*

11. P_2, P_4. *This is a yes/no phrasing and also outside of the group's authority.*

12. F. *This does refer to the content of the charge, but it does not specify who is to act.*

13. P_1. *This is a mystical phrasing. It is not clear what this question is about.*

14. P_2. *Two-valued question.* P_1 *might also do as it is not clear what "blowing the whistle" means, or about what.*

15. P_3. *This assumes that the sales people need training. There is no evidence to support this.*

The task force has worded their question, for the moment: "What can Van do to convince advertising to coordinate their efforts more closely with those of the sales department?" There are some problems with this wording. In the first place, *convince, coordinate, efforts,* and *more closely* are fuzzy terms and need operational definitions. The question is useful because it guides the group to some kind of problem between sales and advertising, and it specifies that Van is to do something. The task force must now gather some facts to see whether they can make the problem more specific. They have some allegations, but they have no data, so at the moment, there is no problem.

The consultants can, of course, see what they can do about writing operational definitions for the fuzzy words in the question, while the task force looks for data about (1) the relationship between Van and the head of advertising; (2) the relationship between advertising and the development of sales leads; and (3) the actual state of sales in the company.

Memo: C-5
To: Consultants.

Your next problem is to help the task force evaluate some facts. Here are some statements by members of the task force reporting results of their independent investigations. Classify each statement according to the following scheme.

R = Useful because it relates to one of the three issues that the task force is investigating and because it can be checked.

Q = Probably not useful because even though it is relevant, it cannot be checked.

I = Irrelevant to the problem, so it doesn't matter whether it can be checked.

Most of these statements are not completely clear. There is some useful material and some that is not useful in each of them. You are to decide on the balance. Classify each statement according to the criteria, and then, using Chapters 5 & 9 as guides, write a brief memo to the task force in which you advise them of the extent to which they can depend on the facts. (In essence, you are preparing a memo or a short speech using a criteria pattern. You will need to refer back to these facts throughout your work on this problem.)

1. Porto Bar advertising copy is written by Phil McCann and Mac Zuss. They have been with the company for ten years. McCann used to work in production, and the head of production says that McCann really knows the technology of Porto Bars. Zuss, according to the production superintendent, is a "fool" and out of touch with current designs. Zuss draws the pictures, and McCann writes the copy. I am told that Zuss does what McCann tells

him to do. They seem to work independently of Lou Quarm, the head of advertising.

Classification _____ Criticism _____

_____

_____

2. Here is the organization chart. I found it in the company policy guide. There doesn't appear to be any formal connection between production and merchandising at the vice-presidential level. I think sales and advertising are also

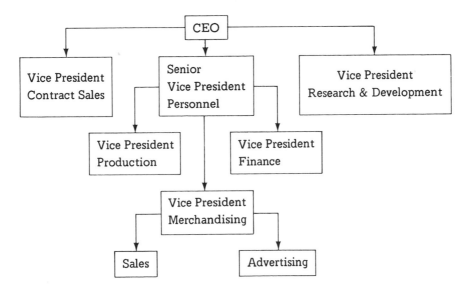

disconnected. I get the impression that contact is made informally between divisions. The industrial engineer who handles communication systems for the vice-president of finance says that one of the problems with the company is that the divisions are not formally articulated. For example, the people in shipping are complaining because there is no way they can get information regularly from sales about big orders coming up so that they can get set to ship them. The problem may be on a higher level than we think. What we have may be just a symptom.

Classification _____ Criticism _____

_____

_____

3. I heard that when Lou Quarm first came here, he had a thing for Lena Genster, who was Van's secretary at the time. There was a big fuss when Lena didn't get her promotion and she filed an affirmative-action suit, and I think Lou testified against Van at the hearing. It was very messy, and Lena

made some claims about Van being against Hispanics. Patsy Buck in the grievance office in personnel says that Van will probably never move up in the company because of that mess.

Classification _____ Criticism _____
_____
_____

4. I checked Van's calendar and he lists meetings with Lou. He has two a week on the average. They are on the premises, not two-martini lunches. Van's secretary says she thinks they meet one time in Lou's office and one time in Van's. She doesn't know what they talk about, and she never gets minutes or notes for the files. She says that there are a lot of complaint letters from salespeople. She has read through them, but she won't give me any. I couldn't get to Van to authorize me to go through the files. The secretary had to write a summary, though, and she showed me that. The last paragraph reads, "Most of the salespeople who complained said that prospects did not even know that Porto Bar was a competitor of Drinkomatic because the ads didn't give any details. They say Drinko ads show the components and ours do not. Some of the salespeople say the ads are confusing the customers, but I think the ads are fooling the salespeople."

Classification _____ Criticism _____
_____
_____

5. OK, so we have some complaints from salespeople. Are they typical? Are they from salespeople who are actually selling. I have had to troubleshoot for salespeople for ten years now, and I know that the ones who are not selling are the ones who blame it all on the main office somehow. We also don't know where advertising gets the data it uses to design the ads. I talked to Sally Forth, who used to work in advertising. She's section head at Grabit and Hyde now. She told me that when she used to write copy here, they just put her in a room with a fully assembled Porto Bar unit and told her to "be inspired," like a method actor. She said she never had enough information to do a decent job of writing. She got fired because she went to the production superintendent to get data.

Classification _____ Criticism _____
_____
_____

6. I want you guys to look at this chart I got from Carol Leiner, the comptroller.

Salesperson	Years with Company	# Complaints Filed	Sales to 9/30 This Year	Sales to 9/30 Last Year
A	2	6	$ 181,000	$ 208,000
B	6	6	79,000	91,000
C	10	0	306,000	248,000
D	3	3	130,000	128,000
E	14	0	370,000	364,000
F	4	9	61,000	148,000
G	4	2	155,000	112,000
H	7	0	196,000	192,000
J	9	0	416,000	328,000
K	4	15	41,000	88,000
L	3	3	216,000	222,000
M	4	0	235,000	122,000
N	6	7	88,000	267,000
P	13	0	456,000	416,000
Q	2	2	184,000	196,000
R	1	1	31,000	No record
S	15	0	644,000	643,000
T	9	1	312,000	318,000
U	1	22	38,000	No record
V	8	0	276,000	274,000
Warehouse A			1,956,000	1,954,000
Warehouse B			1,746,000	1,884,000
Warehouse C			1,785,000	1,884,000
Jobber 1			656,000	775,000
Jobber 2			3,788,000	2,455,000
Jobber 3			2,112,000	3,717,000
Contract sales			11,860,000	11,944,000

Leads from advertising totaled 2,440, and we turned, all told, 189 of them into sales, for about $1,879,000. There are no data on leads and conversions this year. Total sales for last year were $36,262,212.

Classification _____ Criticism _____

7. When Ava Reece headed advertising back in 1973, she held meetings twice a year with the salespeople. We are turning less than 10 percent of our leads

into sales in recent years, but before 1973 more than 30 percent were converted into sales. Ava used to meet with the salespeople to show them how to capitalize on inquiries, but Lou discontinued the meetings when he came in.

Classification _____ Criticism _____

8. I handle the training of all salespeople. Each one of them has to go through production and learn how all the components are made. They can all read blueprints, and they know something about materials. Most of them could function as mechanical engineers. They all have college degrees for S and C, and they are technical school graduates and worked in production before they became salespeople. They get a good deal. Salespeople get a 15 percent commission, and they get 24¢ a mile and $55 a day per diem when they consult for the vice-president of contract sales, along with $100 a day. It's not such a bad thing to be in sales for good old P'Bar.

Classification _____ Criticism _____

9. In the first ad for Portobar in 1954, there were no people. This picture ran in *The New Yorker* and was produced at the Sturm and Drang Agency. The company ran these institutional ads til about 1958.

Classification _____ Criticism _____

10. Personally I think the problem is one of attitude. We have conflict between the two departments and all over the company there is a thing like a feudal kingdom. Nobody gets along with anybody. We've got to get Van and Lou off their high horses and get them together. Companies can't run well when the brass clangs—you know what I mean? I was talking to a secretary upstairs in one of the vice-president's offices and she says there are tensions around this place you wouldn't believe. I mean it is bad, really bad.

Classification _____ Criticism _____

V.G.

Debrief; Memo C–5
The management consultants' report on each of the items is detailed. Here it is.

1. R. *This seems to be related to the problem, although it involves some secondhand testimony. The opinion of the production superintendent has some value, and understanding how advertising copy is produced may have some use.*

2. Q/I. *It is hard to know what to do with this. The company policy guide is not dated. We don't know whether it is still in use. Furthermore Van ruled out contact with anyone on the vice-presidential level. The information about the shipping department can be checked, but it is not related to* this *problem.*

3. I. *People are always interested in gossip. Fixing blame is a way to cop out. The less said about this item, the better.*

4. R. *This is information that can be checked, and it is related to the problem. Van can be asked if he actually met with Lou and what they talked about, and if the task force gets access to the files, they can find out precisely what the salespeople are complaining about.*

5. Q. *There are some useful aspects about this item, but it really is personal testimony. The little narrative on how advertising used to be produced is interesting, but it has a gossipy quality to it, and it is certainly not relevant to what is going on now. When a group is asked to check out present conditions, even though it may be easier to find out what the past was like, they should not spend much time on reconstructing history.*

6. R. This may be the key item. *It might be interesting to stop here and see if you could work out a presentation using a comparison pattern on the similarities and differences between this year and last. There are some things that need to be checked. For example, in the nearly fifty times this experience has been used in classrooms and management training sessions, only six groups ever stopped to total the figures to see what the state of affairs actually is. Did you stop to total up the columns and make the comparison? Did it occur to you to go back to the original description of the company and total up the expenses and then inquire where the money came from? Did anyone ask how many salespeople were dismissed last year and how much business they accounted for? This is important information, and it should be analyzed thoroughly.*

7. R. *This is important information that can be checked. It is the first link in how advertising works to get sales. It is not clear whether advertising weakens the sales pitch or the salespeople are not pitching effectively, but by going back to the files mentioned in Item 4, you might be able to pin down the nature of the difficulty.*

8. R. *More important information. We now have some firsthand information about how the salespeople are trained and what they ought to be able to do. The information on their salaries may or may not be important, but it is specific.*

9. I. *Another interesting piece of history not related to the problem.*

10. I. *This is useless talk. It is distracting and contains no facts.*

As you can see, we have few hard facts in the case. Perhaps it would be a good idea to stop and review what you think the task force knows. For one thing, there is a considerable amount of information in Item 6, which must be teased out. This is the time to find a statistical consultant who can show you how to examine the figures to find out whether Van's suspicions about the connection between sales and advertising are accurate. In the light of inflation, are sales really dropping? (Chapter 8 introduced you to the important issue of being able to handle changes in the economy.) You know that there is a record of contact between the heads of the two departments, but you have not confirmed the contacts, nor do you know what they were about if they really happened. You know that some problem has been mentioned in connection with the production of advertising copy; some people have expressed suspicions about how it is done.

There are complaints from salespeople about advertising, but you do not know yet what the complaints are about. You may never know. You may never get access to the files. You know something about the qualifications and training of the salespeople, but you do not have information about individual salespeople.

The task force tried to reword the question. They tentatively asked, "What can Van do to ensure himself a consulting voice in preparing advertising copy?" They rejected the question because it was premature. There was still no real evidence that the problem involved advertising copy as such. Next they tried, "How can Van and Lou cooperate to ensure that advertising is of maximum use to salespeople and that salespeople are trained to make maximum use of advertising?" Of course, you know they rejected that question because it violated the charge: it proposed a solution for advertising, when the instruction was to propose a solution for Van. They finally agreed that their question was "What can Van do to improve the way sales and advertising cooperate to make advertising useful to sales and to train salespeople to make the best use of advertising?" They preferred that wording because it specified that Van was the person to act, and it did not presume that advertising was at fault.

The task force tried to examine its data to discover what questions it needed to ask next.

Memo: C-6
To: Consultants
From: Van

Following is a list of questions sent to me by the task force. I am not going to be able to answer them all. I intend to tell the task force that the secretary's estimate of the nature of the complaints was accurate. I get the impression that the salespeople are comparing Porto Bar advertising with Drinkomatic and that they are evaluating P'Bar as second best. Here are the questions they asked me. Which *five* of them do you think I ought to answer. Put an *X*, next to the ones you think are the most important—and five only, please.

V.G.

_____ 1. What caused the tension between you and Lou?

_____ 2. What are the specific differences between Porto Bar and Drinko-matic ads?

_____ 3. What is the policy of top management when there is trouble like this between divisions?

_____ 4. What qualities of Porto Bar do salespeople think are most persuasive?

_____ 5. What procedures does advertising use to design copy?

_____ 6. What methods do similar companies use to coordinate information between sales and advertising?

_____ 7. Have we had articulation problems in the company before? If so, how have they been solved?

_____ 8. What personal problems do you have that get in the way of your dealing with Lou?

_____ 9. How do successful salespeople use advertising and with what effect?

_____ 10. What do you and Lou stand to lose if you do not solve this problem?

Debrief: Memo C-6

Here is what the management consulting team said about the question:

1. *This question is a matter of gossip. Also, you aren't even sure yet that there is tension.*
2. *This is an important question. We have allowed hearsay to direct our thinking so far. It is time to look at the ads.*
3. *The group has been directed not to refer the issue to top management. This question, therefore, is academic.*
4. *This could be useful information, provided we draw it from salespeople who really can demonstrate that they use advertising well.*
5. *This is another issue on which we have been relying on hearsay. The group needs to find out how advertising does its work so that it can recommend questions for Van to raise with them.*
6. *There may be nothing in the answer to this question, but if the problem existed elsewhere and a solution was found, it might be applicable to our case.*
7. *It is probably best not even to make an inquiry on this issue, as it might alert top management, which is precisely what Van does not want.*
8. *The task force should be told to cease and desist from their prurient interests.*

9. *The problem is with the word* successful. *The question is repetitive and will be answered under Question 4.*
10. *When things go badly, everyone gets fired. The question is wasteful.*

Van has decided that he will answer questions 2, 4, 5, 6, and 7. The idea of thinking through important questions has been discussed in Chapter 2. It is not useful simply to gather piles of information. Data must be targeted on important issues. Here is a summary of the answers that the task force got to the five questions deemed important.

2. Drinkomatic ads display components. In some ads the components are labeled, but even in the institutional ads, there is more than a suggestion that the bars can be assembled to order. Neither ad lists prices for its components, and Drinkomatic lists no price at all. Porto Bar art seems more professional; Drinkomatic seems a bit cluttered. Following are copies of two of the most recent ads in trade publications for the two companies.

4. Eight salesmen, whose complaints were very specific and whose sales records were very good, were questioned, and their responses were summarized:

   a. Portobar can be adapted to individual suites in the same apartment building. You don't have to buy one installation for all the suites. Drinkomatic production facilities will not permit this versatility, but if people can agree on one design, Drinkomatic can probably produce it for less cost than Porto Bar.

   b. Porto Bar's cost is about 11 percent below Drinkomatic on components and add-ons, however. If someone wanted a really fancy unit, Porto Bar would be cheaper. Porto Bar also has more options. The base price of the "stripped-down" Drinkomatic unit is $980. Portobar units of equivalent size costs $1,250. However, Porto Bar is built of more durable materials.

   c. The Port Bar unit is not bolted to the floor and can be taken out if the tenant moves. Porto Bar uses a spring-base system to keep the unit against the floor. Drinkomatics are actually permanent installations. In most leases, tenants are prohibited from removing anything fastened to floors or walls. Also, Drinkomatics are more expensive to connect to

PORTO

BAR

for

CLASS

LIVING

FROM $1,250

Inquiries to: Porto Bar, Box 80, Cohen City, CO 99999.
Call 800-555-9999.

they add up to

DRINKOMATIC

the home bar

you design

refrigeration and running water, and once installations are made, they are permanent as well, whereas Porto Bar has an option called Party Pleasure, which permits the bar to be used for meals and connected temporarily to water for parties.

    d. The salespeople agree that most of these issues do not occur to the client unless they are mentioned by the salespeople, but that the Drinkomatic ad suggests that Drinko units have a versatility that they actually do not have, whereas Porto Bar ads give very limited information. Customers tend to regard the two units as identical and go for the least expensive if they have a chance.

5. Copywriters spend two weeks in production, where they are oriented to current Porto Bar capabilities. Advertising has a sample unit with all of the features, but there is no formal program guiding advertising personnel through these features. There is no connection with sales or salespeople at all. Thus advertising personnel do not know the information provided in Item 4. Van claims to have periodic meetings with advertising to acquaint them with these features, but there are no data about what is actually discussed. Van says he uses the meetings to talk about problems the salespeople are having getting the message to potential customers, and Lou seems to understand, but his understanding is not reflected in the design of the ads.

6. Drinkomatic advertising is designed by the sales department and is farmed out to agencies once the salespeople decide what they want. They change layouts and copy frequently to sustain the message of price and versatility that Drinkomatic salespeople want to get across. An informant at Drinkomatic says that morale is very low in what passes for an advertising department over there, but no one cares because the salespeople are happy.

7. Just as a sidelight, management at Porto Bar has made it clear that they don't want arguments settled on the executive level; they don't even want to hear about them. The last time two department heads got into a battle, they were both fired and most of their staffs departed shortly thereafter. It is in the best interests of the task force to keep information about the issue away from the vice-presidents.

The next problem is to set some goals and discover limitations on the decision-making process.

Memo: C-7

To: Consultants.

From: Van

The following is a list of statements by the task force about goals and limitations. Please check them carefully and classify them as follows:

        A = Specific goal statement.

        B = Valid restriction or limitation.

        C = Fuzzy goal statement

        D = Excessive restriction or limitation.

V.G.

_____ 1. Our solution should become company policy so we won't have to go through this kind of thing again.

_____ 2. The best thing that could happen would be for Lou and Van to bury the hatchet and work things out.

_____ 3. We should test our solution through the simulation network on our computer.

_____ 4. Whatever we do, it can't cost any money.

_____ 5. Advertising copy should be used by the salespeople.

_____ 6. Lou and Van should feel good about working together to accomplish company goals.

_____ 7. To prevent further occurrences we should solicit a policy statement from the vice-president for merchandising to cover ways to resolve differences between the departments under his supervision.

_____ 8. Salespeople should understand the relationship between advertising copy and sales presentations.

_____ 9. Our solution should protect Van's job.

_____ 10. The solution should give sales control over the production of advertisements because the purpose of advertising is to generate sales.

_____ 11. Our ad copy should be as effective as Drinkomatic's.

_____ 12. Van should have final say over all ad copy.

_____ 13. We should be able to get Lou replaced.

_____ 14. We should get someone to get Drinkomatic's ads in advance and counter them.

_____ 15. We should have our advertising done by an outside agency the way Drinkomatic does.

Debrief: Memo C-7

    1. D. *This has been ruled out by the charge. Not a valid goal.*

    2. C. *The statement is a cliché. It is fuzzy.*

    3. D. *This begs the question and is irrelevant to the issue.*

4. B. *There has been no budget specified for the project; therefore there should be no money involved in a proposed solution.*
5. A. *This is exactly what we are after.*
6. C. *How would we know if this happened? It is fuzzy.*
7. D. *This violates the terms of the charge.*
8. A. *Another statement of exactly what we are after.*
9. B. *He is, after all, the boss. We know that if he goes down, the task force goes with him. His job should be protected.*
10. D. *This might be desirable, but it is not within the scope of the group's authority.*
11. C. *We really don't know that Drinkomatic's ads are effective.*
12. C. *We don't know what "final say" means or whether it is necessary.*
13. C. *This is not possible or desirable or any of the group's business.*
14. D/C. *It is not clear whether this is a goal or a limitation, but it appears to be illegal.*
15. C. *This is a proposed solution; it is not within the authority of the group.*

Now you can become part of the task force, instead of a consultant. You have just about all the information the people on the task force have. We know what Van's counterpart in the real company did. Here are some of the proposals that were offered at the final session of the task force. Examine them carefully and remember that each one you select will have to become an operations plan in which you decide who is to do what, when and where, with what resources, and with what criteria for evaluation. This should help you select concrete proposals. Classify each of the following suggestions as if you were a member of the task force (or, if you are working as a group, the task force itself). Use the following classification code:

S = Satisfactory. Should be included in the solution.
F = Fair. It sounds like a good idea, but it appears to need rewording, specification, or more detail.
V = Violates the limitations and should be rejected.
X = Does not help accomplish the goal and should be rejected.

_____ 1. Get all the information we can about how Drinkomatic salespeople use their ads, and get our own salespeople to use our ads the same way.

_____ 2. Find an intermediary to sit down with Van and Lou and teach them how to work together. Once they work out their differences, they will probably do a better job of coordinating their activities.

———   3. Set up some kind of training program where the sales-people who appear to know how to use our advertising can train the newer or less effective salespeople in how to use it.

———   4. Write some kind of memorandum or suggestion report to Lou about what the salespeople need to have in their advertising. Document everything in it very carefully, and have Van carry it to Lou and try to discuss it with him.

———   5. Send a memo to the vice-president detailing the problems in the two departments and requesting that the vice-president for merchandising hire a consultant to work things out.

———   6. Try an end run: take some of Lou's employees to dinner, and try to get them to understand the needs of the sales department. Try to keep Lou out of the thing because of his hostility to Van.

———   7. There really aren't enough facts yet to make a proposal. What we need now is to do a study of the optimum articulation possible between departments in a company like this. We should set up a study group composed of people in the two departments.

———   8. The production manager could serve as a mediator between Lou and Van.

———   9. If we could get the salespeople trained properly, we might not even have to contact Lou.

———   10. The problem is clearly with advertising, and there isn't a damn thing we can do about it over here except tell the salespeople to do their own bushbeating!

Here is how Van evaluated the proposals:

1. *F.* Not bad, assuming they really do use their advertising well. It is always useful to take good ideas from a successful competitor. However, it does not address the charge.

2. *X.* This really doesn't address the sales–advertising problem as the facts reveal it. This is more a personal thing and consequently outside the scope of authority of the group.

3. *S.* This seems to be exactly what we are after. There are regular sales meetings that are already funded. We could just plan an agenda for one of them.

4. *S.* This seems to be an effective way of reaching Lou. At least the ideas will be available, and if he reads the document and responds, we may have something going. And we can use the data we put into the written document in planning for the sales meeting mentioned in Item 3.
5. *V.* We have been trying to avoid outsiders. We know the dangers of bringing in the brass.
6. *V.* This assumes Van knows what advertising should include. It is also sneaky and can backfire badly.
7. *X.* This is a cop-out. We have all the facts we are going to get, and now we have to do something.
8. *V.* Intermediaries have been ruled out. Furthermore it is still not established that the problem comes from personal difficulties between Van and Lou. Isn't it interesting how an idea will persist even in the absence of facts?
9. *S.* May beg the question but focuses on a valid issue.
10. *X.* Clearly a cop-out.

The problem the task force now faces is to implement the plans for the two "solutions" that they have proposed and Van has approved. The following tasks need to be done. Act as the task force and do them. Summarize your results in a report (written and oral) to Van.

1. Find some motivations for Lou to read the document that Van will send to him. In Chapter 3, you will find information about how to analyze audiences.
2. Prepare the outline of the presentation to Lou. In Chapter 4 you will find information about the various patterns. Use a set pattern for the presentation and confine it to three main points. Try to keep the whole thing within four typewritten (elite, double-spaced) pages, so that it can be read orally in less than ten minutes.
3. Check Chapter 5 to discover what supports you will need to assume your burden of proof in your proposal to Lou. Answer the following questions:
   a. What, exactly, are you suggesting to Lou? What is the problem you are confronting him with? How will you document the existence of an impairment that affects him?
   b. What supports will you need? Check the facts—definitions, examples, statistics, and citations—according to the standards provided in Chapter 5. What experts will you need to

call in to help provide information? Check Chapter 2, and carefully prepare a set of questions that you will want to ask of experts in order to get the information necessary to your document. What kinds of answers will you want? To what use will you put the answers? If there are communication experts available, see if you can get an appointment and ask them some of the more general questions. (Questions about how advertising can be used by salespeople, for example, can be presented to local experts.) There is more information about the Porto Bar in this chapter. You might want to check ahead and see if you can pick up anything useful.

4. Plan the sales meeting. Read Chapter 8 and act as a manager.
   a. What resistance do you expect from the salespeople? How will you overcome it?
   b. Using the criteria pattern in Chapter 4, prepare a statement on how you will select the salespeople qualified to offer the instructions at the sales meeting.
   c. From Chapter 6, figure out a way to tell the salespeople who are not performing well the "bad news" about why they must come to the meeting, what they must learn, how they will be evaluated, and what will happen to them if they do not improve.
   d. Interview local authorities and find out what you will need in order to train salespeople in how to use advertising. (Have your instructor pave the way for you by making appointments.)

5. See if you can develop an operations plan and a budget.
   a. What tasks must be done for a sales meeting starting Monday at noon with a lunch and ending Wednesday at 4 P.M. There will be sessions from 1 to 5 on Monday, dinner and entertainment Monday evening; sessions from 9 to 12 and from 1 to 5 on Tuesday, a working lunch Tuesday with an address by Van, and a dinner Tuesday followed by a reception for company officials, at which the new company movie will be shown; and sessions Wednesday from 9 to 12 and from 1 to 4, as well as a working lunch. All meals not specified will be "salespeople on their own," and the company will pick up the bill. Assume that slides will be shown at each working session.
   b. Acting as manager–coordinator, take care of everything but

the contents of the meeting. Get budget estimates on hotel rooms, travel and lodging, meals, and entertainment, and estimate the per diem for salespeople for meals not covered by the company, including those en route. Itemize a budget for two salespeople coming from each of the following cities to your town: Seattle, Los Angeles, El Paso, Little Rock, Tallahassee, Richmond, Philadelphia, New York, Chicago, and Minneapolis. Each warehouse will send one representative from Denver, Salt Lake City, and Indianapolis, and each jobber will send one representative from Hartford, Detroit, and Nashville.*

c. Fill out a detailed plan answering who is to do what, by when, where, and at what cost in order to get this show on the road.

You can use your groups as management teams to work out this problem. Working through the details of the problem should give you an idea of the difference between administrative tasks and leadership. If you think you have the information you need, you can also generate a plan for the contents of the sessions and prepare an evaluation plan to provide an estimate of the success of the meeting.

Here is an advisory from a management consulting firm that worked on the project. They offer some advice to managers about problem solving and the presentation of ideas. The report is written in very informal terms. Read it carefully and compare the advice in it with the information you have received so far in this book. In the rest of this exercise, you will be asked to work your own way through detailed projects that will take you into various aspects of company operations. We will spare you the technical details of production and much of the agony of fiscal management, but we must warn you that those problems will be serious ones for you on a real job. The advice offered here should be useful to you as you attempt the experiences that follow.

CONSULTANT ADVISORY

The problem with what the task force has been doing is that it is very difficult to try to solve a problem for another person. There is no such thing as "involun-

---

*If you contact local establishments be sure to tell them you are doing a classroom exercise.

tary improvement." People cannot learn if they are dragged in kicking and screaming. Van had some things he wanted Lou to do. Van was not very specific about what he wanted. There was a great deal of temptation for the task force to talk directly to Lou and tell him how to improve his advertising, but that would have been wasteful. People waste a great deal of time giving unsolicited advice. No matter how good the advice might be, if it goes into the wastebasket it was a waste of time to offer it. When you try to get people to do something your way, you must persuade them of why they should do it.

The problem could get emotional. If the salespeople aren't bringing in the orders, Van could get pretty riled up, and the people upstairs in the executive suite could go on the warpath. Emotions are expensive luxuries. Managers are expected to keep cool. It doesn't help for Van to blame Lou. He can't afford to make a public demonstration where someone important might see him. Eventually this problem may have to go upstairs. If it does, both men are in trouble. That might be the way to persuade Lou to cooperate. Just remember that the man who sang that great song about dreaming impossible dreams was a fool who fought windmills. About all you can do is what is possible, no matter how good other ideas may seem. It is too bad you can't make the world the way you want it, but then, if it were the way *you* want it, someone else wouldn't.

People sometimes lie. They don't mean to. The case with Van and Lou is filled with unintentional lies. There is no evidence at all that they are hostile to one another, but everyone thinks they are. We have been on this case for four weeks now, and we have seen no signs of hostility. We have also seen no signs of contact. Maybe the problem is that they are just so lukewarm to each other that they don't want to work together. How can we get them to admit it?

The answer may lie in politics. Most of the people we have contacted on this problem are politically naive. They don't know much about power. They don't know that power plays sometimes work, but that no matter how much power you have, there is always someone with more. One way to get power is through groupthink. There have been signs of groupthink in the task force. They keep going back to personal explanations, they keep trying to refer the problem upstairs, and they seem entirely unwilling to admit that Drinkomatic might be beating the pants off Porto Bar. There seems to be little interest in finding out exactly what Drinkomatic is doing.

Anyway, we hope the solutions work.

OTHER PROBLEMS

In the following experiences, you will be the task force. You will receive a memo asking you to deal with a problem from start to finish. You will not be able to get any more information beyond what you have in the memo. Use the patterns on the following pages to help you organize your ideas. In each case, you will have to prepare a proposal and present both an oral and written version of it to the writer of the memo. Preparation of both Form A and Form B is required for each task. Each memo represents a task. You may devise your own tasks as well.

Form A. Problem Checklist. (Fill out in detail.)
Who says there is a problem? _____
What reasons does he or she offer? _____
    Is this a regular problem? _____ How do you know? _____
    Is this an emergency? _____ How do you know? _____
    Is this a future projection? _____ Is it important enough to worry about? __
_____
    What is your authority to deal with the problem? _____
    Where did you get your authority? _____
What is the problem, exactly?
    What is not happening that should be happening? _____
    How do you know? _____
    What is happening that should not be happening? _____
    How do you know? _____
    Who is being hurt? _____
    What is the nature of the injury? _____
    How serious is the impairment? _____
    What might happen if it is not dealt with? _____
    How soon must we have a solution?_____
    What symptoms do we want to eliminate? _____
    What causes do we want to alter? _____
Phrase the question, the answer to which will be the basis of your final report:
_____
Make sure that you add a "compendium" of your facts. Makes notes with your factual information to indicate why you think you can rely on it.
How will you change your question in the light of your facts? _____
What additional information do you need to answer the question?_____
Can you get it? _____Where and how? _____
How will you know when you find a solution? _____
What limitations do you have in finding a solution?_____
    Financial? _____
    Practical? _____
    Personnel? _____
    Logistics? _____
    Legal?_____
    Moral? _____
    Other? _____
What are the possible courses of action?_____
Which one do you reject and why? _____

Which ones do you accept and why? _____

How can you evaluate the effectiveness of your solution? _____

Form B. Solution Report Form. (Fill out in detail.)

Who is involved in the solution? _____

What will each person do? _____

In what space? _____

With what equipment? _____

By when? _____

Under whose supervision? _____

At what cost? _____

You can use a grid to specify the "total picture" as follows:

Person	Job Title	Duties	Location	Equipment	Deadline	Supervisor	Cost

Prepare the budget. Specify sources of funds (if possible).

How will we evaluate success? _____

What is the best that can happen with our solution? _____

What are the odds that it will happen? _____ How do we know? _____

What is the worst that can happen with our solution? _____

What are the odds that it will happen? _____ How do we know? _____

What is the most likely thing that will happen with our solution? _____

What are the odds that it will happen? _____ How do we know? _____

Who must we persuade to accept our proposal? _____

Why this person? What is the nature of his or her authority? _____

What do we know about the approving authority to which we must adapt? ____

What is the essential message we will transmit? _____

What pattern will we use? _____

What will be the headings of our presentation? _____

What supports will we insert? Where? (Prepare the outline.) _____

Attach the written presentation.

Attach the notes or outline for the oral presentation.

If you choose to develop your own problem to work on, these forms will permit you to work through each of the chapters of the book and apply what you have learned. There are a number of local problems with which you can deal. Your instructor can guide you in the selection of practical questions. One very practical application of this process is to serve as consultants to Junior Achievement groups in your community.

Memo

From: Ed Mann, Executive Vice-president

To: Task Force

You did so well on the task you did for Van that I though you could help us out on some problems we are having. As you know, economic conditions are not the best these days. Our product, Porto Bar, is not necessary to life. It is a luxury item. We are OK right now. Our company is in the black and we are paying dividends. We are planning some diversification, and in a few years, we will be able to enter other markets with goods more vital to consumers. We need some help with internal problems now, however.

We are going to ask your advice on some important issues, mostly involving personnel and how they relate to one another. We are concerned with the problem of narcissism. (See Christopher Lasch, *The Culture of Narcissism.* New York: Norton, 1978.) We think that employees are so concerned with their personal comfort that they are unable to work in ways that will help the company succeed.

I am attaching some notes from research and development that you might find useful before you approach the tasks I am assigning you.

E.M.

EM:hs
Attachment

Advisory on Hypothesis Making
To: Task Force
From: Sy Yentist, Research and Development

When you recommend a course of action, you are generating a hypothesis. A hypothesis is a "best guess" about what would happen if something were done (in this case, your proposal.) When you are asked to generate a hypothesis, you go through the steps of analyzing a problem and recommending a solution. You support your arguments on behalf of your proposal with data, just as a scientist supports his or her findings in testing a hypothesis. The idea is to anticipate your mistakes before they happen.

One way to handle anticipating the future is to divide your proposal into steps and try to estimate the consequences of each step. If Murphy retires, then we will not replace him and Schmidlapp will take over. What is likely to happen if Schmidlapp is in charge? Will there be an impairment? What might we do to prevent it? Is there any alternative to Schmidlapp? Sometimes you can get together enough tangible data to have the computer make your prediction for you, but this doesn't happen very often when you are dealing with human problems. When you deal with humans, you have to reason out the possibilities as best you can. There are five basic ways you can try to predict the unknown:

1. If several events have one and only one circumstance in common but generally have the same results, you can guess that the event they have in common brought about the result. For example if you discover every

time your billing department uses a particular program, the same error appears, you might conclude that the program ought to be changed. If you discover that Bill has an accident with every machine he has worked on, you might decide that Bill is accident-prone. You must be sure, however, that you can argue that the circumstances are causally connected. Don't get trapped in that gin-and-soda, whiskey-and-soda, rum-and-soda trap. It is the alcohol, not the soda, remember?

2. If several events have similar outcomes, but if one circumstance is missing and there is a different outcome, you can guess that the circumstances that was deleted is the cause of the different outcome.

3. If several events have a common circumstance and come out the same, but when the circumstance is removed they come out differently in the same way, then the combination of circumstances in common and the differences can be alleged to be the cause.

4. If adding something gets the same outcome consistently, then the addition can be alleged to be a cause.

5. In dealing with humans, if you can find what similar people did in similar circumstances, you might have a useful conclusion if you can get an operational definition for *similar* that makes sense.

You will have some problems looking at people. People don't like to be studied. They don't like to be tampered with. And if you study them secretly and they find out, you will be in real trouble. Whenever you study people, you affect the way they act, so you are not studying them in a real sense.

When you generate a proposal, you are taking a risk. You need to figure out what the consequences will be if you are wrong, and what the consequences will be if you do nothing.

Finally, every argument you make has some component that must be taken on faith. The notion that you can reason from data must be taken on faith. The idea that democracy is a good system of government must be taken on faith. At some point, you will need to rely on agreement rather than proof.

This may not be all you need to know about the scientific method, but it should get you started. Good luck.

S.Y.

Memo
To: Task Force
From: Ed Mann

We have been operating under a Management-by-objectives formula here for the last four years, and we have required all supervisors and executives to prepare a yearly set of objectives for their departments and divisions. They, in turn, attempt to have their employees develop their own objectives. For example, sales had as its objective a 2 percent increase last year, production was to cut costs by 1 percent and so on. Most of the objectives set have to do with increasing income or cutting costs. A number of the employees, however, have been complaining that we will never achieve company objectives if we don't set some objectives about interpersonal relations. Sy Yentist has done some research on this and he has discovered the following:

1. Employees get along better when they are associated with successful projects, but if you try to get employees to get along well, it does not ensure that projects will be successful.
2. Employees work best when they have a hand in planning their work.
3. Our employees have complained that the reward-and-punishment structure has made them uneasy. They claim that rewards are distributed unfairly to people who make the boss "look good." They claim that mistrust is generated by the system. Furthermore they claim that most supervisors are not very skillful in telling people bad news.
4. When MBO systems are passed on to employees, there is very little choice offered. Many employees claim that when they try to set objectives for improvements in the *quality* of their work, their supervisors turn them off with the complaint that they don't want to deal with intangibles.
5. There are a number of rumors flying around the company about supervisors and executives in trouble because they did not meet their MBO goals. There is no real information about either the goals or the level of accomplishment.
6. It appears to me that our employees do not communicate well with each other. Their social patterns seem awkward, and I think there really is a lot of mistrust, not because of setting objectives but because of the way we are doing it without taking their intangible needs into consideration.

This report has made me uneasy. I would like you to come up with the outline of a plan for communications and interpersonal training for all employees. I want, first, a priority list of the ten most important things you think employees need to know about interpersonal communication.

Second, assume that I can release employees for two hours a week on company time for training. Using one week (two hours) for each of your ten items, make me a proposal for the contents of each two-hour unit. You will have a maximum of ten minutes in which to state your case—and I want the details of what you recommend that we teach and some good reasons for doing it. I also want a summary of each presentation, in writing, but covering no more than two pages (8½ X 11, double-spaced, elite).

E.M.

Mann is asking for brief project proposals with an oral defense about the major issues in interpersonal communication in the organization. Groups can be formed to prepare proposals, and these can be presented at an open hearing. You have the option of *defining the audience* to which they are to be presented. It might work best if each group uses the others as an audience. The groups can then use some real data as they prepare their audience analyses.

Memo
To: Task Force
From: Ed Mann

We have been operating here under a supervisor-based employee-evaluation system. We start with job descriptions, and we let the supervisors do the merit ratings by answering the following questions:

1. How well does the employee accomplish the tasks specified in the job description? (We have left the definition of *well* to the supervisor.)
2. How well does she or he get along with her or his colleagues? What disruptions have you recorded?
3. What special skills does the employee have?
4. Does this employee satisfactorily reconcile his or her personal ambitions and goals with the company mission?

Based on these data, we ask the supervisors to make recommendations about advancement, termination, compliment, or reprimand.

We think the employees ought to participate in the process. Some of the items are meaningless because the words make no sense. Do the following, please:

1. Try to define operationally *well, get along,* and *special skills,* and try to rewrite Question 4 so that it makes sense.
2. Design a simple rating form that you think employees could use to rate themselves and their colleagues.
3. Try the rating form on yourself. Test it on your skill in doing the job requested in this memo.
4. Prepare a proposal and be ready to defend it.

E. M.

When questioned about some of the details, Mann said that he wanted to see how a pilot form might work. The experiment in rating yourself is important, he said, because it will give you an insight into the honesty with which such a form can be used. Mann also wants you to write a set of instructions for the use of the form and to test them out. He offers you some examples taken from the form that President Carter used to evaluate his employees in 1978. He believes these are not useful terms, and he wants you to be more precise, and provide criteria for observation and evaluation.

Exhibit: Ineffective Rating Form, Sample Items
1. Level of effort made by this employee:
   Below Capacity   1   2   3   4   5   6   Above Capacity
   (How do you figure out what the employee's capacity is?)
2. What is the employee best at? (Rank 1 to 5)

_____ Conceptualizing	(We have problems of operational definition
_____ Planning	here. Also, some of the employees may not be
_____ Implementing	called on to do all these things. Furthermore,
_____ Attending to detail	if someone is "best" on one of these items, it
_____ Controlling quality	may not mean that she or he is very good. Finally the instructions are ambiguous. What does *1* mean)?

3. How mature is this person? Immature   1   2   3   4   5   6   Mature
   (When you use a numeric rating scale, how do you go about comparing people? Is there any standard?)
4. How bright is this person?   Average   1   2   3   4   5   6   Very Bright
5. How much supervision does this person need? A lot   1   2   3   4   5   6   Little
6. List this person's three major strengths and weaknesses.
7. List this person's three major accomplishments.
8. List three things about this person that have disappointed you.

Van suggests that someone can make a presentation about the weaknesses of this sort of instrument and identify the possible impairments in its use. The proposal that goes along with it could specify what the components of a good evaluation instrument might be, that is, what could be honestly evaluated.

Memo
To: Task Force
From: Ed Mann
In line with our evaluation program, we want to improve the way we assign employees for training. We have been using the following items:
1. Describe the behavior that requires improvement. Why is it an impairment?
2. What is the nature of the task on which the employee is below standard? How do you identify the standard? What does a substandard performance look like? What does a superior performance look like?

3. Does the employee know that the task is not being done properly?
4. Is the employee capable of doing the job properly?
5. Describe the behavior that you want of the employee. Compare it with description in Item 1. What is the deficit?
6. How would you implement retraining? Provide step-by-step instructions for improvement.

I would like you to try this out. First, have each member of the task force apply this instrument to the task force leader, and second, have your task force leader apply it to each member of the task force.

I also want you to develop some plan for informing the employee about his or her deficiency in performance. This is a "bad news" interview. Write a set of policy guidelines and regulations for the use of supervisors. Present your policies as a proposal.

Sy Yentist offers you some notes:

1. Supervisors should never criticize what they cannot correct. If the employee is incapable of doing the job, she or he should be dismissed. In addition, the supervisor should never pick on intangibles, only overt behavior that can be altered.
2. Supervisors often request change by telling people to "speed it up," "do better," or some such cliché. It doesn't help employees to be told that they are not performing well if they do not know what "well" is.
3. Performance can be improved only if objectives are set in concrete terms.
4. An employee will not try to improve until he or she is convinced he or she is not doing well. This requires a persuasive speech to an audience of one.
5. Employees must understand how they will benefit if they improve and how they will lose if they do not improve.
6. Employees must have a chance to propose an alternative to whatever is proposed by the supervisor.
7. There ought to be a clear-cut reward for improvement and a clear-cut punishment if there is no improvement.

E.M.

The next memo is based on Chapter 8. Career-path assignment is an important element in employee-evaluation programs. Porto Bar wants to discover employees who have potential for management positions. They are looking for leaders.

Memo
To: Task Force
From: Ed Mann
We want a proposal for a technique designed to spot leadership ability in employees. The first thing we want is a statement of what a leader does when she or he is not leading. Use your task force as an example, and see if you can spot and describe "acts of leadership" performed by people other than the leader. What we want to avoid is mistakes in promoting people. We have discovered that seniority is not an effective way of finding leaders; sometimes we put people in supervisory positions, lose their skills in their jobs, and then find out that they are lousy leaders as well. Following is an instrument used by a number of companies to distinguish leaders from followers.

Leader Scale: This form must be used by an observer. 1 = Accurate description of the person evaluated; 2 = The individual sometimes does this; and 3 = This behavior is almost never observed. A score near 20 means that the individual has a dictatorial style; a score near 60 means he or she is more democratic. (Use this form only on leadership acts. The problem, of course, is that the form measures how well someone leads. You must improve on it.) The form is adapted from a form presented in David R. Frew, *Management of Stress.* N.Y.: Nelson-Hall, 1977.

1. Expects people to follow instructions unquestioningly.
2. Exerts tight control.
3. Expects disciplined behavior.
4. Does not subdivide tasks.
5. Refuses to share leadership. Exerts individual control.
6. Takes full responsibility for success or failure and expects rewards and accepts punishments.
7. Maintains constant attention after assigning tasks.
8. When leadership is delegated, maintains a close watch on subleaders.
9. Expects leadership to come from the top.
10. Does not pay much attention to employee suggestions.
11. Bases decisions on statistical data.
12. Rarely shares leadership.
13. Criticizes performance behavior.
14. Quickly develops reward and punishment systems.
15. Suppresses spontaneous acts of leadership.
16. Is impersonal in maintaining discipline.
17. Stays with the book in defining good and poor performance.

18. Acts as if subordinates are extensions of himself or herself.
19. Does not trust subordinates to understand tasks.
20. Appears to regard himself or herself as superior to subordinates.

Follower Scale: This form is to be used by the employee. Give yourself 3 points if you agree with the statement, 2, if you are uncertain or have mixed emotions, and 1 if you disagree. (I don't know how to interpret this one. They don't say what the scores mean.)

1. I expect my supervisor to give me explicit instructions before I start to work.
2. I do not question the orders my boss gives me.
3. I work best when I can understand the rules and regulations completely.
4. My supervisor is responsible for my behavior.
5. I like short jobs so I can improve through repetition.
6. I will not accept orders or instructions from anyone other than my boss.
7. When the boss tells me I am wrong, I regard it as his or her fault because he or she probably gave me defective instructions.
8. It is the responsibility of my supervisor to evaluate me.
9. My boss must be superior to me, otherwise she or he would not have been promoted.
10. When I finish a task, I wait until it is approved before starting the next task.
11. I cannot perform well when I have general guidelines.
12. If I do something wrong, it is not my fault because my supervisor told me to do it.
13. I do not like to undertake new and different tasks.
14. I expect rewards for a job well done.
15. I expect some kind of discipline when I fail.

There ought to be a better way, task force! What is your proposal?

E.M.

Memo
To: Task Force
From: Ed Mann
Here's an interesting problem in human relations. Employees make excuses to cover themselves when they do not perform well. Following are the fifteen excuses we receive most frequently around here. I'd like to have a recommendation about how a supervisor can check the validity of each excuse. Who can he or she check with, and what questions can he or she ask in each case? I'd also like some advice about how to deal with the excuse under two conditions: first, if the supervisor discovers it is valid and, second, if the supervisor discovers it is

invalid. How would the supervisor talk to the employee about it? Remember that if anything looks like an exception, everyone who knows about it will want to take advantage of it. Here are the excuses:

1. I have not been feeling well today.
2. Someone close to me died.
3. I am having a lot of trouble with my spouse (kids, mother, father, and so on).
4. Someone is very sick at home.
5. I have been really worried about paying my bills, and I haven't been able to concentrate.
6. I misunderstood the instructions. I don't think you told me right.
7. The assignment was unfair. You always ask me to do too much. You never ask him or her to do things like that.
8. You couldn't pay me enough to do that job.
9. The people in my department don't like me. They pick on me.
10. You are prejudiced against me, and what you say about my work is unjustified.
11. I can't understand why we even have to do this job.
12. My supervisor is making sexual advances, and I don't like it.
13. They expect more from me in my department than they expect from people in other departments.
14. They expect more from me than they do from other workers in my department.
15. No one ever gets punished. Why are you picking on me?

I'd like to end up with a detailed scenario for supervisors to use in handling these things.

E.M.

Chapter 6 will help you a great deal on this one.

The next set of memos you are going to get will involve you in making some value choices. You will work best if you specify your criteria for decision before you start looking at the details of the evaluation task.

Memo
To: Task Force
From: Ed Mann
Write me a set of qualifications for this job. Provide me with some criteria for judging applicants.

Editor: House Bulletins   Salary Range: $19,000–24,000/year

1. Maintains liaison with company divisions, departments, and executives to obtain information appropriate for general dissemination.
2. Uses facilities of duplicating room to prepare announcements. Disseminates announcements at direction of vice-president for personnel.
3. Publicly requests information about employees and their accomplishments, births, deaths, community honors and activities, and other items of importance about individual employees and disseminates them in a monthly personnel bulletin approved by vice-president for personnel.
4. Releases information about company, its activities, and its employees to press and media at direction of vice-president for personnel.
5. Maintains records of company benefits and consults with employees about same persuant to regulations by vice-president for personnel.
6. Produces the following documents according to schedule established by vice-president for personnel: emergency bulletins, procedural changes, bulletins as required, and monthly house organ by the tenth of the month.
7. Provides editorial service to executives with approval of vice-president for personnel.
8. Supervises activities of duplicating room.
9. The following employees will be supervised by the *Editor of house bulletins:*
   a. Two B-5 secretaries (60 wpm typing, office machines, 90 wpm shorthand).
   b. One C-3 clerk.
   c. Two C-3 machine operators (trained on all duplicating machines).
10. Maintains liaison with vice-president for personnel on budgeting, employee evaluation, pay revisions, hiring and dismissal, and all necessary revisions of tasks.

What I want from you is a statement of how we can look at résumés and applications to select the kind of person we want for this job.

E.M.

Memo
To: Task Force
From: Ed Mann
I am attaching the job description for "field representative: sales." I had personnel prepare some descriptions of candidates. I want you to do two things for me. First, examine those descriptions because I think a number of them are in violation of the Equal Employment Opportunity Act. Please make a note of

any detail you find in the descriptions that might disqualify them. Second, try to sort out the specific qualifications of each applicant and list them for me. Omit all material that is in violation of equal opportunity regulations. I think it would be a good idea if you would select three of them to invite to the home office for interviews. Give me a short paragraph telling me why you selected the three you did, and a paragraph explaining why you rejected each candidate, telling me why you selected the ones you did. I will need a separate paragraph on each one. If you like, you can also draft a memo to personnel for me explaining to them how to omit illegal information from their subsequent reports to me.

Job Description: Field Representative (Sales)   Salary: $10,000/year + 15% commission on gross sales + $100/day per diem when on technical assignment.

1. Maintains liaison with home office to receive and integrate product information.
2. Keeps all catalogs maintained and current.
3. Transmits required report forms weekly to sales department.
4. Calls on potential customers as directed by sales department.
5. Develops customers to call on based on personal assessment of potential.
6. Keeps posted on activities of competing companies and transmits information to sales department.
7. Develops and proposes suggestions for product improvement.
8. Executes contracts under company policy for the sale of Porto Bars.
9. At direction of vice-president for special contracts or sales manager, serves as engineering consultant for special-design Porto Bars, for major sales, or for installation plans for major sales and provides technical help as directed.
10. Provides estimates for trade-in value of old units and arranges distribution of secondhand units. (There is no restriction on profits made here. Salesperson accrues all funds over and above minimum-base trade-in price).

E.M.

Candidates:
Buck Carew   Age 39   Certificate: Clark Technical School, Boston, Mass. Worked on production line at Porto Bar for nine years. Promoted to line supervisor on final assembly of main units four years ago. Served as chairman of task force that designed technical service manual for troubleshooting installation. References from production superintendent say he is "generally quiet, a strong

person, very skilled in production, and very knowledgeable about the details of the product."

Ellie Vader   Age 22   Graduate, B.S., North Dakota State, Fargo, N.D., in mechanical engineering. Member of debating team, women's pep club, runner-up for Miss Red River, worked part time as shortorder cook at MacDonald's, West Fargo, where supervisor called her work "OK." Reference from Professor Ignatz says "Miss Vader is a charming young woman, sometimes not attentive to detail but able to handle problems. She is good at human relations. People like her."

John Quill   Age 30   Graduate: B.S. in agriculture, Ohio State University, Columbus, with honors. Worked six years as supervisor in greenhouse in Greensburg, Pa., where owner calls him "self-contained, able to work on his own, not very talkative but very competent." School reference from Professor Griffle says, "Quill keeps to himself and gets a great deal of work done. You really don't have to check on him."

Bertha DaBloose   Age 28   Two years at Juilliard School of Music. Currently a performer (singer–piano player) at the Kitty Kat Klub in Kenosha, Wis., where the owner refers to her as "more serious than most of these chicks, and she keeps studying how to do things on her own. She can fix most of the stuff around here. She's amazing about how she knows electricity and plumbing, and she is some looker." School reference calls her "moderately talented, personable, a credit to her race."

Izadore Schutt   Age 45   Graduate: Technion University, Haifa, major in mechanical science, with honors. Has been working as a salesman for Drinkomatic since coming to the country five years ago. Prior to that time, worked as a maintenance engineer in the tank repair shop for the Israeli army. Provides no references from Drinkomatic, claiming hostility from supervisor, but displays pay stubs showing very high commissions.

Glenda Meetcha   Age 23   Graduate: B.A. in economics, Washington State University, 2.77 average (4.00 = A). Served as entertainment editor of school paper, member of social sorority. Worked part time in bursar's office during school. Supervisor calls her "reliable." School reference from Professor Gruggle says, "Glenda is a very nice person. She has good social skills and is smarter than her average shows."

Barbara Seville   Age 30   Certificate: Anne Crocker School of Business (proprietary school). Has worked for nine years as secretary–administrative assistant to shop superintendent at Blowhard Design Corp., manufacturers of bar sinks, beer taps, and various bar accessories, a major supplier to Porto Bar. Supervisor calls her "very sharp and capable. She learns technical routines very quickly and I could rely on her to look after things in the shop while I was out." School reference from Miss Dake says, "She was sometimes too outgoing and noisy, but she always did good work and graduated at the top of her class."

Manual Labore   Age 45   High school graduate. Has held jobs as taxi driver, furniture finisher, lathe hand, and most recently as custom carpenter for the Flutz Furniture Company, manufacturers of custom office furniture. He has also been a part-time insurance salesman for a major casualty insurance company and has been averaging about $300,000 a year in sales. His supervisor at the insurance company says, "His sales are above those of most of our full-time people. He is quite a salesman, honest, hard working, and very alert." His supervisor at the furniture company says, "Manny can be trusted to follow instructions good."

Marcus Absennet   Age 30   Graduate: B.A. in liberal arts, Dartmouth College, 2.4 average (4.00 = A). Member of ski team, candidate for Olympic ski team, member of Delta Tau Delta fraternity, member of burlesque review company. Has been employed as a salesman for the Drabnik Dodge–Plymouth Company in Coshocton, Ohio. His supervisor says, "If I had had more salespeople like him, I would not have gone bankrupt, and if the company had people like him selling, they would be in better financial shape. Marc has been pushing out an average of seven new and nine used cards a month for the last five years. His customers come back, and he can even hustle service. He is absolutely the best salesman I have ever seen." School reference from Professor O'Goshe says, "Absennet is somewhat sporadic in his work. He disappears for days at a time but always gets his term papers in on time. I had occasion to question whether he really did his own work once or twice, but I could not find anything to indict him on. Frankly, I didn't like him, but everyone else seemed to."

Dan Cashane   Age 25   Graduate: B.A. in philosophy, North Carolina State, with honors. Member of the wrestling team. State champion weight lifter. Has been working as bartender–bouncer at major resort hotel in Atlantic City and studying law at night school. Plans to finish law degree within the year. Job supervisor calls him "just the right man for this kind of job." School reference from Professor Miggle calls him "steady as a rock, an all-around good guy."

Memo
To: Task Force
From: Ed Mann
Now that you have decided which people we are going to interview, why don't you prepare three questions we can ask each one. Tell me what each question is supposed to accomplish and what kind of answer the interviewee could give that you would consider a good answer. This is not as easy as it looks. You will have to anticipate what the respondents might say. You may want to try to role play the situation to see what kinds of answers are possible to the various questions you think up.

E.M.

Memo
To: Task Force
From: Ed Mann
I have a really messy problem for you. We are going to have to cut costs to meet some real problems in the company. One of the things we are going to have to cut is company benefits. We have approached the union, and they will make their recommendations about what can go. I want recommendations from you (complete with about five minutes of argument for each suggestion) about how to cut about $1.25 million from the following list of benefits.

1. Major medical. Covers 100 percent of emergency and hospital care up to $5,000, with a $750,000 lifetime limit and $100 deductible, as well as 85 percent on all other medical care, including physical exams, routine visits to the doctor, and prescription drugs. The premium we pay is $625,000/ year. We also buy extended counseling and psychiatric coverage for 50 percent of consultation with psychologist (certified) or psychiatrist at $88,000/ year.

2. Dental and optometric care at 80 percent after $100 deductible. Cost $374,000/year. (On both of the above plans, figure you lose about 10 percent of the benefits for every 5 percent you cut from the premium. Employees pay a flat $75 for their share of the coverage. Figure employees would have to go up 50 percent on premiums for every 10 percent cut in benefits if they want to maintain benefits, but we would require 100 percent employee participation to retain benefits.)

3. Employee education program pays 100 percent tuition for courses relevant to job assignment and 50 percent for courses taken for enrichment, with a $500 annual maximum for a given employee for a lifetime total of no more than $3,000. Cost has averaged $264,000 over the last three years, and em-

ployees have taken enrichment courses over job-related courses at a factor of 3:2.

4. Vacation, one week added per year, up to three weeks' maximum annually for clerical and hourly rated employees and up to four weeks annually for supervisory and executive employees. Average cost, $1,100,000. We also give holidays: Christmas, New Year's, July 4, Thanksgiving, Good Friday, Veteran's Day, Labor Day, Memorial Day, and employee's birthday at a cost of about $188,000 per holiday.

5. Sick leave at one day for every three months' employment to a maximum of thirty days/year with full coverage and half coverage until disability retirement is negotiated. Cost was $477,000 last year, plus $214,000 premium for disability and accident coverage.

6. Pension (cooperative company share of 5.7 percent matching employee contribution, with social-security-waiver equalization program for extra shares vested after ten years), provides retirement after twenty years or age sixty, whichever comes first, without penalty, computed at 1.87 best three years' salary average; lump-sum settlement and death-benefit privileges. Cost was $1,315,000 last year. Every $114,000 lopped off the premium would require a 9 percent increase in employee's share to maintain present benefits or would reduce retirement increment figure by .19.

7. Emergency medical care in company infirmary, including heart and blood pressure program—$135,000/year. Alcohol and drug counseling—$68,000/year. Round-the-clock nursing service and first-aid center—$44,000/year. (Forty-one employees in alcohol and drug counseling; infirmary has been used for an average of three cases per day.)

8. Subsidized company cafeteria serving breakfast, sandwich/soup/salad lunch, and coffee breaks (Danish), with vending machines for off hours—$428,000. If employees paid cost plus 10 percent for the service, the cost to the company could be cut by half. Employees currently save about 40 percent over similar costs outside.

9. Annual awards banquet, Christmas party and summer picnic, intramural bowling league, and sponsorship of little-league baseball team—$111,000.

10. Company-award bonus system with prizes for suggestions that cut costs and improve production—$921,000/year. (Suggestions valued at $235,000 in worst year to $2 million in best year, with average about $840,000/year.)

11. New ideas/suggestion box awards—$91,000/year.

12. Ombudsman and grievance office for nonunion personnel—$71,000/year.

13. Life insurance, declining term at increment of $6,000 per each year of employment up to $120,000, converting to paid-up insurance policy of $15,000 at twenty-year retirement, with maintenance-of-premium con-

version for employees who leave the company—$877,000/year. Employees may not take over premiums privately if they remain with the company.
14. Children's college tuition benefit at $2,100/year maximum for four-year maximum term—$274,000/year.

E.M.

You may be tempted on this one to ignore those items that you do not understand. However, this experience gives you a chance to exercise your interviewing skill. If you ask questions of experts in your community about some of the items you do not understand, you will find that you can get enough information to do this problem.

As a final note, it is a great deal of fun and superb experience to design your own Porto Bar problems. Create your own company. Try to develop some problems that will enable the next class to try their hand at using what they have learned. Talk to company executives, teachers, and people who work in industry in order to discover some of the ways communication is used in their companies, and use your information to sharpen your own skills.

Index

decision to speak, 64, 65, 66
organization chart, 65–66
questions to ask, 64
Publication, articles for, 295–98
cautions about, 298
discussion, 295
and oral presentation, 295ff.
periodicals, 295
presentations, 296
publication standards, 298
steps in preparing, 297–98
topic types, 296–97

Q

Questions, and opposition to speaker
confrontational questioning, 155–56
control of, 117
informational speaking, 155
preparation of answers for, 116–17

R

Readings, 20–21
Regulations, 284–87
active voice in, 287
guidelines for, 285–86
nature, 285
Resumes, 40–41, 273–77
data in, 40, 41
example, 274–75
letters with, 274
preparing, 40–41
principles, 276–77
use, 273–74
Repetition, 86–87
and logical vs. emotional presentation, 86
means, 87
and redundancy, 86
Reports. *See* Evaluations and Reports
Riesman, Davis, 187
Robert, Henry, 246

Rules of Order, Revised, 246
Rumor. *See* Gossip and rumor

S

Small talk, 182–83
content, 183
and jokes, 183
occasions for, 182
Social Behavior: Its Elementary Forms, 174
Speaking, presentational, 49–52
fear about, 49
ideas, for appeal of, 50
ideas for, as concerns, 50
information for idea, 50–51
intelligibility, 52
interestingness, 52
organization for, 51
quality of performance, 52
Speaking, reasons for, 17–18
good, advantages, 17–18
poor, disadvantages, 18
Speech, performance in
diction, 122
eye contact, 122
mispronunciation, 121
nonverbal behavior, 122–23
postures, 123
vocalized pauses, 122
voice modulation, 123
voice strain, 121–22
Speech, public, in organizations, 53–58
briefings, 55
employees, negotiating with, 58
evaluations, 54–55
information, 53
inspiration for, 53–54
instructions, 57, 58
organizations for, 57
orientation, 57
professional meetings, 56, 57
proposals, 54
public relations, 56
rebuttals, 58
sales presentation, 58